Today's academic discourse is filled with the word "perform." Nestled amongst a variety of prefixes and suffixes (re-, post-, -ance, -ivity?), the term functions as a vehicle for a host of contemporary inquiries. For students, artists, and scholars of performance and theatre, this development is intriguing and complex. By examining the history of theatre studies and related institutions and by comparing the very different disciplinary interpretations and developments that led to this engagement, *Professing Performance* offers ways of placing performance theory and performance studies in context. Shannon Jackson considers the connection amongst a range of performance forms such as oratory, theatre, dance, and performance art and explores performance as both a humanistic and technical field of education. Throughout, she explores the institutional history of performance in the US academy in order to revise current debates around the role of the arts and humanities in higher education.

SHANNON JACKSON is Associate Professor of Rhetoric and of Theatre, Dance, and Performance Studies at University of California, Berkeley. Her first book, *Lines of Activity: Performance, Historiography, Hull-House Domesticity*, received honourable mention for the John Hope Franklin Prize at the American Studies Association. She has also published in a number of journals including *The Drama Review*, *Theatre Journal*, *Text and Performance Quarterly*, and *The Journal of Dramatic Theory and Criticism*.

Professing Performance

Theatre in the Academy from Philology to Performativity

Theatre and Performance Theory

Series Editor
Tracy C. Davis, *Northwestern University*

Each volume in the Theatre and Performance Theory series introduces a key issue about theatre's role in culture. Specially written for students and a wide readership, each book uses case studies to guide readers into today's pressing debates in theatre and performance studies. Topics include contemporary theatrical practices; historiography; interdisciplinary approaches to making theatre; and the choices and consequences of how theatre is studied, among other areas of investigation.

Books in the series

Jacky Bratton, *New Readings in Theatre History*
Tracy C. Davis and Thomas Postlewait (eds), *Theatricality*
Shannon Jackson, *Professing Performance: theatre in the academy from philology to performativity*

Professing Performance

Theatre in the Academy from Philology to Performativity

Shannon Jackson

PUBLISHED BY THE PRESS SYNDICATE OF THE UNIVERSITY OF CAMBRIDGE
The Pitt Building, Trumpington Street, Cambridge, United Kingdom

CAMBRIDGE UNIVERSITY PRESS
The Edinburgh Building, Cambridge, CB2 2RU, UK
40 West 20th Street, New York, NY 10011–4211, USA
477 Williamstown Road, Port Melbourne, VIC 3207, Australia
Ruiz de Alarcón 13, 28014 Madrid, Spain
Dock House, The Waterfront, Cape Town 8001, South Africa
http://www.cambridge.org

First published 2004
Reprinted 2006

Printed in the United Kingdom at the University Press, Cambridge

Typeface Plantin 10/12 pt.   *System* LATEX 2ε   [TB]

A catalogue record for this book is available from the British Library

Library of Congress Cataloguing in Publication data
Jackson, Shannon, 1967–
Professing performance: theatre in the academy from philology to
performativity / Shannon Jackson.
    p.   cm. – (Theatre and performance theory)
Includes bibliographical references and index.
ISBN 0 521 65189 1 – ISBN 0 521 65605 2 (pbk)
1. Performing arts – Study and teaching (Higher)   2. Performing arts.
I. Title.   II. Series.   ′.071
PN1576.J33   2004   791   ′1 – dc22   2003055729

ISBN 0 521 65189 1 hardback
ISBN 0 521 65605 2 paperback

For Michael

Contents

Acknowledgments   *page* x

1   Discipline and performance: genealogy and
    discontinuity   1

2   Institutions and performance: professing
    performance in the early twentieth century   40

3   Culture and performance: structures of
    dramatic feeling   79

4   Practice and performance: modernist paradoxes
    and literalist legacies   109

5   History and performance: blurred genres and
    the particularizing of the past   146

6   Identity and performance: racial performativity
    and anti-racist theatre   176

    Notes   220
    Select bibliography   239
    Index   248

Acknowledgments

The idea for this project began, appropriately enough, during my transition from graduate student to assistant professor. As it does for most of us, the transition involved a change of institutions. It was during that process that I became more acutely aware of the institutional construction of knowledge and wanted some kind of how-to manual. What I offer in this book turns out to be less of a how-to; after all, the variety of institutions makes the idea of a manual impossible. This book does, however, offer a way of thinking about institutional variety. At base, *Professing Performance* asks colleagues, scholars, and students to allow the recognition of difference and contingency to structure our professional and disciplinary lives. At a time when disciplinary wars have hit the professing of performance with a certain amount of virulence – resulting in self-righteous declarations, oppositions, and exclusions that push the bounds of both collegiality and reasonable argument – it seems important to learn to welcome institutional variation.

A number of individuals served as necessary interlocutors at Northwestern, Harvard, and the University of California at Berkeley (my three sites of employment) and at the symposia, scholarly organizations, and other speaking engagements where I have shared this material. For critiques, citations, patience, and perspective during many manic conversations, I particularly want to thank Phil Auslander, Sally Banes, Larry Buell, Judith Butler, Charlotte Canning, Anne Cheng, Dwight Conquergood, Marianne Constable, Elin Diamond, Jill Dolan, Harry Elam, Marjorie Garber, Mark Griffith, Bill Handley, Barbara Johnson, Caren Kaplan, Loren Kruger, Jeff Masten, José Muñoz, Peggy Phelan, Della Pollock, Martin Puchner, Joseph Roach, Miryam Sas, Rebecca Schneider, Kaja Silverman, Eric Smoodin,

Anne Wagner, Lynn Wardley, Linda Williams, Stacy Wolf, and William Worthen. Tracy Davis deserves particular thanks for her detailed readings and generous stewardship. Vicki Cooper at Cambridge University Press has been a model editor as well. My research assisstants – Kristina Hagstrom, Laura Levin, and especially Renu Cappelli – were diligent and insightful up until the very end. Parts of Chapters Two and Three were previously published in *The Drama Review* and *Modern Drama* respectively, and I am grateful to their editors for granting permission to reprint.

This book is dedicated to Michael Korcuska, the person with whom I learned to face the personal and geographic hazards of institutional transition and with whom I now happily share its personal and geographic rewards.

1 Discipline and performance: genealogy and discontinuity

"Differentiation is one strategy that disciplines employ to protect themselves against incursion and self-doubt. But how about the opposite strategy: emulation, imitation, envy?" Marjorie Garber[1]

"It is not easy to say something new." Michel Foucault[2]

Coming to terms

"Isn't 'performativity' the latest thing in 'English' theory?"

It was one of those over-determined moments in the life of a theatre academic. I had been asked as a faculty member in an English department to participate on a panel responding to a production of the American Repertory Theatre. The question came from a dramaturg – the in-house academic of the theatre profession – as we ate dinner before the ART's subscriber event. The director of the production also sat at the table, looking slightly amused.

"Yes, it's actually pretty trendy," I said, picking up my fork and being fairly certain that neither of them really wanted to hear about the trends.

"Perform-a-tivity," repeated the director, and then once again, "per-form-a-tiv-ity. That's what they call it?"

"Yeah," said the dramaturg, "I hear it alot."

"So maybe I should start using that," the director was laughing, "No, I'm sorry; I'm not a director. I'm a Performativity Coordinator."

We all laughed. I took another bite of food, hoping that the conversation was finished.

"So what do . . . what does . . . they mean . . . that mean?" the two asked one on top of each other.

1

I continued chewing. I swallowed.

"Well," I began, dreading what would follow, "the concept of 'performativity' within literary studies is a reworking of the ideas of this guy, J.L. Austin . . ."

This guy, *this guy* . . .?

". . . and he was, well, a kind of philosopher called a speech act theorist. He wrote a book called *How to Do Things With Words* . . ."

Did they want to hear this? I found myself staring at the table while I talked.

". . . and there he argued that words are not purely reflective . . . that linguistic acts don't simply reflect a world but that speech actually has the power to *make* a world."

Reductive but brief. I looked up and was somewhat comforted to see that the two had been listening. The director nodded casually and picked up his fork again.

"Oh," he said, "you mean like theatre."

This type of exchange is fairly familiar in theatre and performance studies. In what follows, I want to work from similar moments – as well as even more bizarre and friction-ridden ones – in order to understand the varied forces that produce such conversations. At dinners, in deans' offices, in department meetings, at academic conferences, in office hours, in rehearsals, such interactions testify to an awkward and emergent period in the study and practice of theatre and performance. I happen to believe that it is necessary both to analyze the dispositions that produce that awkwardness as well as to embrace awkwardness as a condition of emergence. The conversation is familiar in part because it incarnates the scholar-versus-artist divide that persistently shadows a variety of disciplines in the humanities and arts. The provisional resolution at the end of the conversation is perhaps less familiar, entrenched as scholar/artist binaries are epistemologically, professionally, even socially in delineating amongst those of us who have decided to make performance a lifelong preoccupation. Certainly other academic fields face similar theory/practice conundrums and navigate internal divisions within themselves – splits between sociologists and social workers, art historians, and studio artists, political scientists and activists, literary scholars, and "creative writers." One of the tasks of this book will be to trace how the link between scholars and artists has been alternately disavowed and celebrated, touted and feared, re-termed and re-organized – in institutional controversies, in "new" intellectual frameworks, in genre debates, in curricula, in artistic movements, in performance history itself.

There is more percolating in this exchange than scholar/artist or theory/practice oppositions, however. When the dramaturg asked about the trend of the word "performativity" in "English theory," he presumed that he was asking about a literary concept with some bearing on, or interest in, his own world of theatre studies. The nature, indeed existence, of either that bearing or that interest is still uncertain. P-words of various sorts – couched amongst various prefixes and suffixes – circulate in the contemporary academic discourse of various disciplines in the humanities and social sciences. The specific intellectual roots of performativity to which I referred are located within a genealogy of speech-act theory, a philosophical school that distinguished the performative from the constative function of language and explored how certain types of speech (e.g. promises) enact their world-creating power in the moment of utterance. Such an orientation has tremendous implications for the discipline of theatre studies, though the nature and direction of those implications have been less well-developed and occasionally received with indifference from both literature and theatre scholars. The director's delightfully assured come-back in the phrase "like theatre" would have been roundly contested by J.L. Austin himself who argued against an alignment between speech-act theory and theatre, famously characterizing theatrical language as "hollow or void" and as "parasitic upon its normal use."[3] As I explore in a later chapter, Austin reproduced a neo-Platonic notion of derivativeness to add a kind of "anti-theatrical performativity" to the long list of anti-theatrical prejudices that have vexed Western intellectual history. For that reason, scholars within theatre and performance studies have been as suspicious of the language of performativity as they are intrigued by its theoretical potential.

At this point in the differently emergent and partially overlapping fields of theatre and performance studies, it is worth trying to place the vocabularies, goals, assumptions, and objects of inquiry of various critical schools in conversation with each other. Any rapprochement requires some excavation, however, especially of how hybrid intellectual histories get elided by the sledge-hammer dichotomies and false consensuses that surround certain keywords. The fact of the matter is that speech-act theory is only one of the many disciplinary strains that contribute to the intellectual ferment surrounding performance, even if it is the orientation most emphasized in literary and rhetorical studies. Scholars drawing from anthropology, sociology, art history, folklore, and media studies have developed vocabularies of performance to understand artifacts and events ranging from parades to television, from story-telling to religious ceremonies. The aspects of performance that these scholars emphasize can be quite different; the theoretical models that they derive may be incompatible, and even the reality principles that they assume may appear to undermine each other. Scholarship looks uninteresting to some when there is no abstraction, ungrounded to others when there is no description, romantic when there is no consideration of structure, incomplete without an account of production, determinist without a theory of agency, naive when it assumes a real historical referent, apolitical when too theoretical, apolitical when it is not theoretical enough. Such are the opportunities and hazards of interdisciplinarity. Comparisons amongst different types of performance discourse show this complexity and, more importantly, encourage vigilance against various kinds of synecdochic fallacies in cross-disciplinary inquiry – moments when scholars assume that one body of texts adequately represents an entire field.

This book asks how and why all of these kinds of judgements are made and what kinds of enabling illuminations and disenabling blindspots they produce. While my argument develops differently over the course of each chapter, there are some relevant issues and themes that serve as discursive touchstones for the project as a whole. First of all, this book takes seriously Michel Foucault's unsettling notion of "genealogy" in the fabrication of intellectual history, an approach that has appeared throughout Foucault's work. Before his elaboration of this concept in *Language, Counter-Memory, Practice*, Foucault's early archaeology of knowledge found that "the problem arises of knowing whether the unity of a discourse is based not so much on the permanence and uniqueness of an object as on the space in which various objects emerge and are continuously transformed."[4] The non-unity of discourse is thus, for Foucault, a principle operating assumption. Consequently, my analysis acknowledges the value of assuming the discrete stability of something like "performance" – and related terms such as "theatre," "speech," "drama," or "dance" – while simultaneously tracking the discursive dispersal and decidedly indiscreet saturation of such references with that which they claim not to be. The effort to account for "theatre and performance theory" – to invoke the title of this series – is an examination of the referents in a "unity of a discourse" that paradoxically requires an awareness of "their nonidentity through time, the break produced in them, the internal discontinuity that suspends their permanence."[5]

My contention, however, is that an account of scholarly development offers only a partial accounting of the space in which knowledge is produced. Hence, I have also found it necessary to focus on what might be called the "institutional genealogies" of knowledge formation. The modern university is itself a formidably complex and self-contradicting array of institutional practices. Its modes of knowledge production are propelled by the vagaries of institutional power, pedagogical process, and occupational structure as much as by felt desire and intellectual curiosity. In addition to such consideration, I also take seriously critiques of the professional intellectual and of the role of the arts and humanities in higher education. As it happens, such critiques are particularly resonant for (and made more resonant by) comparison with the discontinuous cluster of knowledges that come under the term performance. Consider, for instance, John Guillory's critique of the class status of the intellectual and the assumption of the knowledge-worker's progressivism.

While it has always seemed necessary to define intellectuals by their inclination to dissident political stances, it has also been possible to ground the analysis of intellectuals in the socioeconomic domain by positing a constitutive distinction between intellectual and manual labor, a distinction that for good historical reasons implicates intellectual labor in the system of economic exploitation. It is quite difficult on that basis to demonstrate how the fact of intellectual labor becomes the condition for the innate tendency to progressive or even leftist politics that is assumed to characterize intellectuals. . . . What troubles such an account is certainly not its "optimism of the will" to use Gramsci's phrases, but rather an unfounded optimism of the intellectual, an analysis of intellectuals in which identity is defined by generalizations about their innately progressive political nature or tendencies.[6]

The suggestion that the phenomenon of the intellectual rests upon an opposition to manual labor reflects back on the conversation that opened this introduction. As much as the opposition between "theory" and "practice" is erroneous, as much as both terms have a hugely complicated set of references, it would be disingenuous to ignore the fact that this conversation took place across different occupational positions. I will suggest that the enmeshment of "practice" and "production" in performance-related fields is one that blurs and hence exposes the opposition between the intellectual and the manual on which so much humanistic knowledge-making relies. This is just one of many moments where an awareness of the institutional genealogies of knowledge help to give a keener, albeit more confounding, picture of the internally discontinuous status of performance knowledge in the academy.

This predicament relates to another issue that will return throughout the book – what might be called the hyper-contextuality of performance. The *enmeshment* to which I referred above characterizes not only the occupational life of performance but also its intensely contingent status as a research object, a radical contextuality that makes it difficult to locate as a research object at all. The production and reproduction of knowledge is, to some extent, a formalist operation in de-contextualization. To the extent that the discernment and dissemination of knowledge requires boundedness and containment, performance has faired unevenly in the academy. The imprecise boundaries of the theatrical event made it difficult to know where the research object ended and its relevant context began. The intensely intimate, varied, social, and inefficient character of performance pedagogy make it less amenable to mass reproduction on the grand scales of a modernizing university. For Foucault, of course, every knowledge formation resists such structures. For me, however, performance tends to flout the conventions of knowledgeability more explicitly. If Foucault's project and that of cultural materialism more generally is to expose the contingencies of apparently pure forms, then we have in the case of performance a form that knows contingency all too well, indeed, was too manifestly enmeshed in context to effect the disavowal of materialism even when it was trendy to do so. As such, performance sometimes calls the bluff of more recent critical turns toward material analysis as well as more recent calls for innovative pedagogy.

In the rest of this chapter, I want to think more specifically about the notion of disciplinarity as it affects the study and practice of theatre and performance. In theatre, in performance studies, and in related fields such as dance, rhetoric, visual arts, and cultural studies, participants continually enjoy and endure the paradoxes of interdisciplinary exchange. Sometimes these encounters happen self-consciously. Indeed, origin narratives behind the formation of performance studies are filled with interactions between theatre directors and anthropologists, between folklorists and psychoanalytic critics, all working to graft a conversation based in avowedly different modes of knowing. At other times, these encounters happen less self-consciously, often in situations where epistemological consensus is assumed only to be thwarted by the return of repressed difference. I want to examine such instances of intended and unintended boundary crossing even as I critique assumptions of where such boundaries lie. In the current context, the term *interdisciplinary* serves sometimes as a facile index of the "new," opposing itself to a *disciplinarity* retroactively construed as old. As such, these terms function as fundamental, if not always helpful, pivots on which questions of theatre and performance studies turn. By extension, questions of interdisciplinarity broach the obscure operations of boundary formation, asking what is inside and what is outside – which may or may not line up with the question of what is "in" and what is "out." An analysis of interdisciplinarity asks what kinds of knowledge formations are considered multiple and which are considered singular. What gets labeled generalist and what is specialist? universal and particular? different and the same? What may seem *inter*-disciplinary in one locale can be experienced as solidly *intra*-disciplinary in another. Indeed, a historical, institutional, and theoretical consciousness of disciplinary formation demonstrates how variable and contextual the boundaries of knowledge can be. It also reveals how very difficult it is to say something new.

After introducing the range of debates and the range of associations attached to the term "performance," I situate its study historically in a changing modern university. Focusing on the issue of "interdisciplinarity" in theatre and performance studies allows a point of entry into a number of other contemporary concerns – debates about scholars and artists, about canons and counter-canons, about professionals and amateurs, and about movements in feminism, multiculturalism, and "theory" of various guises. The problem of interdisciplinarity further provides

a way of analyzing the relation between disciplines and institutions, a saturation between scholarship and employment that
is not always transparent. The chapter concludes by offering a
vocabulary for analyzing the epistemological glitches that such
debates leave in their wake – a set of conceptual tools that will
reappear in the case studies of subsequent chapters.

Discontinuous performances

At this point, it is worth reflecting briefly on the framing of disciplinary debates in theatre and performance – the two terms
that title the editorial series in which this book appears. In the
United States, disciplinary change has clustered around two institutional narratives at New York University and Northwestern
University, what Jon McKenzie calls the "Eastern" and "Mid-
western" strains of performance studies.[7] The more oft-repeated
origin story involves Richard Schechner and a cohort of thinkers
at NYU. The narrative focuses on Schechner's generative interactions with the anthropologist, Victor Turner, who took the
study of performance beyond the proscenium stage and into the
carnivals, festivals, protests, and other cultural rituals of an intercultural world. As Peggy Phelan notes, this Performance Studies
story is an intriguing one in which "two men gave birth."[8] It is
also a heroic story of disciplinary breaking and remaking, one
framed by the language of the rebel, the renegade, and later,
incorporating new schools of critical theory, the subversive and
the resistant. Key moments in this "Eastern" institutional narrative note the avant-garde experimentation of the 1960s, the
transfer of location and orientation of the *Tulane Drama Review*
to New York's *TDR*, the hiring of an interdisciplinary faculty of
anthropologists, folklorists, musicologists, and dance theorists at
NYU's Tisch School of the Arts, the Performance Studies name
change in 1980, and the hosting of the first meeting of the eventually incorporated Performance Studies International at NYU
in 1995. Another notorious moment in that history occurred at
the 1992 meeting of the Association of Theatre in Higher Education where keynote speaker Richard Schechner called for the
abolition of theatre departments, for the Kuhnian adoption of a
performance studies "paradigm" shift, and for an acknowledgment that the art form of theatre had become "the string quartet"

of the new era.[9] A decided irony, noted by many, was that field practitioners continually invoked the language of rebellion and subversion while simultaneously seeking institutional solidity and professional security.[10] Others were distressed to hear that an articulation of epistemological transformation – something to be expected in any field – needed to cast theatre and performance in oppositional terms. While the scholarly rhetoric called for cultural inclusion under the performance umbrella, the institutional rhetoric sounded much more adversarial. As I hope to show, this kind of irony is not specific to performance studies but can be seen as symptomatic of a larger set of paradoxes in the institutionalization and employment of the arts and humanities at the end of the twentieth century.

The development of Northwestern's department of Performance Studies proceeds from a different direction. To some, its narrative is less often recounted. To others, of course, it is the only one that matters. There are occasional stories of men giving birth – though Wallace Bacon and Robert Breen are a generation older than Schechner – and of performers meeting anthropologists – though the figures might be Dwight Conquergood and Mary Douglas. The institutional landscape of such stories is quite different, however. The department of (Oral) Interpretation had a decades' long existence in a very different institutional milieu – that is, inside a School of Speech, one that also housed distinct departments of Communication Studies, Radio/TV/Film, and Theatre. Thus, unlike the progenitors at NYU who broke from a prior institutional identity as Theatre, Northwestern's department had considered itself something other than Theatre for its entire institutional existence. Oral Interpretation was most often positioned as an aesthetic subfield within Speech, Communication, and/or Rhetoric. Its proponents drew from a classical tradition in oral poetry to argue for the role of performance in the analysis and dissemination of cultural texts, specializing in the adaptation of print media into an oral and embodied environment. Northwestern was unusual for devoting an entire department to this area. Most of that faculty's colleagues and former graduate students would find themselves in the oral interpretation slot of a larger Communication department – in the Midwest, the South, the Southwest, the West, and on the East Coast. This made for a dispersed kind of institutional network. It also meant that the decision to shift nomination and orientation to Performance Studies occurred within that network rather than exclusively within a department. The division within the National Communication Association was renamed Performance Studies, and field practitioners around the country followed suit. Thus, while it is large-minded of McKenzie to note regional variation in the formation of Performance Studies, the East/Midwest focus on two departments actually obscures central figures and deliberative societies in other parts of the United States.

If these two stories show that institutional contexts differently constitute disciplinary identity, they also imply that the history of a discipline changes depending upon where one decides to begin. One way to resituate this two-pronged story of a late twentieth-century formation is to cast Performance Studies as the integration of theatrical and oral/rhetorical traditions. This framework necessarily invites reflection on a longer history of separation between the theatrical and the rhetorical or, as it often appears institutionally, between Theatre and Speech. There are many ways one might take up this relationship and, after Foucault, pursue its "non-identity through time."[11] One might note classical antagonisms and alliances in the history of poetics, rhetoric, and the performer/orator, investigating nineteenth-century discussions on the role of elocution and argumentation in higher education, attending to the cultivated antipathy between proponents of theatre and proponents of oratory at the turn-of-the-century, attending to the cultivated alliances between proponents of theatre and oratory in their shared effort to distinguish themselves from the solidifying profession of literary studies. Such reflection might also include the transformation of speech under the influence of social science, the transformation of theatre within an arts and liberal arts education, the return of rhetoric in a new form under the legitimating paradigms of Theory in the late-twentieth century, the return of performance in a new form under the legitimating paradigms of Theory in the later twentieth century. Whatever corner of the rug one decides to pick up, whatever moment in time one decides to posit as a relevant origin, such investigations can only be done with an awareness of the contingent, slippery, and decidedly contextual nature of knowledge formation. Behind a story of disciplinary docility there is no unitary knowledge formation from which "new" epistemologies break. This also means using Foucault to temper the Kuhnian language of "paradigm" in order to suggest a "genealogical" awareness of the partial and entangled relationships amongst knowledges that are too conveniently opposed and aligned.[12] The predecessors of one's current allies turn out to be antagonists. The predecessors of one's current antagonists were once allies. Somewhere in this history that many of us unwittingly share, there are too many alliances and oppositions to imagine unbroken chains of continuity or radical breaks from the past.

What institutional critic Gerald Graff says of debates within and around the field of literature seems appropriate to the predicament of theatre and performance: "teach the conflicts."[13] This means not only acquainting students with various points of view, something that is already difficult for many, but also developing a more historical and complicated sense of what those conflicts are. Indeed, such teaching might also mean recognizing how conflicted the terms of opposition are, acknowledging that the various "sides" of an argument may share less-emphasized concerns and institutional genealogies. In this spirit, this book works from the notion that performance studies and theatre (along with adjacent and related performance forms such as oratory, performance art, folklore, and dance) might be usefully understood within a shared, if internally discontinuous, institutional history. Consequently, I will use the term "performance" generally to describe instances of performance pedagogy in the American university since the nineteenth century, distinguishing subsidiary forms such as theatre, dance, and oratory when necessary and using the phrase "performance studies" to refer more specifically to scholarship and scholars that self-consciously composed a late twentieth-century intellectual formation. Despite my general belief in the historical and epistemological connections amongst these various terms, "conflicts" of various sorts will abound.

The vagaries of the interdisciplinary encounter are compounded by the vagaries of the term "performance." In a cross-disciplinary conversation, interested parties may engage in a conversation only to find that performance means different things to different people. The confusion derives from the fact that performance has been a site of epistemological anxiety in many societies for quite some time; Western intellectual history's centuries' old anti-theatrical prejudice is only one case in point. Consequently, performance scholars who have worked to make sense of current interdisciplinary trends in light of contemporary and historical theoretical movements have had quite a job to do. Scholars continually find themselves rehearsing and revising various kinds of intellectual histories, recounting trajectories from Bakhtin or Bateson, from Turner or Goffman, from Dewey or Austin, from Derrida or Lacan, from Butler or Sedgwick. Depending upon a prior disciplinary affiliation, some may emphasize certain figures over others. To those who proceed from literary studies and linguistic philosophy, J.L. Austin is a rediscovered intellectual predecessor; Richard Bauman figures more prominently for folklorists just as Kenneth Burke does for social theorists, Victor Turner for anthropologists, Judith Butler for queer theorists, and so on. Marvin Carlson required an entire book – *Performance: A Critical Introduction* – just to describe the possible paths of intellectual influence.[14] Any attempt to be comprehensive will inevitably exclude thinkers or craft chronologies that miss important connections.

Rather than offer a corrective intellectual history, I hope to provide ways of negotiating this discursive complexity and of accepting it as a condition of performance research. Joann Kealiinohomoku's attempt to make sense of the way "dance" has been abstractly interpreted offers an illuminating example of a larger problem in disciplining performance. In preparing an essay entitled "An Anthropologist Looks at Ballet as a Form of Ethnic Dance," Kealiinohomoku reread "pertinent writings by DeMille, Haskell, Holt, the Kinneys, Kirstein, Le Meri, Martin, Sachs, Sorell, and Terry."[15] What she says of the contradictions in dance scholarship can be said of those found within performance more generally:

This survey of the literature reveals an amazing divergence of opinions. We are able to read that the origin of dance was in play and that it was not in play, that it was for magical and religious purposes, and that it was not for those things; that it was for courtship and that it was not for courtship; that it was the first form of communication and that communication did not enter into dance until it became an "art." In addition we can read that it was serious and purposeful and that at the same time it was an outgrowth of exuberance, was totally spontaneous, and originated in the spirit of fun. Moreover, we can read that it was only a group activity for tribal solidarity and that it was strictly for the pleasure and self-expression of the one dancing.[16]

The kind of malleable historicization outlined by Kealiinohomoku generates a reciprocally malleable conceptualization. Different approaches and contexts emphasize certain kinds of associations while in turn the connotations of various terms influence what histories get told. Such flexibility helps to clarify how scholarship within and without the fields of dance, theatre, and performance work with different operating assumptions.

In order to create a compass for navigating this complexity, consider the range of connotations that have galvanized performance research in the past and in the present. First, an etymological angle yields one particular type of emphasis. The word *performance* derives from a Greek root meaning "to furnish forth," "to carry forward," "to bring into being." In this guise, the term foregrounds not only instances of making but also the active and processual aspect of that making. To extend the etymological tack, the word *theatre* derives from a root meaning "a place for viewing," emphasizing the spectacular qualities of a thing beheld as well as a vision-based locus of reception and interpretation. A second angle yields another network of connotations derived from the many artistic registers at which performance operates. This tack propels different strains of conceptual thinking. Performance conventionally employs bodies, motion, space, affect, image, and words; its analysis at times aligns with theories of embodiment, at times with studies of emotion, at times with architectural analysis, at times with studies of visual culture, and at times with critiques of linguistic exchange. Consequently, one visual analyst who speaks of sutures and gazes may struggle to translate that perspective to another who speaks of uptakes and perlocutions. Moreover, none of these associations are themselves internally consistent. One "theorist of embodiment" may derive from phenomenology, another from social theory, and another from kinesthesiology, all of which may operate with different notions of identity, agency, and bodily integrity. For one scholar, concepts of space may be synonymous with an abstract public sphere while for another it is enmeshed quite literally in architecture's study of material entrances, exits, thresholds, and barriers. The many registers of performance thus have many registers of meaning. As a result, interdisciplinarity at the site of performance can feel like an epistemological conundrum of imponderable proportions.

Connotations of a third type are also attached to performance, associations that are not based so much in etymology or in the various media of the form. Rather they are a reflection of the term's location in a philosophical history as well as in a contemporary theoretical context. They also reflect not simply how varied but also how contradictory performance's referentiality can be. For instance, theorists of various stripes have foregrounded performance as a vehicle of community formation as often as others have emphasized its function as a site of social transgression. Sometimes both of these associations can appear in the work of the same scholar, often without note of the variation. Another area of theoretical emphasis has been the question of repetition in performance. To many scholars, performance's repeatability has been fundamental to its theorizing, whether couched in Richard Schechner's restoration of behavior, derived from Linda Hutcheon's theory of parody, or echoed in Judith Butler's adaptation of Derridean citationality. While such scholars have been quick to add that repetition occasionally entails variation and difference, their point of entry differs markedly from that of Peggy Phelan who argues for performance as fundamentally non-repeatable, as a reiteration whose chief feature is its non-reproducibility. Competing associations revolve around other performance registers, further confounding the quest for theoretical purity. For some philosophers, performance is an intentional realm of purposive action; for others, it is an unintentional realm of spontaneous or habitual enactment. Some theorists, spurred by recent cultural theory, link performance to innovative realms of creation and resistance; others, reproducing new versions of older Platonic condemnations, link performance to derivative realms of conformity and tertiary imitation. Finally, the occupants of many theatre departments use a language of the actual, the real, and the authentic to distinguish their practices of artistic production from a presumably "less real" practice of scholarly research. Their rhetoric contrasts starkly, sometimes obliviously, with the long-held assumptions of theatre's fakery, artifice, and inauthenticity that still circulate in most other wings of the university. In sum, performance is about doing, and it is about seeing; it is about image, embodiment, space, collectivity, and/or orality; it makes community and it breaks community; it repeats endlessly and it never repeats; it is intentional and unintentional, innovative and derivative, more fake and more real. Performance's many connotations and its varied intellectual kinships ensure that an interdisciplinary conversation around this interdisciplinary site rarely will be neat and straightforward. Perhaps it is time to stop assuming that it should.

"Old" genealogies

The notion of interdisciplinarity depends, of course, on a notion of disciplinarity. Since a central mission of this study is to deploy institutional history in order to resituate debates in theatre and performance studies, I would like briefly to consider the history of disciplinarity in the emerging American university. "Teaching the conflicts" of theatre and performance studies is sharpened, concretized, and complicated by a larger understanding of modern knowledge production. The concept of an academic discipline is actually a fairly recent formation. It emerges in concert with the rise of the modern university, an arc whose beginnings historians place in the late nineteenth-century.[17] A number of social factors converged slowly and unevenly to redefine American higher education. Earlier understood as an elite education based in a classical tradition, university reformers sought a more democratic institution based in a vernacular and (in the United States) "practical" education oriented toward the professional ambitions of a rising middle class. The unevenness of this shift was determined by a number of factors including region, religion, university traditions, alumni influences, and the individual preoccupations of university faculty and administrators. The enrolment of a non-aristocratic group of young white men challenged the self-conception of the university in some ways. The admitting of white women and students of color to some institutions challenged it in other ways as did the rise of all-black colleges and the changing self-definitions of all-female institutions. Ivy League universities such as Princeton, Harvard, and Yale differed from each other in their acceptance of democratic ideals, sometimes touting a new civic ideal for the university toward its public, other times expressing alarmist concerns over the lowering of university standards.

The profile of higher education underwent a significant change as the result of the Morrill Federal Land Grant of 1862. This act created the phenomenon of the "land-grant college" – what would be referred to as the state university – and sought to enable young people from a variety of backgrounds to attend college with public support.[18] The democratic ideals of the land-grant college rested not only on demographics and on public financing but also on a "practical" emphasis. Inspired by the potential for applying scientific innovation to "real world" concerns, land-grant universities and changing modern universities sought to create a curriculum that applied scientific research to the arenas of industry and agriculture. While midwestern colleges initially emphasized agricultural innovation, the language of practical knowledge and of applied education permeated various wings of the university, providing a discursive vehicle with which to legitimate or to de-legitimate the utility of a variety of educational fields. The opposition between practical and liberal arts curricula fueled heated conversations in all-black colleges; often historicized as the Washington-DuBois debate, interested parties disagreed about which kind of curriculum would further racial advancement.[19] The language of the practical made its way into some wings of the Ivy League universities and not into others. As the only Ivy League school that also claimed the funds and the identity of a state institution, Cornell University particularly sought to temper the traditions of a classical education with a use-oriented focus on agricultural and industrial education. This emphasis in turn affected the genealogy by which theatre appeared on campus; it is perhaps no coincidence that Cornell's theatre department first established itself in a revamped machine shop.

Other factors contributed to the changing identity of the modern university, factors that did not always dovetail with democratic or pragmatic goals. While the term "professional" could sometimes justify a utilitarian curriculum in higher education, the term also occupied a wider and more flexible discursive sphere. The late nineteenth and early twentieth century saw the rise of "professionalism," or what Andrew Abbott calls "the system of professions," in a number of arenas.[20] In traditional fields such as law and medicine, in newer fields of employment such as social work, and in changing occupations such as academia itself, the term professionalism was also synonymous with the concept of "expertise" and denoted an arena of rigorously trained experts. The modern concept of "discipline" thus arose when the discursive strain of professional expertise met the exigencies of a restructuring university. This meeting sustained a social transformation in the occupation of "the intellectual" – a figure who increasingly required university training and affiliation – and altered this figure's relationship to the acquisition and dissemination of knowledge.[21] Bruce Kuklick summarizes:

> During the late nineteenth century the university as we understand it, the social organization defining the modern professoriate – came into existence. Amateur intellectuals, those without an institutional base, all but disappeared as the university came to be the sole focus in the production and distribution of knowledge. Various areas of study hived off from older and vaguer 'departments' of inquiry, and scholarly disciplines were established as limited fields of knowledge in the university, distinguished by special techniques and an accepted set of doctrines. Academic departments grew up, and disciplinary integrity was defined by the number of positions in a given field the university would finance. Teachers were trained and placed in this field by an intensified apprenticeship leading to the doctorate and an appointment as a college professor.[22]

Kuklick's language repeats the fundamental assumptions of contemporary doctoral training, a model that is so common-sensical now that its historical contingency is barely recognized. His language also finds a progressive narrative behind this shift, attributing "vagueness" to earlier "amateur" intellectual formations and the status of a "grown up" to later ones. Indeed, the concept of the amateur switches during this period from a largely salutary term based in the love of certain pursuits to a largely derogatory term.[23] While intellectual vagueness is retroactively measured from the standpoint of a present context's sense of its own integrity, the turn into the twentieth century was nevertheless distinguished by the quest for highly distinct forms of knowledge. A nineteenth-century "humanities" curriculum that in hindsight looked like an amalgam of philosophy, literature, rhetoric, and moral inquiry began gradually to divide itself into separate fields with their own departments, professional societies, hirings, curricula, standards, and self-justifications. Attributions of "amateurism" and "professionalism" were thus newly deployed to delineate and confer value upon increasingly higher degrees of specialization. A variety of fields profession-alized during this period – Literature, Philosophy, History, Art History – spurred by the emphasis on specialization and by a uni-versity structure that rewarded disciplinary distinction in both senses of the word. While there still existed university professors who worked as "generalists," the recognition of that generalism could be greeted with suspicion and, like the term "amateur," could connote vagueness and imprecision. Of course, the term specialist depended upon the concept of generalist in order for the rigor of the former or the expansiveness of the latter even to be registered.

The movement toward disciplinary specialization was also spurred by the influence of foreign university models. American administrators and faculty looked with eyes both wary and fasci-nated to the creation of the new research universities in Germany. Opposing themselves to arenas of vocational testing and training, German universities received substantial state funding to create an educational structure that serviced, as much as possible, the research careers of its professors. Teaching schedules and curric-ular mechanisms were geared toward facilitating further faculty specialization; when professors taught, their classrooms provided arenas for their focused questions and a body of students who aided their exploration. The goal of student training was coinci-dent with the unadulterated pursuit of knowledge; such students trained for careers inside the university itself.

University schooling was in fact little connected with professional prac-tice or knowledge. The two level examinations reflected in part a dif-ferentiation between education and professional training that emerged between 1780 and 1860. These years saw the rise of the *Bildung*, a con-cept variously defined as 'cultivation,' 'a combination of taste, learning, and judgement,' . . . *Bildung* entailed a resolutely anti-professional ped-agogy. Preprofessional studies were ridiculed as *Brotstudium* (literally, bread studies). The professors executed their assault on professional-ism with vigor.[24]

Germany's research professors adapted a scientific discourse of legitimacy to other arenas of inquiry in order to tout the no-ble and rigorous pursuit of pure knowledge. The disingenuous

element of the *Bildung* model rested on its anti-professional discourse, a disavowal that still persists in faculty self-descriptions
today. Despite their own rhetoric, Germany's faculty were of
course an intensely professionalized body, substantially influenced by the conventions of rigor, expertise, hierarchy, ap-
prenticeship, and specialization that circulated throughout the
discourse of professionalism more generally.[25] The professorial
disavowal would persist in future rationalizations of research and
graduate training, denying the legitimacy of a pre-professional
education unless it happened to fulfill the occupational requirements of a professional academic.

The first American university founded on the Germanic model
was, most famously, Johns Hopkins University. Ivy League as
well as land-grant colleges began to adopt aspects of this model.
Historians of the American university interpret this change with
differing amounts of celebration and ambivalence. Frederick
Rudolph's study notes that "the collegiate tradition in the United
States could not find new inspiration in the spirit of the German
university without some loss to the collegiate way."[26] Rudolph
chooses to interpret the combination of influences within a nationalist frame. The state universities that began developing as
research institutions, he writes, "would combine in a typically
American institution that Jeffersonian emphasis on excellence
and learning which had become the special commitment of Johns
Hopkins and the Jacksonian emphasis on numbers and on the
practical which had become the special commitment of the land-
grant colleges."[27] Here Rudolph reroutes the Germanic influence through an American presidential history, casting the research emphasis as a return to a Jeffersonian tradition rather
than as an imitation of a European model. Whether or not the
international influence was acknowledged or disavowed, American universities integrated the research model in various ways
and appealed to its disciplinarity for intellectual legitimacy. They
thus participated in the occupational transformation that would
eventually place the concept of "Research" in the forefront of
a faculty member's job description and professional evaluation.
For a variety of reasons and with notable exceptions, theatre
and oral performance initially tended to find more welcome institutional homes in land-grant universities such as University
of Iowa, University of Wisconsin, and Indiana University. The

newer universities responded to the modified "practical" orientation of these fields. Moreover, as such universities simultaneously began making a play for disciplinary distinction, they found that they could secure prestige more immediately by cultivating newer fields.

Before returning to a more contemporary context, it might be important to keep some of these historical qualifiers in mind. Current debates about the academic legitimation of performance, theatrical and otherwise, need to be situated within larger histories of the university. Remaining cognizant of such changes is both a reminder of how relatively recent our "old" models actually are and a warning to remain vigilant about the complex and often contradictory ways that performance has found its way into the academy. Turn-of-the-century American administrators and faculty debated constantly the role of both "new" and "traditional" skills in higher education, arguing for or against them within competing "practical" and "research" models of the new university. On the one hand, rhetorical performance and the acquired competency in verbal arts were part of an *old* form of liberal education in the nineteenth century before the modern concept of the research university fell into place. As such, performance was and can still be framed as a hyper-traditional form of pedagogy that underwent significant change, reassignment, devalidation, and reinterpretation as the university's identity and mission changed. On the other hand, performance in its theatrical guise was a *new* disciplinary field at the turn of the century, one of many arguing for itself within individuating terms. It bubbled from within a newly professionalizing field of literature at certain universities. At others, it grew out of an aesthetic strain in rhetoric or in the fine and performing arts, and at others, its design and technical elements were emphasized to rationalize its location inside schools of industrial and practical arts. With varying degrees of intensity, the would-be discipline of theatre indiscriminately borrowed the language of disciplinary specialization, of practicality, of scholarly rigor, of democracy, or of civic ideals. At some universities, the Germanic influence oriented programs toward the methods of *Theaterwissenschaft*, focusing on theatre as a research object to be analyzed with the fact-based lens of the science-loving philologist. Meanwhile, more programs in the United States focused on theatre as a produced event and with an eye toward the development of the professional artist. Depending upon region, tradition, and the temperament of a university president, theatre's institutionalizers drew from available legitimating discourses, arguing for performance in expedient and occasionally contradictory terms whose institutional consequences still confuse us now.

An awareness of the various transformations of the twentieth-century university makes the shaky academic position of theatre and oral performance somewhat more interpretable. As fields of inquiry that emphasized theatrical production and technical skills in the verbal arts, performance had a "practical" side that appealed to the Jacksonian discourse of educational utility. Nevertheless, it did not immediately appear to have the scientific character of conventionally applied knowledges, such as agriculture. Moreover, while rhetorical performance could be construed as a training ground for professional competence in law and business, theatre's model of "practice" did not come with the clear capitalist promise of economic advancement. In other words, theatre's version of the practical did not appear all that pragmatic. At the same time, theatre and rhetorical performance could also have a stake in the humanistic dimensions of the university, the commitment to *Bildung* and cultural expansion that legitimated departments of English, Art History, Philosophy, and more. The tendency, however, to associate theatre with a debased and feminized form of culture kept it from being a full participant in pedagogies of acculturation. Furthermore, the emphasis on practical production – however economically impractical – spawned a fettered and cumbersome method of knowledge making, one that did not match the pure and ascetic conventions of scholarly research. Similarly, and discussed further in Chapter Two, classrooms for oratorical performance increasingly became defined as a technical arena – akin to, and eventually replaced by, the composition class; with such a move, performance's technicality became opposed to the mind-expanding classrooms of a cultural education. Of course, these larger transformations varied from university to university. In pockets, alternate pedagogies remained; some professors in the oral performance of literature worked to sustain an arena that taught technical skills alongside the cultivation of a *Bildung*-like cultural consciousness. In the mid-twentieth century, furthermore, certain colleges around the country formed with the express intention of developing an arts-based pedagogy, a phenomenon that I consider in Chapter Four.[28]

While admitting variation, it is important to take into consideration the larger social currents that structured if not determined the development of our fields and subfields. These and related institutional concerns of the *Bildung/Brotstudium* dialectic give more traction to current one-dimensional discussions of "theory" and "practice" in both theatre and performance studies. They demonstrate the historical contingency of this opposition as well as the skewed referentiality of the terms. They also suggest that the associations attached to these paradigms can be neither blithely opposed nor blithely unified. The attempt in so many theatre and performance departments to integrate the realm of the scholar-academic and the realm of the artist-practitioner is, amongst other things, an attempt to reconcile historically different occupational structures. Consequently, the relationship between theory and practice, between research and production, between scholarly and "non-scholarly" skills, requires a careful understanding of the very heavy institutional, industrial, cultural, and professional forces weighing in on such terms, on the institutional missions that they legitimate, and on the behaviors that they produce.

"New" genealogies

The current interdisciplinary discussions in the fields of performance are also structured by another historically specific influence – the restructuring of higher education based on intercultural, feminist, and non-Western critiques of its exclusions. Variously labeled "the canon wars," "the culture wars," "identity politics," and/or "multiculturalism," different aspects of a liberal arts curriculum came under scrutiny during the last two decades of the twentieth century. Attempts to expand the gender, racial, and global representation of undergraduate texts were met with defenses of traditional canons and academic "standards." Conservative thinkers such as William Bennett, E.D. Hirsch, Harold Bloom, Dinesh D'Souza, and Roger Kimball painted a nightmare vision in which great works of Western intellectual history were replaced by the lesser works of white women and writers of color; this is what Gerald Graff parodied as the "Great *Color Purple* Hoax."[29] Issues of interdisciplinarity came to the fore during this period, often supported by critiques of the canon, often castigated by defenses of the canon.

The emergence of Performance Studies in the United States was enabled, albeit unsystematically, by these adjacent movements in feminism, multiculturalism, theory, cultural studies, as well as disciplinary critiques, canon wars, and a host of other concurrent debates. While such movements spurred a variety of curricular reforms within and outside theatre departments, Richard Schechner's discourse targeted the field and departmental structures of theatre itself. As such, the phrase "performance studies" often served as a touchstone for a larger epistemological shift that promised or threatened to transform theatre's institutional status in the US academy, one that promised or threatened to transform the epistemological and political status of the arts and humanities more generally. When performance studies scholars called for an expansion of favored objects of study from drama to performance, the rhetoric sounded quite familiar. When Schechner told the ATHE membership to consider performance beyond "the enactment of Eurocentric drama," he echoed the anti-canonical arguments that were circulating in other disciplines. Similarly, Dwight Conquergood told the readers of speech communication journals that performance was key to understanding marginal cultures and their acts of resistance. Later, in Great Britain, Baz Kershaw's discussion of "the radical in performance" cast theatre as limited and conservative and performance as subversive. In all of these scenarios, performance studies aligned itself with the canon-busters, calling for the recognition of heretofore excluded people and cultural forms.

The most pained reactions against performance studies tended to accept these alignments without accepting their value system. In an essay entitled, "The Death of Literature and History," Richard Hornby castigated *The Drama Review*'s frame of reference and, under Schechner's editorship, the appearance of "articles about figure skating, folk drama in Spain, and an avant-garde performance artist in Germany" without regard for "traditional theatre."[30] Working from an affiliation in Oral Interpretation, Ted Wendt published a parallel lament on the de-privileging of oral interpretation by the frame of performance studies, a process that he argued participated in the de-valuing of literature in favor of marginal forms of cultural expression.[31] In both cases, Hornby and Wendt echoed the language of the culture wars, casting inter-disciplinary expansion as disenabling relativism. "The difference between figure skating and a production of *Hamlet* is not triv-ial," wrote Hornby.[32] The statement played into the humanist conspiracy theories of the 1990s in theatrical form. As humanist conservatives warned of the replacement of Shakespeare by Alice Walker, so their counterparts in the performing arts worried over the replacement of Shakespeare by Tonya Harding.

In most of these discussions of the relation between theatre and performance studies, there is a recurrent pattern of sense-making which elides a series of conceptual binaries. Dramatic theatre and oral interpretation are aligned with the dominant, with the canonical, and with disciplinary singularity while performance studies is aligned with the marginal, with the anti-canonical, and with disciplinary multiplicity. These moves conveniently ignore the fact that oral interpretation and dramatic literature have had marginal canonical status in the humanities, effectively treating a relatively subordinate field as dominant through an argument based on analogy rather than on institutional analysis. Given a longer academic tendency to associate theatre with a lower, feminized, and more primitive form of literary culture, the as-sertion of the dominance of the Western theatrical canon rings strangely hollow. The same goes for the field of "oral interpre-tation." The oral performance of literature is not one that most literature professors recognize as part of their field – and have not since the break between Speech and English in the early twentieth century. In sum, dramatic literature was already out-side the literary canon; the oral interpretation of literature was already a marginal cultural expression. Neither "traditionalists" nor anti-traditionalists in theatre and performance studies found it expedient to remember that history, however; they both chose to assume its stability – whether to call for canonical mainte-nance or to condemn a monolithic canonical enemy. In all cases, an appeal to "literature" served to link certain dramatic and oral performances to "tradition" despite the historic location of both on the periphery of the literary.

The elision of binaries such as old and new, disciplinary and interdisciplinary, Western and non-Western, conservative and progressive, theatre and performance, creates more obfuscations than it clears. It threatens, for instance, to ignore the scholarly and institutional efforts of those whose work addresses issues of gender, race, sex, class, and globalization from within the theatre context. An expansion of the genre of drama to the realm of performance may permit the recognition of non-Western cultures. However, if Western/non-Western too easily maps to drama/performance, then the work of, say, an African playwright is relegated to a conceptual blindspot. For some institutions, the adoption of a performance studies perspective went hand in hand with a feminist curricular revision. However, those masculinist origin stories recounted above suggest that it is just as possible to align performance studies with a macho, homophobic quest to dissociate from the feminized realm of theatre.[33] Indeed, the gendered, racial, and sexual relations between theatre and performance studies are intensely varied, contextual, and complicated. No one falls neatly into any kind of good guy/bad guy opposition. The complete elision of double binaries too neatly bypasses a variety of circuitous connections and backgrounded histories.

The class dimensions of theatre and performance studies debates are even harder to assess. It is especially difficult since class analysis returns us to the social role of higher education in a democratic state, to the cultural and economic capital upon which it relies, and to the different professional structures occupied by humanists, artists, and their students. As debates about canonical inclusion and exclusion raged during the "culture wars" of the late-twentieth century, several critics adopted a different view by considering the social location of humanities education more generally. For John Guillory, it was no coincidence that such "wars" took place in the domain of "culture" and that critiques focused on the literary-humanist syllabus. The acculturating curriculum was responsible for exposing students to a realm of philosophical, imaginative, and moral reflection, separate from – and often subordinated to – the domains of knowledge associated with economic advancement. Thus, the earlier twentieth-century legitimation of and by *Bildung* had transmogrified into a liberal humanist legitimation of and by "cultural capital." Canon wars erupted in this sphere partly because the economic stakes were lower. Debates could occur on a cultural front that was both symbolically significant and socio-economically subordinate.

The contours of those debates were complicated further by reflection on the institutional history of higher education and on the status of the "intellectual," considering not only the early twentieth-century genealogies of the "modern university" but also the various turns taken by a professionalizing professoriate in the middle to late-twentieth century. The GI-funded era of the big university contributed to both the centralizing and the marginalizing currents of liberal arts education. The promise of acculturation attracted returning students to the large lectures of the humanist syllabus while the political climate of the Cold War turned to the sciences and engineering for a relevant academic curriculum. Humanities education during the increasingly radical decade of the 1960s inherited this kind of partial and backhanded form of legitimacy while simultaneously changing its political terms. For many, the notion of "relevancy" was redefined, changing from patriotic pre-professionalism to dissident student activism. For some leftists, the space of acculturation became the space of "culture work." Though the sciences and engineering were loudly touted as the arena for the most radical forms of intellectualism, humanist intellectuals sought to channel their domain to serve radical ends. This gesture, however, was internally conflicted. Was the elite history behind the concept of acculturation so easily thrown off by the desire to create an arena of culture work? Might, furthermore, such dissident intellectualism be compromised by the fact that it increasingly took place in a professionalizing university? It was precisely by ignoring rather than addressing these questions that something like a "canon" could be figured as a site of activism. The symbolic inclusions and exclusions of cultural capital could be debated while the class politics of culture's pedagogical location could remain unremarked. The situation thus produced another version of professionalist disavowal in a new generation of academics, something anticipated in John and Barbara Ehrenreich's "The Professional-Managerial Class," developed in Alvin Gouldner's study of the "New Class," and parodied in the notion of the "literary left." The generation of 1960s dissidents who became 1980s academics could cast a suspicious eye on the content of canons while remaining obliviously blind (or self-hatingly in denial) of the professional undercurrents of humanist intellectualism.

Such class politics and histories reflect unevenly on the status of theatre, oral interpretation, performance studies, and other performance-related fields. As fields with a historically marginal status vis-à-vis the literary canon, theatre and oral interpretation had an attenuated relationship to the arena of cultural capital and an uncertain status as humanist forms of inquiry. This made the claim to canonical status resonant at some moments and misdirected at others. At the same time, and as intellectual occupations became further politicized, these fields taught skills in embodied expression that could claim an active pedagogy, an "on your feet" approach to education that underscored the "work" in culture work. Considering this complicated puzzle, it might be fruitful to adopt a both/and approach to reconciling performance in a classed chronicle of higher education. On the one hand, the proponents of performance in all its disciplinary varieties were subject to the same discursive paradoxes that shadowed other fields of both conservative and dissident humanist inquiry. As such, debates around the theatre and performance curriculum had the tone, structure, and institutional position of a canon war. On the other hand, performance exposed the class politics of literary and humanist fields. The ill-fit of its productive pedagogy placed the conventions of acculturation into high relief. To incorporate theatre and performance into the space of "culture" – whether in appreciation or as a form of activism – required not only canonical critique but also the teaching of very different skills.

The same both/and class argument applies, not only to discussions of curricular content, but also to occupational security. As Pierre Bourdieu has argued in *Homo Academicus*, the position of the humanities professor may be subordinated to the purveyors of economic capital, but it is still dominant relative to the conventionally less secure position of the artist.

As *authorities* whose position in social space depends principally on the possession of cultural capital, a subordinate form of capital, university professors are situated rather on the side of the subordinate pole of the field of power and are clearly opposed in this respect to the managers of industry and business. But, as holders of an institutionalized form of cultural capital, which guarantees them a bureaucratic career and a regular income, they are opposed to writers and artists: occupying a temporarily dominant position in the field of cultural production, they are distinguished by this fact, to differing degrees according to the faculties, from the occupants of the less institutionalized and more heretical sectors of the field.[34]

If professors and artists thus usually occupy different sectors, then it becomes clear why it can be so difficult to install the heretical arts into the institutionalized academy. In a limited field of cultural power, professors' dominance (and regular income) is dependent upon the maintenance of professional distinctions. One distinctive, if often conflictual, aspect of performance departments is that they most often hire occupants of both sectors of the cultural field. As such, they experience the tensions and possibilities of incorporated heresy.

Of course, those possibilities more often manifest as tensions. They occur every time a professor and an artist tussle over the symbolic significance of a particular art work – and, with it, jockey for the authority to make such determinations. They occur every time a theatre director seeks academic employment in order to secure medical insurance, and every time a theatre professor castigates this ignoble motivation. They occur every time an artist disdains involvement with a campus production as outside a professional career, and every time a university's promotional policy affirms that disdain. They occur every time a tenured theory professor condemns the "conservatism" of a contracted acting teacher. Indeed, class allegiance is key to understanding many a conflict between the professional artist and the professional intellectual. In performance departments of all kinds, furthermore, a varied array of occupational structures means that attributions of professional and amateur are shifting and complicated. The theatre history professor who directs a campus production may not be a "professional" to a theatre artist. The choreographer who reads Merleau-Ponty is not a "professional" to the theory professor. In these departments, all of us function as the amateur to someone else's professional, each serving as a foil for propping up the identity of the other. Such tensions perhaps too painfully expose the political genealogies of our profession. Even self-nominated "progressive" performance scholars are, like many other scholars, pulled by what Andrew Ross calls the "contradictory political interests" of the New Class: "elitist in its protection of guild privileges secured by cultural capital, but also egalitarian in its positivist vision of social emancipation for all; anti-capitalist in its technocratic challenge to the rule of capital, but also contemptuous of the 'conservative,' anti-intellectual disrespect of the popular classes."[35] These kinds of contradictions help to situate the conflicts in performance as a discourse and as an academic practice. Performance studies is not the only inheritor of New Class paradoxes. The same sensibility can be found in the liberal arts study of theatre where an admirable desire to preserve the imaginative realm of cultural reflection can simultaneously prompt a cultivated disdain for the work-a-day curriculum of the professional theatre artist, one that many scholars have conveniently called "conservative" or "anti-intellectual."

While tracts from the self-nominated "Right" have used similar political paradoxes to condemn progressivism in higher education, others such as those by Guillory, Graff, Ross, Michael Bérubé, and Cary Nelson have used them to encourage more self-reflection on the part of left-leaning academics. Surely it is possible to scrutinize relationships of class, gender, race, and occupation in presumably progressive education without assuming an anti-progressive position. Ross's critique of left narratives of the intellectual might also apply to narratives of the performance avant-garde.

[T]heories of the new class, or the professional-managerial class, have taken their toll on those intellectuals' traditions that rest upon the codes of alienated dissent or social disaffiliation. Humanists and social critics, especially, have always been loath to share the term 'intellectual' with less bona fide word brokers, and with number workers. Increasingly positioned by the contractual discourses of their institutions and professions, they have had to forsake the high ground and recognize the professional conditions they share, for the most part, with millions of other knowledge workers. The loss of this high ground has been much lamented, especially when linked to romantic left narratives about the 'decline of the public intellectual,' who, in the classical version, is a heroicized white male, and who if he is like C. Wright Mills, still rides a Harley-Davidson to his university workplace. Professional intellectuals who are not self-loathing have come to insist that it is necessary to examine their institutional affiliations in order to transform the codes of power that are historically specific to their disciplinary discourses.[36]

As an "anti-discipline" born in the 1960s and consolidated in the 1980s, performance studies participates in that era's brand of professional disavowal. As such, its language of subversion co-exists uneasily next to the language of institutionalization. Once again, it is important to note that such a contradiction is not peculiar to performance studies – and might just as easily occur in a literature, philosophy, art history, or theatre department. Thus, what Jon McKenzie identifies as the "liminal norm" in performance discourse – the impulse to link a p-word to instances of transgression, resistance, and liminality – can be seen as symptomatic of a broader thought-structure in late-twentieth-century disciplinary discussions.[37] It replicates the paradoxes, privileges, and conventions of resistant humanism. The intellectual formation that called itself performance studies can be seen as one amongst many for whom some kind of liminality became a routine way of invoking a dissident status while disavowing an increasingly professionalized one.

Discipline envy

Institutional histories are complicated; the project of interdisciplinarity is thorny; the conceptual vocabulary of performance is wide ranging. Yet all of these factors structure the terms and practices in which we work and in which we imagine we will work in the future. Theatre, dance, and performance scholars in the last decades of the twentieth century spent a great deal of time claiming to be saying something new. As Foucault's essays on the archaeology of knowledge remind us, however, the enunciative moment of an epistemic shift like performance studies is always dependent upon enabling enunciative conditions. Furthermore, the pronounced newness of such a shift is also disputable. Epistemological breaks reproduce conventions of knowledge as much as they alter them, often quietly or unself-consciously repeating aspects of the traditions that they claim to reject.

In the absence of interdisciplinary harmony, one can become knowledgeable about the relationships amongst these factors and develop tools for interdisciplinary vigilance. In the remainder of this chapter, I would like to offer a vocabulary for navigating such institutional and interdisciplinary puzzles. First of all, if there is anything that cross-disciplinary interaction teaches us, it is that attributions of sameness and difference are variable, contextual, and highly charged. Hence, it is important to be wary about the axes of sameness and difference that can present themselves as common sense or that structure interactions in unacknowledged ways. Sameness/difference constructs can work at a number of levels; institutional operations can have the character (and endure the pain) of the most intimate forms of subject formation. As such, one's disciplinary identity occurs, like any identity formation, when one is in the presence of an Other. It is in the contrast, in an encounter with difference, that one comes to understand with more complexity (or to consolidate with more jealousy) who one is and who one is becoming. Such encounters produce a psychic structure that exacerbates what Sigmund Freud called the "narcissism of minor differences."[38] One is moved to speak "as an historian" or "as an anthropologist" at precisely those times when one is speaking to people who are not historians or not anthropologists. Hence, these moments simultaneously contain the possibility for the most intense kind of self-evaluation *and* the potential for the most vociferous forms of self-delineation and disciplinary retrenchment. For some, such encounters force people to realize that they *have* a distinctive approach or perspective, that what had been a normalized, unquestioned procedure was actually a unique and contingent method of analysis. For others, such encounters serve simply to reconfirm the superiority of their own perspectives or approaches. Faced with recalcitrant Others whose perspectives and reality principles do not easily assimilate, a subject might be just as likely to foreground and reify difference. In this increasingly paranoid scenario, less similar terms are further opposed. Heretofore unnoticed attributes of one's own identity now become symbolic of one's difference, sufficiency, and uniqueness. And, when perceived power differentials unbalance the encounter, an "everyone is unlike me" strategy can easily augment into what Sverre Sjølander calls an "everyone but me is an idiot" stance toward interdisciplinary interaction.[39] And, like any identity formation, one's structural position and relative institutional power will probably influence which of these options one takes. In the university context, the relative distribution of economic and cultural capital creates the uneven power field in which such choices emerge.

The energy behind the quest for self-differentiation can also quite easily flip into an opposite, and equally aggressive, quest for resemblance. A subject's encounter with an Other can take shape as an excessive *we are all alike* model of cross-disciplinary interaction. In this alternatively narcissistic scenario, superficial characteristics are misrecognized as indicators of similarity. The use of the same keyword, an alliterative link between less similar words, an easy definitional equation, all assure the subject that disparate inquiries, methods, and objects belong under one umbrella. This kind of orientation – what might be called a *narcissism of minor samenesses* – becomes even more urgent, furthermore, when the principle of sameness is one's own umbrella. Unevenly propelled by intellectual power differentials, the "we are all alike" model quickly transmogrifies into an "everyone is just like me" model. Here, the components of one's own identity – one's own approach, one's own objects of inquiry, one's own reality principles, one's own department – are held up as the unifying solution to everyone else's confusion. In the evangelical urge to craft a new knowledge formation – such as performance studies – the risk of a narcissism of minor samenesses is probably even more acute. Varieties of p-words can be assumed to cohere, indeed must cohere in order to establish epistemological legitimacy, renegade and otherwise.

Issues of sameness and difference face another register of complexity when such Self/Other constructs meet the multiplicity/singularity dyads of interdisciplinary thinking. While interdisciplinarity is conceived as a realm of the multiple – and opposes itself to disciplinarity's realm of the singular – it turns out that perceptions of multiplicity and singularity are variable and site-specific. They rely on shared and reproducible assumptions of what is already different and already the same. Thus, a mode of inquiry may be comprised of various components that, over time and through exercises of disciplinary self-instruction, come to feel like attributes of the same field. Meanwhile, the same attributes might be received from a different perspective to represent quite different fields of inquiry. For instance, a theatre department's conventional mid-century division of academic labor often included historians, dramatic literature scholars, and director/artists. While these orientations occupied the same field within theatre, each mirrored a different network of methods, skills, and reality principles, networks that appeared separately in History, English, and Art departments. The question of whether such clusterings constitute divisions of labor within the Same or are interdisciplinary indicators of Difference is far from clear. In a more recent context, attributions of multiplicity and singularity were further confused. While one might assume a trans-historical equivalence between generalism and interdisciplinarity, certain kinds of interdisciplinarity appeared quite specialist to certain eyes. Similarly, while a multicultural movement sought to value multiplicity, it received the specialist appellation (often "special interest") from conservative thinkers for whom Western intellectual history was paradoxically more general. Rather than approaching this puzzle with the hope of absolutely assimilating or absolutely differentiating selves, others, and their internal attributes, it is perhaps more useful to operate knowing that heterogeneity and homogeneity are never absolute but shift with altered perspective -- and political interest.

An analytic knowledge of academic institutional structures and of the history of academic institutions facilitates such destabilizing, and hence illuminating, alterations in perspective. It is probably no surprise to most critical theorists to hear that narcissism and paranoia -- in both their productive and paralyzing forms -- go hand in hand with interdisciplinary interaction. In addition to the multiplicity/singularity construct, the psychically complicated conundrums of sameness/difference also interact with other terms of alliance and opposition, dyads such as "old and new" or "inside and outside." Significantly, such terms and psychic mechanisms emerge and maintain their potency by acting in concert with institutional structures and histories. They become most forceful in naturalizing the organization of knowledge, especially when such structures and histories are disavowed. Recognizing their influence thus assists in defamiliarizing normalized categories of knowledge, even categories that neither self-proclaimed progressive nor conservative scholars are always interested in interrogating. Historical knowledge questions the ease with which delineations of old and new are mapped. Sometimes movements cast as traditional turn out to be relatively recent and once transgressive formations. Other times, movements cast as new turn out to reproduce many of the conventions and structures that they claim to transcend. Institutional structures further affect what we perceive to be inside and outside our own lines of inquiry, tacitly dividing our understanding of what is internal to our field and what is external. Comparative and historical analyses of different universities reveal the contingency of such constructs. Since each university found its own way of responding to the utilitarian, disciplinary, and demographic pressures of the twentieth-century university, each positioned theatre and performance somewhat differently as well.

Institutional structures also entail differences of institutional power, an unevenness that affects who borrows from whom in an interdisciplinary encounter, whose histories are foregrounded, and who takes credit for interdisciplinary innovation. These factors can take shape in a number of ways. First, all parties may be subject to the vagaries of the synecdochic fallacy, the tendency to assume that one approach or movement or piece of scholarship can represent an entire discipline. In this scenario, a single famous author stands in for many. A body of texts serves as shorthand for much larger traditions of scholarship. Subfields are misrecognized as entire fields. One variant of the synecdochic fallacy occurs in the selective appropriation of a borrowed discipline in order to stage a break with one's own. The result is a selective "it's new to you" attitude toward a method or an argument that does not remember that such methods or arguments are old to someone else. The fallout of these synecdochic fallacies and these "it's new to you" trajectories will be different based on the relative power of borrowed and borrowing fields. Members of a field whose reputation and cultural capital is solidly rooted in the university may feel more able to experiment without threatening their institutional position. Such scholars' forays into adjacent fields may spice up their own work, give it a new angle or a new object, without seeming to require an investigation of the borrowed discipline's wider discussions and legacies. In this scenario, one scholar's tradition is transformed into another scholar's innovative experiment. Members of a less established field may be just as subject to synecdochic misrecognition; however, as a wide range of cultural theory makes clear, subordinate subjects usually do a better job of learning the ways and wiles of the dominant. Nevertheless, the "borrowing up" performed by scholars in less powerful fields – whether done for experiment or, more often, for intellectual legitimacy – can also remain ignorant of larger inter-locutionary contexts.

These and related topics will be expanded and re-positioned in the various chapters that follow. Each addresses a particular network of epistemological dilemmas and opportunities via a selected theme and a range of case studies. Together they offer different ways of conceiving and interpreting genealogical continuities and discontinuities in the disciplining of performance. I have selected moments on a loose chronological plane, examining key intellectual developments in philology, new criticism, cultural studies, deconstruction, new historicism, and post-structuralist theory throughout the twentieth century in order to locate "the space" in which performance's epistemological objects emerge. Chapter Two focuses most explicitly on the nature of "institutionalization" as it impinged upon the early formation of theatre studies at the beginning of the twentieth century, using the figure of George Pierce Baker as a springboard. By looking more specifically at how the conventions of professionalization and curricular legitimation affected the development of theatre, rhetoric, and performance, I interrogate terminologies and expose paradoxes that still affect and afflict the status of performance in today's university. Chapter Three considers the intellectual genealogies of the 1940s and 1950s in order to resituate performance's relationship to "cultural studies." While the latter interdisciplinary field is conventionally invoked as a recent and "trendy" intellectual formation, an examination of its earlier history in Great Britain reveals early alignments between the study of drama and the study of "culture," shaky allegiances that nevertheless challenge assumptions of what is old and new, traditional and "cutting edge," in theatre and performance studies scholarship. The association of performance with a kind of anti-intellectual "literalism" and pre-professional "practice" provides the foundation for Chapter Four, using it to speculate more generally on the legacies of philosophical and artistic experimentation of the 1960s and 1970s. This chapter continues Chapter Two's excavation of the role of art production in performance curricula while simultaneously examining discourses in the visual arts and in deconstructive philosophy that complicated the conceptual status of performance in several disciplines. In Chapter Five, I consider the connections and disconnections between performance and the writing of "history," particularly focusing on the epistemic impact of cultural anthropology and new historicism in the 1980s. Situating the so-called "cultural turn" next to debated practices in theatre historiography and alongside the institutional story of performance studies, this chapter foregrounds less-remembered intellectual genealogies in literature, performance, theatre, and anthropology while considering the gender politics of their disavowal. Finally, Chapter Six takes a sustained look at theatre and performance next to the provocative and multifaceted paradigms of performativity as the twentieth century gave over to the twenty-first. While offering a fuller account and revision of the terms that opened this chapter, I also interrogate the conflicted and contradictory effects of the "culture wars" and "identity politics" on performance practices and performance theorizing.

I have found the case study approach to be selective but essential to tracking the internal discontinuities of theoretical, disciplinary, and institutional processes. While this kind of specificity is necessary to understand epistemological contingency, I do try to abstract key concepts and invite application and revision through other examples. Nevertheless, there are obviously many issues and sites that I do not address in this book. I focus most explicitly on higher education in the United States, noting international influence and variation only selectively. Many of the institutional and disciplinary dilemmas are thus distinctive to or exacerbated by an "American" location; surely the utilitarian celebration and humanist skepticism of a term such as "practice" becomes particularly virulent in its capitalist context. Additionally, though I consider the history of a range of performance forms in higher education, this book emphasizes the institutional histories of theatre, speech, and performance studies in the context of literature, cultural studies, and the general humanities. My ardent hope is that other scholars contribute to the larger story of performance's genealogy in the academy, importing and resituating the arguments that I offer here by analyzing parallel movements in greater North America, Europe, Asia, Africa, South America, and Australia and by mapping more specific institutional histories of dance, visual art, folklore, and of key wings in the social sciences.

Performance and performance-inflected vocabularies have an overwhelming number of meanings, connotations, and intellectual legacies. This kind of discursive flexibility interacts with a larger field power – namely the forces of gender, race, sexuality, and class – in diffuse and exponentially complicated ways. Each of my analyses considers such factors while being acutely aware of their variation. In order to characterize some structures within this discursive plenitude, I have found it helpful to focus on what might be termed the "flexible essentialism" of performance, that is, its tendency to inhabit the essentialist as well as anti-essentialist side of any conceptual binary. Terms such as performance or theatre are often used as metaphors for representation and, in other contexts, are invoked to ground the "real." While a history of Western thought associates performance with the figural, the allegorical, and the copy, a host of critical theorists in the late twentieth century used performance examples to characterize the literal, the stable, or the naïvely authentic. These divided tendencies are only exacerbated in a university context, where performance has been the site of some of the most intensely anti-essentialist theoretical speculation and where, conversely, its artistic practitioners often invoke the term to stall theoretical musing. As a result, the disciplinary genealogies of performance tend not to have one feminist reading nor one implication for an anti-racist politics. Attributions of masculinity and femininity in the study of theatre can cut both ways and change with definitional relation. Sometimes, theatre's association with artifice and deception reproduce classical stereotypes of the feminine. Sometimes theatre's practices of collectivity and publicity align it with a masculine performance of democratic citizenship. Sometimes theatre is equated with high-brow elitism; other times, its proponents and its detractors emphasize theatre's infrastructural and technical dimensions to create a classed portrait of industrial labor. White women and people of color may find themselves equivocally positioned by theatre's theoretical flexibility, for a performance frame can simultaneously open the door to non-dominant forms of cultural production while at the same time submitting those forms and those cultures to the most insidious modes of stereotyping. Theatre and performance further change their gendered, race, sexed, and classed associations depending upon the disciplinary, interdisciplinary, regional, and university context. Attributions of femininity vary if theatre is opposed to film or to literature, to technology or to folklore. Its class allegiances change depending whether it is located in a liberal arts college, a technical school, or a research university. In the disciplining of performance, there are no clear good guys or bad guys, no single silver bullet with which to receive and resolve a critical, political, and occupational puzzle. As the referent for theatre changes, furthermore, the nature of the anti-theatrical prejudice changes with it. Indeed, "the anti-theatrical prejudice" is not a singular thought-structure but itself, multiple, opportunistic, and a constantly moving target. For that reason, a case study approach offers the most responsible way to test analytic approaches, to de-mystify our field's defense mechanisms, and to imagine our field's future.

An awareness of variation and contingency adds more dimension to the interdisciplinary puzzle. It serves as a warning against assuming the normalcy and naturalness of one's own present-day institutional context, forcing a heightened awareness of epistemological complacency. It suggests that an institution's common-sense unions and divisions conceal histories of disavowed difference and disavowed connection. There is a great deal of heterogeneity within sameness and a great deal of similarity within difference. There are also many older legacies repeated within new movements, and a great deal of change within apparent reproductions of tradition. As hard as it is to say something new, it is perhaps (*pace* Foucault) equally impossible not to. Our understanding of disciplinary and interdisciplinary operations should shift with historical perspective and institutional location, a slipperiness that might in turn unsettle easy alliances and convenient oppositions in our current ways of talking about ourselves. The challenge is to make the harder alliances and to devise new types of self-description. Whether falling across axes of multiplicity and singularity, traditional and non-traditional, inside and outside, our conventional assertions of disciplinary sameness and difference can be disrupted by a consciousness of institutional history. That consciousness confronts some of the occupational hazards of inhabiting an emergent field by guarding against its reinvention of the wheel and by loosening the selective vocabularies that threaten to inhibit the breadth and depth of that emergence. Finally, it provides a variety of templates for the kind of arguments that theatre and performance scholars need to make, preparing us for those vexed and confusing conversations (remember the department meetings, the office hours, the conferences, the rehearsals) where invoking an historical allusion or noting an unacknowledged connection will make the difference in getting some pedagogical work done.

2 Institutions and performance: professing performance in the early twentieth century

"Our professional protocols of value [are] being squeezed by a system whose ideal image of itself promotes theoretically sophisticated, interdisciplinary work in extraliterary studies but whose material base is shrinking . . . it was roughly twenty years ago that Richard Ohmann pointed out, in *English in America*, that the profession of English studies thought of itself as doing criticism and theory but was in actuality devoting half of its courses to introductory composition." Michael Bérubé[1]

"What a deal: by honoring our own history we get to lead the hottest trends." Joseph Roach[2]

To profess performance

In 1905, Professor George Lyman Kittredge, Chairman of the English department at Harvard University, dropped a note to his colleague Professor George Pierce Baker. The latter had been concerned that one of Kittredge's new hires might have designs on the teaching of "the drama" and thus designs on Baker's own curricular territory. Kittredge sought to mollify Baker's anxiety. "You may feel quite secure," he wrote, "as to any cutting into your special field."[3] The sentence reproduced the content and form of an all-too familiar interaction between empowered chairman and paranoid colleague. And, as is often true of such interactions, it also revealed a hint of intellectual condescension within its gesture of institutional assurance, one that left flexible whether the word "special" had the connotation of the extraordinary, the narrow, or the peripheral.

Similar kinds of anxieties can be found in the archives of other key figures in the early institutionalization of performance in the American academy. As such, they anticipate the kinds of

defensive anxieties that contemporary proponents of performance find themselves enduring. George Pierce Baker and
other white academic American men – Brander Matthews at
Columbia, Thomas Dickinson at Wisconsin, Frederick Koch
at North Carolina, Thomas Wood Stevens at Carnegie Tech –
figure prominently in what Joseph Roach calls the "myths of origin" of theatre studies. "What is striking at first glance is how
very different these pioneers' objects of study were," says Joseph
Roach, "Different, yes, but they are all in some way focused
on performance."[4] Roach uses their unified eclecticism in part
to make an argument for "performance" as a conceptual and
methodological turn with which theatre might "lead the hottest"
trends in a current academic climate. Roach's invocation of these
names is strategic; they are the figures who are heroically and
sometimes melodramatically chronicled in the struggling, perpetually marginalized field of theatre studies. Written for an
audience of theatre history scholars, Roach's polemic brings
comfort to those who are dubious about "trendiness," suggesting that theatre studies has been doing performance studies all
along. The hottest trend, according to this argument, is really
traditional; the new is old after all. At the same time, Roach's
recognition that each of these disciplinary pioneers was quite
"different" is potentially somewhat less comforting, for the imputed sameness of "theatre" across objects and histories underwrote the formation of the discipline in the first place.

In this chapter, my first goal is to investigate these genealogies
of disciplinary difference and the relationship of that difference
to performance. While I focus on one of Roach's figures, George
Pierce Baker, I will also suggest that there are even more "myths
of origin" and much more "difference" with which to contend.
The discipline of American theatre studies offers one discontinuous genealogy of performance, but, as Paul Edwards has shown,
a rhetorical genealogy in Speech and Oratory plots another route;
a dance orientation might suggest a different set of moves, according to Alexandra Carter.[5] Each of these performance fields
has a different notion of what history needs to be honored, and
the behaviors to which each refers – whether performed in a
classroom, in a theatre, or in a gymnasium – endure different
types of curricular and extra-curricular legitimation. While incorporating these strains of performance study, I also investigate

their fundamental connections to other fields, such as English, Architecture, and Art Practice, that are reputedly not about performance at all. If a current performance paradigm sees sameness in disciplines that were once-different, an historical genealogy of performance must also emphasize how now-different fields were once-the-same. Rather than defending or rejecting terms such as "drama" or "art" or "speech" or "literature," I am most interested in thinking about how such concepts become discursive touchstones for attributing and withdrawing value at different moments in the academy. Often this is about re-casting what we already know about disciplinary history into a differently aimed kind of argument. As it turns out (and as Roach knows well) "honoring our own history" turns out to be a messy business. It is unclear whether "honoring" is exactly the right verb; it is less clear who is included in the "we" behind the possessive "our," and multiple claims of possession make the assumption of ownership next to impossible. In such a context, instances of anxiety and defensiveness proliferate.

As I argued in the previous chapter, paranoid and/or narcissistic delineations of sameness and difference are exacerbated by fields of institutional power. Hence, my second goal in this chapter is to track some of the institutional processes that both reflect and reproduce these power fields. What kind of work must proponents do to install an academic field? What particularly does it mean to advocate the study of performance in American higher education? Investigating issues of performance's institutionalization is lamentably not always the same as investigating developments in performance scholarship. It can be somewhat jarring to realize that there is a difference. This is the kind of realization that one begins to have in graduate school. Here, and depending upon the type of program, students learn not only about theory or history, not only about image or embodiment, but also about conference participation, about audition processes, about job interviews, about portfolios, head-shots, and curricula vitae. The realization is advanced further with an academic appointment where one contends with departmental divisions, school divisions, job placement, graduation requirements, building infrastructure, curricular breakdowns, and departmental divisions of labor. Usually such questions are compartmentalized somewhere else in the mind of an academic. They are categorized as "my service," as "my committee work," and as opposed to "my research" (or, more insidiously, "my own work").

This chapter takes a closer look at a more defined network of histories and processes. My hope is to consider the early twentieth-century institutionalization of performance in order to illuminate some contemporary concerns about what it means to profess performance in the early twenty-first century. Along the way, I seek to de-familiarize, if not exactly to dislodge, the occupational processes that we sometimes vilify, sometimes celebrate, and sometimes decide to ignore. Occasionally, this is also about re-familiarization, about seeing our behaviors and everyday processes as both structured by and structuring larger questions of value and authority. The first sections use George Pierce Baker's early career to examine the emergence of academic careerism as well as to trace rhetorical and literary philological trends that antedated, and in some ways anticipated, Baker's turn to theatrical performance. The final sections examine the institutional, gendered, and classed contingencies of that turn. Throughout, I connect this multifarious history to contemporaneous figures in higher education and to current debates. At the same time, I also consider what I earlier referred to as the "ill-fit" of performance within certain kinds of legitimating discourses in order to highlight, and perhaps to challenge, the conventions of legitimation itself. The educational practice of performance can disrupt historical and critical accounts of educational practice more generally. Sometimes performance counters understandings of ideological trends in higher education; other times it troubles conventional interpretive frameworks and modes of categorization. Tracking this kind of ill-fit – and performance's attempts *to fit* – thus adds another dimension to a larger body of scholarship on the idea of the university as well as on the employment of the arts and humanities.

In many ways, the early story of theatre's institutionalization is also a story of racial and gender privilege. This is not to say that white female educators and intellectuals of color did not take an avid interest in theatrical performance. Prominent black intellectuals such as W.E.B. DuBois and Alain Locke experimented with performance at Fiske and Howard Universities.[6] Spelman's status as a premiere black women's college allowed the incorporation of theatre as a means of racial uplift.[7] Young dramatists such as Josephina Niggli found ways of using Frederick Koch's folklore-based program at the University of North Carolina to stage Mexican-American experience.[8] Meanwhile, female teachers of various races promoted theatre education in child and community development. However, the institutional voice for academic performance largely belonged to professors who were white and male. Discussions of departmentalization, curriculum, professionalization, and academic legitimation took place in an administrative arena dominated by white men. It was also subject to the blindspots, value judgments, and projected anxieties of such a sphere. As it happens, the phenomena of theatre and performance provide a means of exposing those anxieties and showing their effects in the institutional process of disciplinary formation.

Mr. Baker's profession

In my opening anecdote of 1905, Chairman Kittredge and Professor Baker inhabited an English department that was in the midst of a transformation in the field of literary studies and in the organization of higher education. As such, they were also negotiating the interpersonal conflicts and inter-office paranoias that drive and derive from occupational changes. Baker's background was similar to many of his contemporary pro-performance colleagues at other universities. Though twenty years later Baker would become the founder of the oft-renowned Yale School of Drama, at the turn-of-the-century, he was a teacher of Rhetoric in an English department. He was a professor who began with dual interests in literary research and in oral pedagogy. His interests transmogrified from a focus on argumentation to a curious fixation on the oral performance of the drama, proceeding apace down a slippery slope that went from the oral performance of Shakespeare, to the oral performance of "drama exclusive of Shakespeare," to the promotion of campus play production, to the writing of new plays by the students themselves. The same year as his exchange with Kittredge, Baker had published "The Mind of the Undergraduate," a document that condemned the apathetic indolence of the typical Harvard student who had no "original ideas" and displayed "absolute imperviousness to the ideas for which he is supposed to be taking the course."[9] Baker would later characterize his involvement with academic drama as facilitating the needs of students who were "stirred to expression," suggesting that he found in theatre a means of solving the problem of student apathy and of tapping an otherwise dormant student desire.[10]

To consider performance in this era of higher education is useful for a number of reasons. US colleges and universities grappled with their relationship to a changing American society. They argued over access to higher education for women, for newer immigrants, for African-Americans, and for the children of both the industrial bourgeoisie and working classes. For numerous historians of higher education, this was a pivotal period. It solidified a nineteenth-century shift in the content of academic knowledge from a classical to a vernacular curriculum, backgrounding the study of Greek and Latin in favor of an ever-expanding list of fields in cultural and scientific study. It also ushered in the era of "professionalism," an economic and discursive formation that differently but pervasively inflected both professors' sense of their students' educational goals as well as their own sense of their positions as "career academics." With increased enrolments and a booming US economy, it was also a time when the economic capital and architectural image of the university expanded. Harvard University president Charles Eliot is the administrative figure to whom higher education historians continually refer to illustrate these changes. In 1869, Eliot devised a curricular program in what he termed "liberal culture," ostensibly to promote the widest range of vernacular learning in a context that also attended to the ethical development of a new generation of American citizens. Along the way, he changed the delivery and dissemination of his college's courses, installing the "elective system" in order to match a democratizing curriculum with a democratic structure of selection.[11] Next to his active role in redefining the instruction of higher education, he was also extensively involved in the business of higher education. As such, his situation anticipated the network of interests – and conflicts of interest – that contemporary critics now call the corporatization of the university. Eliot attracted funders, oversaw infrastructural expansion, instituted standards for faculty evaluation, balanced budgets, counted enrolments, and remained accountable to a board of trustees and economic authorities that called itself – in a once-classical, now fiscal, turn of phrase – The Corporation.

Professionalization meant that the always conflicted position of the academic came to inhabit another type of conflicted situation with which we are now quite familiar though not necessarily reconciled. To give this transformation more dimension, consider Barbara and John Ehrenreich's Marxist critique of what they famously called the "professional-managerial class." The Ehrenreichs include "college professors" in what they identify as an emerging PMC, one broadly "consisting of salaried mental workers who do not own the means of production and whose major function in the social division of labor may be described broadly as the reproduction of capitalist culture and capitalist relations."[12] As salaried mental workers, college professors are aligned with engineers, journalists, social service providers, clerical workers, medical workers, and others who gained their identity by accessing specialized knowledge and by claiming their authority as "experts." The Ehrenreichs identify a paradox in that, despite their role in the reproduction of capitalist relations, PMC members often invoke an "anti-capitalist" rhetoric. Take the college example. As the demographics of the US university changed, new students increasingly saw a college education as an opportunity for class mobility and economic advancement. While this shift was "progressive" from one perspective, from another it also over-determined the social role of higher education. Many academics, meanwhile, worked to maintain a separate professional position outside relations of capitalism and commerce, sometimes by adopting explicitly socialist language, other times by calling for the safe preservation of moral and cultural inquiry. Humanities professors in particular tried to create a separate sphere of cultural capital while simultaneously legitimating themselves curricularly and institutionally within professionalizing terms. This made for a messy, complex, and occasionally self-contradicting context for humanist self-definition. As PMC members, humanities professors would argue for occupational "autonomy" – e.g. "academic freedom" – while remaining enmeshed in a university's relations of production and while teaching students who would enter capitalist occupations. As "professionals" outside of the capitalist industries that they simultaneously reproduced, the idea of "technical knowledge" would be variously defined. Sometimes this discourse supported a salaried humanist's own claims to rigor, advanced training, and expertise. Other times it characterized a pedagogical ground, whether "manual" or "pre-professional," whose character and goals were opposed to a humanistic project. The PMC critique adds more complexity to a chronicle of higher education. The opposition between "research" and "practice" may designate a difference in the curricular orientation of a college course, but it does not necessarily designate a difference in the social role of any particular kind of college professor.

"Now about your personal prospects," President Charles Eliot wrote an advisory letter to his faculty member, George Pierce Baker. Baker also happened to be Eliot's nephew by marriage. "I believe that you are in a fair way to get promotion at Cambridge in time. If your publishers can tell you just where your books have been introduced, I should like to know the facts. They might be useful with the Corporation."[13] Eliot wrote in 1895, ten years before Kittredge's discussion of that "special field" and before Baker's interest in the theatre had taken hold. Eliot obviously had a personal interest in Baker's personal prospects. Nonetheless, his note illustrates the enmeshment of both men in the professionalizing class of higher education. As a salaried mental worker, Baker would need to characterize and quantify his contribution to knowledge. This early example of Baker's participation in the modern organization of knowledge anticipated the characteristic structures of the PMC as the Ehrenreichs defined them, specifically:

a) the existence of a specialized body of knowledge, accessible only by lengthy training
b) the existence of ethical standards which include a commitment to public service and
c) a measure of autonomy from outside interference in the practice of the profession (e.g. only members of the profession can judge the value of a fellow professional's work).[14]

Baker's evaluation for promotion in 1895 reflected the beginnings of this process of professional structuration. Beyond notifying the Corporation of "where [his] books have been introduced," colleagues at various universities throughout the nation were asked to submit a written assessment of Baker's work. While brief and perfunctory by contemporary standards, this was an early version of a process that confirmed the existence of specialized knowledge by requiring specialists to evaluate it. As a member of what might be called the "professorial-managerial class," Baker thus endured the anxiety of the "peer review" on which professionalism depends and enjoyed the relative intellectual autonomy that such peer reviews ensure.

That this kind of evaluation happened within the context of an English department was also noteworthy, especially because the professional status of the English professor was somewhat uncertain as the century changed. At most research universities, the field of "English" would become the most powerful field in the increasingly unempowered domain of the humanities. As the field from which so many performance professors reportedly broke free, it is useful to examine the marginally dominant status of this domain in order to better understand the counter-identity project of performance in the same period. Literature was in danger of not faring very well within professionalist modes of legitimation. As Lawrence Vesey, John Guillory, Gerald Graff, and others have argued, these fields thus had manifestly to make themselves "rigorous," to become knowledges based in evidence. Emerging literature professors worked to define their object of knowledge with clear rules to replace nebulous belletrism and to fend off their association with the feminine. German philology entered and/or was imported precisely to lend the study of literature this necessary positivism, a specialist training in historical research, etymology, and the accumulation of facts that pushed to develop a science of the literary and thus to assure all involved that literature professors had an object of study. Such manifest rigor warded off feminizing discourses of delegitimation that derived from the university's changing demographics of class, ethnicity, and gender. Philology kept literature from appearing to be a sentimental field that appealed only to the co-eds. To give this some contemporary institutional significance, Graff and Guillory both situate current training in "Theory" on a historical plane with philology (with New Criticism in between). Of course, philology and most critical theory are very different in the content of their intellectual assumptions and in their espoused gender politics; nevertheless, they occupy a similar structural position from the perspective of professional history. They both serve a similar function in the mechanics of professionalization and scholarly "training" within the arts and humanities. It is this kind of coincidence that exposes the interdependence between the production of ideas and the production of professionalism.

How did these transformations manifest themselves? Richard Moulton, Professor of Literature at University of Chicago from 1892 to 1919, provides a statement on the kinds of rationales that lay behind the move to scientific literary criticism. "In the treatment of literature the proposition which seems to stand most in need of assertion is, *that there is an inductive science of literary criticism.* As botany deals inductively with the phenomena of vegetable life and traces the laws underlying them; as economy reviews and systematizes on inductive principles of commerce, so there is a criticism not less inductive in character which has for its subject-matter literature."[15] Moulton felt compelled to assert defensively that "there is" an object of study and used the scientific analogy to do it. (It is perhaps no coincidence that this passage also anticipates the specialist tendency to make nouns – e.g. "system" – into verbs.) Differentiating between judicial criticism and his own inductions, Moulton used the example of Ben Jonson. "Judicial criticism can see how the poet was led astray: the best of his disposition induced him to sacrifice dramatic propriety to his satiric purpose." Inductive criticism by contrast did away with judgments and sought to track only the facts of influence and transformation, pictured by Moulton as a literary approximation of the biological laboratory. "Induction has another way of putting the matter: that the poet has utilized dramatic form for satiric purpose; thus by the cross-fertilization of two existing literary species has added to literature a third including features of both."[16] Contemporary critics might have different responses to this discursive legacy, identifying and disidentifying at once. Academic humanists today often still need to confirm to our science colleagues that we have a subject at all – and, moreover, that it requires skill, training, and discipline to do it. Many might also side with Moulton against evaluative, hierarchical, taste-based judgments of cultural forms. At the same time, many might not respond to the language of science (of species and fertilization) nor to the quest for objectivity in a critical project.

By 1905, Chairman George Lyman Kittredge emerged as one of the foremost practitioners of literary philology in the United States. At the same time, the rise of his reputation as a researcher coincided with a shift in the administrative organization of the

American university, one that dispersed power into discrete departments, one that granted the "department chair" a relatively
large amount of institutional control.[17] As such, the moment
when Kittredge dropped his chairman's note was also a moment
when the promoter of a then "trendy" intellectual movement –
philology – was simultaneously in the midst of exercising a position of intellectual and organizational power. Kittredge is now an
oft-chronicled figure in the disciplinary history of literary studies
and hence *its* "myths of origin." His reputation for introducing
dispassion and objectivity into the field of literature is legendary.
In graduate school conversations, students who dared to question the appropriateness of the literature professor's interest in
"mere facts" famously endured his disdain. "'I am interested,'
was the withering response, 'in nothing but facts.'"[18] Kittredge's
orientation was castigated by some even as it secured his national fame. As with contemporary anti-theoretical backlashes
now, many worried that philology's success in establishing the
profession of literary studies de-centralized the appreciation of
literature itself. As one skeptic wrote, "We are inclined to doubt
whether he considers it any part of his function to import to
his students a love of literature."[19] Nevertheless, the accumulation of historical knowledge clarified a researcher's contribution,
making President Eliot's process of faculty evaluation that much
easier.

Interestingly, this same detractor who questioned Kittredge's
love of literature also imagined another kind of dire future. "And
it is when you see the newly fledged philologist at work, teaching
composition (and which he has never practiced) . . . it is then
that you begin to recognize that something is out of joint in the
state of Denmark."[20] This writer unwittingly revealed competing assumptions about the role of the English department. While
at some moments, its role was to extend a love of literature, at
others it was to teach the much more mundane basic skills of
composition. Presumably someone who "loved literature" and
someone who had philological aspirations would be equally as
frustrated by the task of teaching composition. The statement's
blindspot illustrates a much bigger disavowal. As John Guillory
has argued, the teaching of basic writing testifies to the social role
of the English department in the production of a skilled managerial labor force, a function that remains the *impensé* of the
literary professoriate.[21] Here is one of many moments when all

involved – both theoretically rigorous researchers *and* morally righteous literature lovers – elected not to notice the participation of English in the reproduction of capitalist relations.

What does this discussion about love, about literature, about professionalism, and composition have to do with performance? Dramatic literature, especially drama "exclusive of Shakespeare," risked associations with the feminine, the primitive, and the commercial in a way that threatened the profession of literature's redefined story about itself as a masculine, hard science. Whether theatre could transcend these associations was still debatable in the early twentieth century. Hence, the condescending assurance and hedged institutional protection of a trendy philologist like George Lyman Kittredge vis à vis a professor like George Pierce Baker. As Michael Quinn and Marvin Carlson have noted, philology's relationship to drama was relatively problematic for many a German professor.[22] Both Quinn and Carlson emphasize the significance of *Theatrewissenschaft* as a research paradigm in Europe, one whose processes set the terms and conventions of what would become theatre historiography. Back in the United States, the adoption of philological methods was more scattered, sometimes done begrudgingly, other times mimicked in spite of a scholar's own anti-philological pronouncements.

Baker's writing career illustrated the ambivalence. In 1895, he had two books to offer for "peer review," one on techniques of argumentation derived from his rhetoric teaching, the other an annotated edition of John Lyly's *Endymion*. The latter reflected the impact of philological trendiness on his own thinking, or at least, on his own perceptions of what he should be thinking. Kittredge, then at the beginning of his relationship with Baker, was exceedingly complimentary, writing as one who imagined a future for his young colleague.

Dear Baker, I have put off thanking you for your *Lyly* until I should find time to read the introduction with something of the care which it evidently deserved. . . . I hasten to offer my warmest congratulations on so thorough and scholarly a piece of work . . . Of course there are details in which I'm not convinced, but, throughout, your reasoning seems to me, with very few exceptions, quite cogent, and nobody can say that you haven't made clear the distinction between facts and hypotheses. In a word, I have only one regret – that the book, with its masterly introduction, isn't in *my* series instead of in Holt's. Your command of the details of your subject is amazing.[23]

Kittredge's invocation of "thoroughness," his discourse on "details," and his riding assumption of the importance of a fact/hypothesis distinction testify to the effects of scientific models on "masterly" humanist knowledge formations. That "no one could say" that Baker did not tow the line in this domain suggests that Kittredge had wondered whether Baker could do it. Reflecting an emergent circle of literary professionals, Richard Moulton himself was called upon to respond to the book and did so: "Baker has rendered a distinct service to literary study by editing this work, a type of a class of literature not generally accessible. I appreciate further the research that has gone to produce that life of the author."[24] Moulton and others in his peer review agreed with Kittredge, confirming Baker's promising status as a would-be expert.

The reaction of another colleague to the same book illustrates that scholastic debates about the fashion and future of literary studies were being waged in Harvard's English department. Barrett Wendell, Baker's early mentor and eventual author of an eclectic body of scholarship in rhetoric, composition, Shakespeare, and literary history, was the first professor to introduce a course in "drama exclusive of Shakespeare" at Harvard and hence was cautiously sympathetic to Baker's emerging interests. In 1895, however, he gave an unenthusiastic response to "the Lyly."

In its way, the *Lyly* seems to be admirable. Its way, too, is that from which, as a professional scholar!, you should expect distinction . . . While I heartily admire it, though, I cannot honestly say that it gives me pleasure as a reader. . . . I am overwhelmed with facts; and have no imaginative impulse to make me feel how these facts differ from those of antiquity and of our own time . . . You know me well enough to understand how coyly I try for such a type of scholarship as shall not only possess the minute accuracy which is now the fashion, but also vivify its facts with bold constructive imagination which shall not fear to state its faith . . . Imagination you had in the old days. You have been right, perhaps, in checking it. Professionally you are certainly right . . . I heartily hope, though, that you will not end with work like this.[25]

Wendell's references to the lack of pleasure, to the lack of vivification, to minute accuracy, to the necessity to check an imagination, exemplified anti-philological reaction. They also anticipate the terms in which the "new" trends of "Theory" would be criticized one hundred years later. Wendell's use of the term "professional" and "distinction" testified to the change in institutional practice, one that could be defensively characterized as part of a "fashion." All of the terms together in a paragraph that digressed into what "I try for" in scholarship exemplify the narcissistic and paranoid structures of an intellectual climate buffeted by a field of institutional power.

Baker submitted another type of writing for peer review in 1895, namely his book on the practice of argumentation. The coincidence provides an opportunity to incorporate another performance genealogy in literary studies, one that returns us to the "composition" class about which few wanted to think. Being a book that derived from Baker's background in rhetoric, the coincidence also highlights a less well-remembered and decidedly discontinuous rhetorical genealogy in the study of performance, one that in turn plots a different route to alternate "myths of origin." First, I want to back up by recalling the placement of oral performance as a kind of pre-origin in the field of literature, in the practice of theatre, and in the less modern nineteenth-century university. In their introduction to *The Origins of Literary Studies in America*, editors Michael Warner and Gerald Graff describe the emergence of literary studies as a discrete field by painting a picture of its earlier, less discrete, practitioners. In nineteenth-century universities, rhetoric-and-oratory professors were most often responsible for "introducing boys to the golden passages in Shakespeare and the poets." "To be a rhetoric-and-oratory professor," say Warner and Graff, "one had only to know the classics, have a pretty way of talking, and what some at the time referred to as 'a general society-knowledge of literature.'"[26] The rhetoric-and-oratory professor seems, retroactively, quite amateur in the disparaging sense of the term. As such, he shadows the rest of their book, serving as a marker for disciplinary transformations such as a shift from a classical to vernacular curriculum as well as the consolidation of the fuzzy generalist who increasingly served as foil to the literary specialist. Interestingly, to "have a pretty way of talking" is also an index of his generalized amateurism. Elsewhere, the rhetoric-and-oratory professor appears as a "spell-binder," as a mystifying "belletrist," or as a "rearguard" spiritualist. With less and more self-consciousness, the pretty talker is framed historically and in the present as the opposite of everything that the humanist academic would become – the opposite, that is, of professional, rigorous, scholarly, rational, theoretical, disciplinary, modern. Indeed, in some institutions, the denigration or excision of "speech" was fundamental to the intellectual redefinition and professional rise of the literary. Neither Warner nor Graff have much interest in unsettling the feminizing and primitivist associations attached to this spellbinder who "only" talked prettily to boys. Instead, the rhetoric-and-oratory professor functions as a source of amusement in the otherwise disputed "origin" narratives of literary studies.

It might be the Warner of *Letters of the Republic* (rather than the Warner who edited *Fear of a Queer Planet*) who decided not to see any radicality in this homosocial talking scene. And while I am not exactly committed to its celebration either, I am interested in the historical occlusions and institutional effects of personifying "belletrism" in the image of the performing professor. For one thing, this mystifying figure homogenizes a great deal of heterogeneity in the "talking" genealogies behind literature, theatre, and what would continue as the field of speech communication. Paul Edwards's and Margaret Robb's studies of early elocution demonstrate a range of philosophies and practices in the work of expression figures such as Samuel Curry, Charles Wesley Emerson, and Elizabeth Stebbins.[27] All of them attempted to make a claim for the academic professionalism of performance at a moment when performance had become a signal of a maligned anti-professionalism within literary-humanism. That equation persists today. The spectre of a belletrist's amateurish display deflates the professionalist hopes of professorial performance.

The gender politics of these equations occupy other dimensions, for the image of the female elocution teacher participated in the feminization of the belletrist literature professor. While emerging disciplines in the humanities increasingly defined and homogenized all of the talking fields as rearguard in one or more pejorative ways, proponents of the talking fields scattered, divided internally, split off, and re-grouped, sometimes deploying those same pejoratives to differentiate amongst themselves. As with so many fields in the arts and humanities, there was a gendered dimension to this process of scattering and re-grouping. Paul Edwards describes the scrambling moves for self-differentiation as speech teachers tried to construct their professional identities after being marginalized within professional literary societies.

The National Association of Elocution . . . In late November 1914, seventeen conventioneers decide to remain in a Chicago hotel until they could come up with a better idea. They emerged as charter members of the National Association of Academic Teachers of Public Speaking . . . The "Academic" in the Association's first name . . . was thrown in to scare off those elocutionists 'who were not educationally oriented.' . . . It [left] out as well as a lot of private studio teachers, of the sort who occupied the borderland between theater and elocution . . . Academic public speaking would not be English, let alone Oral English – and it would not be elocution.[28]

Like many young college students and faculty, Baker's first encounters with oral performance had been with an elocution teacher. He and his biographer credit Harriette Miller with the development of Baker's vocal technique, training rendered superfluous by its equation with "pretty talking."[29] As speech teachers scrambled to shore up a professional identity, the Harriette Millers of their world increasingly served as an internal foil. To be an "elocutionist" was to be the opposite of professional for an emergent group of speech professors. As Elizabeth Bell writes, this defensively revised equation further marginalized female teachers, for the "growing respectability of speech" was simultanously a move "away from private, women-centered unaccredited academies."[30] Thus, gender hierarchies were not so much tied to one particular form but served as a flexible discourse of legitimacy and delegitimacy. Just as oral performance had served as the feminine to literature's masculine, so elocution served as the feminine to public speaking's masculine.

If elocution was the feminized figure of performance training from which many sought to break free, then Baker's newer adoption of "argumentation" was a more manly type of talking training. Baker titled his book *Specimens of Argumentation*, echoing philological language in order to cast applied argumentation as a rigorous research field. In his 1962 analysis of Baker's pedagogy in argumentation, Harry Kerr (a professional descendant of the National Association of the Teachers of Public Speaking) wrote a recovery article that heralds Baker's "effect on the teaching of argument which is in some ways comparable to his more widely recognized contributions to the theater."[31] Kerr found marginalia scrawled on a copybook in which Baker noted the important "difference between mere ornament and more persuasive graces."[32] Most of Baker's rhetoric students were preparing themselves for entrance in the fields of law and business. As such, Baker's provisional move away from ornament to persuasion demonstrates his pivotal position in a structure that advanced the rise of the professional managerial class and what the Ehrenreich's would recognize as "capitalist relations." It was thus no coincidence that the "persuasive grace" that Baker developed was the seemingly ungraceful notion of the "brief." "Baker decided that the key to avoiding stylistic excesses and achieving cogency and clarity lay in pressing his students to focus first on a carefully prepared plan for their arguments . . . a summary of the facts of the case with reference to points of law supposed to be applicable to them." The brief was "a term which . . . had never before been used in connection with instruction in writing and speaking," writes Kerr, celebrating Baker's professional genius in identifying this mechanism for the dissemination of professional knowledge.[33] Baker's contemporaries were similarly enthusiastic about this element in his research and teaching profile. In reviewing his book, colleagues from various universities promised to incorporate it into their syllabi.[34] In 1895, it looked as if applied argumentation might become Baker's special contribution to the Harvard curriculum. President Eliot was excited by the prospect. Responding to Baker's request that argumentation classes be enlarged on campus, Eliot was cautious but enthused. "Whether it is going to be practicable to enlarge the instruction in argumentation, I cannot tell until I see the Corporation and learn what the prospects are as to the College income. This I know now, that there is no branch of instruction which the Corporation would more gladly enlarge."[35] That the Corporation would "gladly enlarge" such courses also testifies to the more general recognition of the economic link between basic skills and post-graduate employment.

While this kind of technical teaching addressed the perceived professional needs of a changing university, it did not necessarily prove to be a professional success for the professor who provided it. Barrett Wendell began to be concerned that Baker's alignment with skills teaching ultimately would jeopardize his young colleague's professional status. As the writer of a book called *English Composition*, Wendell was in charge of undergraduate courses in college writing, one of the few courses still required in Eliot's otherwise non-restrictive "elective system." To be a teacher of required courses in basic skills turned out to be an infrastructural nightmare. William Lyons Phelps's admiring memory of Wendell also remembers a less than admirable work environment.

For many years, he carried the all but intolerable burden of reading and correcting themes, day after day. His room was filled with these compositions; they were all over the table and on the chairs, and when he lay down on the sofa, to get a little rest, he used a bunch of themes for a pillow.[36]

Phelps's own thoughts about the proper allotment of this kind of work is telling. "It seemed to me that this work was not University work at all, and that any primary schoolma'am would probably have been more efficient in the correcting job."[37] Phelps's ideal division of labor is now familiar, testifying to what James Berlin critiques in the tendency of college professors to define "writing instruction" as something other than their own responsibility.[38] Faced with the overwhelming predicament of basic writing, the professorial managerial class would rather ask someone else – whether primary or secondary school teachers, whether lecturers or graduate students – to sleep on a pillow of freshman essays.

It was no doubt as a result of fitful sleep that Wendell reacted to Baker's book on applied argumentation. Though Wendell had earlier adopted a saucy stance toward the fashion of literary studies, by 1899, he started to change his tune. Trying to discourage Baker's involvement in prescribed argumentation, Wendell used the opportunity to reflect on his own career and to warn Baker about the future of his.

As the writer of *English Composition*, I believe myself to be commonly grouped rather with elocutionists than with scholars. Kittredge's reviews, and Monty's *Specimens*, meanwhile – to say nothing of Child's *Ballads* – have forced respectful recognition not only for them but for their subjects from scholars of the widest rarity and range. You see my conclusion. I honestly believe that in maintaining prescribed argumentation you are unwittingly crucifying yourself. Martyrdom is normally admirable; but is the faith in this case worth martyrdom?[39]

The martyrdom of the basic skills teacher exposes a conundrum at the heart of academic humanism as well as a hypocrisy in the professionalist appeals of the modern university. That this form of teaching could be so central to the university's educational mission and so deleterious to the career of a university professor is still an unresolved contradiction. Attempts to legitimate rhetoric pedagogy took different forms. The pretty talker stopped talking prettily – and became argumentation – or stopped talking altogether – and became composition. However, the infrastructural nightmare and professional martyrdom of basic skills remained. Such repudiations were embedded not only in the gendered metaphors of the "primary school ma'am" but also in classed ones. Consider James Morgan Hart's turn-of-the-century polemic at a key moment in disciplinary formation.

To me rhetoric is purely formal drill, having no more connection with the literature of English than it has with the literature of Greece, Rome . . . rhetoric always savors to me of the school bench . . . It is little more than verbal jugglery . . . Rhetoric exercises are, of course, useful. So are the parallel bars and dumb-bells of a gymnasium. Need I push the comparison farther?[40]

Aligning the school bench with the press bench, the drills and dumbbells of Hart's metaphor equated rhetoric with the vocational, the technical, and even with the manual. By invoking the gymnastic metaphor, Hart also echoed and anticipated another ubiquitous argument against the institutionalization of performance in higher education, one that equated its practices with the extra-curricular domain of exercise and athletics. Rhetoric, in both its compositional and argumentational forms, was not a subject for a professional scholar. From the angle of the President, however, both were useful, too useful in fact to an American university that was beholden to a practical pedagogy as much as a research model of the university. Here was the hypocrisy. Rhetoric was valuable for a student's professional future but of little value to the professional future of the rhetoric professor.

Class, gender, and academic theatre

In the end, Baker decided not to crucify himself on the cross of argumentation. Nor, however, did he construct the research agenda that Kittredge had in mind for Baker's post-*Lyly* career. Instead, Baker turned to theatre as a source of scholarship and as an artistic practice; eventually, he ended up deciding to make a geographic move to Yale. Wisner Payne Kinne's biography of Baker includes descriptions of an early boyhood that anticipates this turn. Kinne chose to quote friends who remember that there was "a certain distinctive quality about his bearing even as a child. There was something grand about George, something superior in his very precise enunciation . . . He was never robust, and things were arranged in the home so that he could be and was an indoor boy."[41] That superior, fragile figure had a particular way of managing his life as "an indoor boy," one that included a luxurious toy theatre. "'I remember George's theatre very well. There was a large closet with a door which opened into the up-stairs bedroom where the audience was seated. George kept his theatre things in the closet and had the toy theatre arranged on a stand in front of the closet doorway. He stood inside the closet, behind the stage, very much like a Punch and Judy operator. He spoke the lines and did everything.'"[42] The image of this deli-cate boy standing inside his closet performing all the parts of his imagined play is useful for conceiving the gendered conventions and gendered threat of becoming a professor of performance.

Rather than chronicling all of the trials and tribulations, the hopes, deferrals, and disappointments that structured this pro-cess, I want to consider a few touchpoints in that shift. While the stories of particular persons and institutions vary enormously, George Pierce Baker's location paralleled that of a number of his pro-performance colleagues and serves as an index of a larger epistemological and institutional fallout around the professing of performance. Less incorporated, however, are the principles under which that disciplinary break happened and, more to the point, how that history resituates disciplinary re-unions that the-atre and performance studies are attempting to effect now. Argu-ing for drama and performance against and so within the already conflicted field of English, of the humanities, and of the modern university produced multiple ambivalences. They affected the professional legacies of philology in performance research, the gendered positioning of the performing professor, and the classed positioning of the performing professor. All of these concerns re-late to each other and have several dimensions, illustrating the disavowals, elisions, confusions, and site-specific structurations of knowledge production.

Writing in 1903 as the first professor of Dramatic Literature in the United States, Brander Matthews of Columbia University published treatises such as *The Development of Drama* that exemplified performance's epistemological predicament and that laid the foundations for the anti-traditional break that would eventually become the tradition of theatre studies methodology. Like Richard Moulton, Matthews addressed dubious interlocutors, attempting to assure them that theatre existed as a research object at all. Hence, he and fellow theatre scholars reproduced turn-of-the-century conventions of historical singularity and progressive continuity, mapping new principles of similarity and difference on which the autonomy of theatre could rest securely. The evolutionary and philologically historicist claims about convention, species, and progression made their way into the formation of period-tracking courses on the drama, attempting to give the same kind of spine, unity, categorization, and evolution to drama that their departmental colleagues were doing in literature. Showing drama to be scientific and systematic was fundamental to the new scholarship, and a key reason behind the note of defensiveness that would (and still does) accompany such a move. Matthews sought to "bring out the essential unity of the history of the drama and to make plain the permanence of the principles underlying the art of the stage . . . Its principles, like the principles of every other art, are eternal and unchanging, whatever strange aspects the art may assume . . . If we could only behold all the links we should be able to trace an unbroken chain from the crudest mythological pantomime of primitive man down to the severest problem play of the stern Scandinavian."[43] Exercising a Moultonian enthusiasm, it was in such a professionalizing university climate that the evolutionary paradigm of "from ritual to theatre" became invoked and later routinized. Thus the primitivism that many in theatre and performance studies now seek to rectify should be remembered for the role that such "progressions" once played in the creation of the object of knowledge. The "from ritual" "to drama" progression is part of an inherited curricular structure. As performance studies scholars seek to undo the ideological, national, and global consequences of such a construct, it is probably equally important to remember its institutional expediency; knowledge was made more teachable, useful, and justifiable to a professionalizing university when it took shape in the clear categories and progressive arcs of a delineated "survey."

While Brander Matthews and like-minded souls occasionally pitted themselves against philological trendiness, they most often borrowed and adapted its methods. In addition to adopting the (non-Foucauldian) genealogical models of genre development, theatre scholars also employed other methodological preoccupations with "facts" and "details." Theatre scholars took philology's emphasis on historical research and on the conventions of literary transmission to rationalize the investigation of such "extraliterary" realms as street lay-outs, building configurations, set designs, managerial structures, actors, and audiences. Indeed, to a philological method acutely preoccupied with the accumulation of "facts," the circumstances of the performed event offered an endless supply of discoverable data. In many ways, theatre's excessive contextuality called literary philology's bluff, for its voluminous data were not always the kind of facts that most literary philologists were interested in or skilled in discovering. Baker's own work made use of the philological impulse. In his next book of scholarship, he approached *Shakespeare as a Dramatist*, choosing inductive over judicial criticism and its language of species and genus as well as its attempt to displace a narrative of genius.

Yet the feeling of the critical untrained public that there should be certain final and permanent standards by which values may be apportioned to plays of different sorts and different periods has an element of truth in it: namely, that throughout all periods plays show common properties which distinguish them as a species of composition from tales, essays, or poems, – the differential which makes them the species play, in the genus fiction.[44]

Baker took a Moultonian line on induction and Shakespeare but gave it a specific theatrical cast, locating the relation of genus and species more discretely within the dramatic arts. Intriguingly, Baker, Matthews, and other American scholars of the theatre did like to acknowledge the influence of philology despite its saturation inside their own language and methods. Nevertheless, the philological impulse could become entrenched in the disciplinary practice of theatre history, a "literary" influence on the field that "anti-literary" theatre scholars would continue to disavow.

The philological genealogy has other contemporary reso-
nances. Like recent conversations in which theoretical influences
are disavowed by reductive characterizations of Theory (and despite a detractor's own theoretical deployments), philology was
something that exerted its influence and enforced conceptions of
rigor on individuals who were not entirely willing to admit the
claim. It was also criticized in much the same set of confused,
non-coincident terms. It was accused of being too scientific, of
being over-specialized, of being jargon-ridden and of compromising the experience of literature. Both theory and philology
have many referents and enter discursively to delineate boundaries of all kinds – American versus European, traditional versus
contemporary, systematic versus chaotic, rigor versus unrigor,
professional versus amateur, scholar versus journalist, fact versus emotion, male versus female. In theatre, references to philology could include all of the above as well as discipline-specific
oppositions such as text versus performance, academic versus
professional, and scholar versus artist. Occasionally, its American critics appealed to nationalist allegiances by accusing its
followers of slavishly imitating the Europeans, more specifically
the Germans. As such, it anticipated many subsequent "Theory" movements accused of being specialist, jargon-ridden, and
ruinous to the humanities – or for being French. There are different, somewhat conflicting, lessons that we can learn from a
defamiliarization of theory and its associations of specialism and
"jargon." On the one hand, new thoughts need new language.
Indeed, as Joseph Roach recalls in his first encounter with the
conventions of theatre history, "traditional" disciplines are filled
with unconventional vocabulary.

What a bewildering vocabulary of arcane terms the young student en-
countered in that first course in theatre history: *thronoi, choregoi, peraktoi,*
proscenium doors, *loci, foci, carros,* wings and grooves, chariot and poles,
lazzi, "heavens," free plantation, denouement, magic if, through-line,
Eidophusikon . . . I can remember my classmates asking (before anyone had learned to describe terms they didn't care to understand by
resorting to the j-word): 'Why can't theatre historians just write plain
English?' The answer then, as it remains today, that the history of the
theatre is too rich in ideas to be comprehended by the lexicon of one
language.[45]

On the other hand, institutional and disciplinary genealogies reveal a constant rotation as new thoughts and new language cycle

in to everyday parlance. One era's "specialization" becomes the next era's "generalism"; ground-breaking theoretical movements look like dunder-headed empiricism to subsequent generations.

The attempt to delineate theatre as a research object was coincident with an attempt to delineate theatre as a curricular object. This meant devising courses that filled out the vast array of dramatic performance that was "exclusive of Shakespeare." In 1902, Baker proposed a larger series of courses that introduced students to the post-Renaissance theatre, even including the more recent experimentation of the stern Scandinavian, Ibsen. While the proposal could rely for discursive support on an appeal to "specialization" and on the genealogical paradigm in the notion of a "series," the chairman initially ignored Baker's idea. At such a moment, when intellectual change met institutional practice, the rhetoric-and-oratory-and-now-drama professor worried. When Baker tried again with Kittredge, the chairman was cordial and contrite. "I thought about your letter weekly. I wrote not at all. Here again, however, there was no real damage done; except to my reputation as a correspondent . . . and I also discovered that I had no suggestions to make that were not too obvious to be worth troubling you with . . . Seriously, though, I am ashamed of being so inconsiderate."[46] Of course, laziness in inter-office correspondences could also mask large-scale epistemological battles.

Ultimately, laxity abated on both sides when issues of field definition and field legitimation came to the fore. Baker's efforts to move the dramatic "page" to the dramatic "stage" challenged emergent literary definitions. By 1905, Baker submitted a proposal to add playwriting to his Dramatic Series, the course in Dramatic Technique that would become the renowned 47 Workshop. The course, which already existed under the auspices of Radcliffe College, involved acting and technical production in its development of new plays. Kittredge objected to the idea in a department meeting, inducing a flurry of angry letters to which he responded with the measured calm of the powerful.

Dear Baker, Thank you very much for writing to me so fully about your course. The information you give in your letter will be of great value to me in advising graduate students at the end of this year and the beginning of next. Pray don't think I have any doubt that your proposed course will be of exceptional utility, as well as uncommonly interesting . . . My purpose in asking to consider the matter further was not to "prejudice the business" but simply to make sure that all possible contingencies had been weighed. . . . It occurs to me, however, to ask you to have an eye to possible misconceptions as to the scope and method of the new course.[47]

Baker's "scope" included contemporary drama, and his "method" would include theatrical production. Neither incarnated Kittredge's hopes for Baker's professional career or for the knowledge domain of the English department. In the end, the 47 course went on the books, but Kittredge and Baker's correspondence became more guarded and less collegial.

The significance as well as contingency of George Pierce Baker's location – as well as that of Brander Matthews – is made explicit by comparing it to another institution. The comparison illustrates that the constitution of knowledge, like performance, is site-specific. While Baker struggled for the next decade to integrate not only dramatic literature but also dramatic production into the Harvard curriculum, at Carnegie Tech the obstacles were reversed. With it being the site of the first US theatre department in 1914, Thomas Wood Stevens found it easier to incorporate dramatic production at Carnegie Tech and harder to incorporate dramatic literature. Stevens was recruited from the University of Wisconsin where he engaged in other brands of theatrical innovation in the "applied" and agricultural orientation of The Wisconsin Experiment. Wisconsin would go on to house a highly-rated theatre department as well as the first curricular, rather than extra-curricular, program in dance. Like other mid-western universities, such as Iowa (the site of the first doctoral program in theatre), the applied orientation of the land-grant college provided a seed bed for more than just agriculture. Carnegie Tech made use economically and discursively of the appeal to the practical in the American pragmatic model of higher education. Instead of an agricultural focus, the "technical" in Carnegie Tech referred to a diverse array of industrial fields. The internal divisions of this university thus set up quite different epistemological divisions from those of Harvard; with them, the relations of sameness and difference amongst and between fields were different as well. In a university that specialized in "science" and "industries," theatre found itself in the school of "applied design" (later the fine arts) and in a building that, as Thomas Wood Stevens remembered somewhat ecstatically, had the words

"Architecture, Painting, Sculpture, Music, Drama" engraved in its façade.[48] Thus, while Baker struggled to have "drama" appear on a course schedule, Stevens enjoyed and endured the privilege of seeing his domain written in stone.

This epistemological location also had epistemological consequences for how "the drama" was conceived as a cultural form. In English departments, drama was classified with poetry and prose as one in a species system of "genres," a system that assumed the literary medium as a unifying principle of sameness. At Carnegie Tech, likeness and unlikeness were drawn in relation to other artistic forms; a relation to architecture, painting, and music that emphasized drama's graphic, material, temporal, sonic, and spatial elements. These two types of institutional location thus conceived the fundamental elements of the drama differently. While drama was a "genre" at some universities, it was a "medium" at others. The difference in institutional location also brought with it a difference in humanistic status. Carnegie Tech's administrators saw the drama not only as one amongst other graphic media but also as a way to usher in the humanities. Drama enabled the integration of what Stevens called "cultural study" into the domain of industrial study. For Stevens, this part of the endeavor was harder to do. "The technical side was fairly simple," he wrote more casually than George Pierce Baker would have thought possible. "The students were to learn the entire work of the theatre by doing the entire work of the theatre . . . the larger problem [was] the combination of the technical training with related work in the humanities."[49] Thus, while drama's technical elements lowered its humanistic status at Harvard; at Carnegie Tech, drama's humanistic status was elevated. The difference offers another demonstration of discontinuities in a performance genealogy. Attributions of technicality and humanity, of genre and medium, were institutionally produced and relationally conceived. To track performance's terms, references, and legitimacy is once again about tracking a "non-identity through time."

Baker's turn to the drama exacerbated a number of gendered anxieties that were already lurking in his institutional context. To consider this exacerbation is to return to the originary site of playwriting outside of the English department, outside of the Yard, and in the women's school of Radcliffe College. It also returns us to a different originary site, the one where a rhetoric-and-oratory-now-drama professor could be found talk-ing prettily to boys. As an historically feminized cultural form, theatre threatened to restore the foppish belletrist, the retroac-tively feminized figure who served as foil to the project of literary studies. Reports suggest that this figure and his "pretty voice" made regular appearances in Baker's pedagogical repertoire, in-carnating the gendered threat of a colleague who was not only a professor of performance but himself a performing professor. One student remembered a class lecture on *The Man of Mode*:

Professor Baker's blue-gray eyes would deepen behind his pince-nez, his face would beam with pleasure, his portly body rock with mirth . . . he would begin to assume the airs and graces of a Restoration fop. His voice would change and take on the mincing tones of Etherege's hero. His hands which he always used swiftly, would begin to race in elaborate circles. Artificial gallantries would be slightly indicated, in a way which seemed so courtly and was so deliciously right that one could have sworn his sleeves were fringed with lace.[50]

By portraying Baker forgetting "all about facts and tendencies," the student reinforced a sense that the performed study of theatre was the opposite of the rigorous study in the humanities. It might well have been that Baker's English colleagues agreed. Baker's in-terest in presenting, not only the drama, but the performance of drama heightened the feminizing potential of the theatre. Addi-tionally, it scratched at a perpetually deferred history that lurked within the attempt to construct the new field of literary studies. The image of a performing professor recalled and reproduced the feminized and amateur display associated with the unprofessional belletrist. This was the queering, the rendering inappropriate, of what we know in theatre as a professor's "dog and pony show." Throughout, the student characterized Baker's performances as "possession" by a "far more entertaining melodrama" than any-thing that came from his "yellowing notes." Such enthusiastic student reaction only reinforced the sense that Baker was becom-ing a repudiated "spellbinder." Furthermore, the same student recalls that the workshopping of student scripts involved content that "pinkened his cheek" and "love scenes that must have dis-turbed everything New England in him."[51] Theatre thus risked distracting students from the new rigor while, at the same time, exposing the latently unrigorous in literature's new quest for le-gitimacy. To perform the drama was, as most any theatre person would contend, a way of incarnating the production. At this moment in the origin of literary studies, however, such professorial performance was an index of unprofessionalism.

As the reference to "pinkened cheeks" suggests, the gendered and sexed dimensions of performance as an academic field were varied, making clear that the "feminization" of knowledge can mean more than one thing. Feminization happened not only when a professor talked to boys but also when he talked (prettily and otherwise) to girls. As Baker's interest in the theatre grew, he initially found a much more hospitable home for his experimentation through sponsorship at Radcliffe College. More and more Harvard faculty participated in the Radcliffe curriculum, a reflection of a larger national current in the expansion of women's higher education. While the move augmented the women's curriculum, it could reciprocally reduce the offerings in the male curriculum both numerically and symbolically. The gendered anxieties of higher education were symptomatic of larger ones as turn-of-the-century women more actively participated in public life and as men scrambled to retain or rediscover the means of maintaining a masculine identity. To the extent that Harvard theatre began at Radcliffe College, the possibility of its intrusion inside the Yard exacerbated already felt concerns about the masculinity of a literature professor. Theatre's historically feminine status was literalized by its institutionally feminine status at Harvard. The threat of the theatre lay not only in its association with display or sentiment, however, but also in its appropriateness. The gendered anxieties around the theatre could thus become explicitly sexual anxieties. Barrett Wendell's tisk-tisking reaction to the possible introduction of playwright John Fletcher in a "girls" classroom demonstrated how theatre's "pinkened cheek" pedagogy could be perceived to cross the line of sexual appropriateness.[52]

Both as a matter of turn, then, and as a matter of business, I find myself unwilling to put my name on the title page of any popular book . . . addressed to women which should contain such sick stuff as I find in any comedy of Fletchers . . . In the matter of study, [Barrett wrote again a day later] I think myself consistent. I was never willing to teach on the old drama – apart from Shakespeare – when I taught at Radcliffe. And one of my objections to the higher education of women by men anyway is that, so far as I can see, it cannot be at once veracious and decent.[52]

The scholarly quest for veracity could actually compromise decency, a potential that was apparently permissible in the homosocial arena of all-male "study" but that was made too explicit by a mixed-sex pedagogical arena. Once again, theatre and co-education reciprocally exacerbated the anxieties surrounding each other.

There was another set of gendered concerns that affected the image of theatre as a form of study. In addition to the spectre of feminized ornamentation and amateurism, in addition to the spectre of sexual inappropriateness, theatre practice could also be associated with a kind of nurturing and unaccredited maternalism. That is, the affiliation of the "primary school ma'am" also compromised theatre's status as a legitimated curricular and research object in higher education. A letter from Elizabeth Hunt to former Professor Baker illustrates:

Having received no reply to a letter which I sent to you some time since, I am going to trouble you once more, feeling certain that it never reached you. I am, you may possibly recall, one of the favored ten who you so kindly invited to take your first 47 Workshop group work on the drama. The work of that year and the previous year's study with you have been the inspiration of my work since with boys and girls. So anxious am I to have my pupils in the Beacon School enjoy the privilege of hearing your lectures that I am going to see if I can get another school or club in Brookline to join with us in undertaking the expense. . . . Awaiting your earliest convenience, and trusting that you will be able to find time to give this to us, I am yours sincerely . . .[53]

Like many male institutionalizers of performance (and there will be more of them as the book continues), Baker had an equivocal relationship with the feminized association and the female bodies that constituted his largest demographic and support system. As women found roles for themselves outside of higher education in schools, reform arenas, and in formations such as the little theatre movement, their work foregrounded the use of theatre as a tool in service, education, and community formation. As Elizabeth Bell argued of women elocutionists, however, the professionalization of academic humanism contributed to a delegitimation of these realms. The new imagined communities of scholarship emphasized professional credentialization and geographical dispersion, eclipsing the local proximities of learning that became the feminized domain of the "little" movements of women, of students, of children, of amateurs. Ms. Hunt's work with "boys and girls" exemplified theatre's status as the domain of the primary school ma'am, a connection that may explain Baker's own "laxity in correspondence." All of these illustrations show that what it means to gender an academic field is itself various. Between belletristic, erotic, and maternal associations, the possibilities for devaluing professorial performance in gendered terms are myriad, wide-ranging, and inconsistent with themselves. In many ways, such inconsistencies and contradictions give "the anti-theatrical prejudice" its discursive force, spawning and diffusing prejudices of all kinds, turning the discursive tables with each counter-argument, eliciting a defensiveness that confuses that which it seeks to clarify.

The potential for self-contradicting diffusion multiplies after incorporating the gendered positioning of the performing professor with a classed understanding of that position as well. Baker's first course in playwriting appeared in the Harvard curriculum in the "Composition" sector of the English curriculum with the title "Technique of Drama." In adopting the classed language of "applied" technique, he quite possibly knew that he was involving himself in a familiarly relentless pedagogical cycle, one that required endless amounts of student contact, one that exchanged "themes" and "briefs" for an equally overwhelming pile of student-written plays. Indeed, despite his own enthusiasm, Baker's move from applied rhetoric to applied theatre had no less potential for self-crucifixion.

The nightmare of a "technical" class was further expanded and literalized in the infrastructure of the theatre. As Baker proceeded down his slippery slope from student playwriting to student production, this English professor found himself confronting the technical and infrastructural demands of the theatre event. English 47, which would eventually adopt the engineering-like label of "workshop," took place in a larger space within Harvard's Massachusetts Hall. Combining playwriting and production into all hours of the night, it exceeded both the spatial and temporal limits of the conventionally scheduled course. It also involved a much wider engagement in "the technical" than any composition course ever had. One description sets up a delighted picture of classed inappropriateness.

Outside, Massachusetts Hall was (and still is) one of the truest architectural joys of the Harvard landscape. . . . Inside it was, at least in the
days when Mr. Baker and his designers worked in it, a fascinating nightmare. Its hollow shell, cluttered with flats and drops which stretched
to the ceiling, and smelling strongly of paint and glue, was a defiant
contradiction of its chaste exterior.[54]

In the last decade and a half of Baker's Harvard career, this world
of "flats and drops" predominated. In many ways, this was an
entirely new education for Baker, a set of experiences for which
childhood play in a toy theatre hardly prepared him. His route to
the theatre had been through acting and literature; the world of
design and technical theatre was new to someone who, as one of
his students noted, "had little visual imagination."[55] Such contingencies would also weigh on his Harvard colleagues. Indeed,
it is hard to decide what unnerved Chairman Kittredge more, the
mincing tones of a feminized fop wafting between classroom walls
or the hammering sounds of a student carpenter building new
walls of his own. The demands of theatrical infrastructure placed
Baker in a new kind of correspondence with his employer. A significant part of his exchanges with Eliot's successor, President
Lawrence Lowell, revolved around architectural issues. Baker's
attempts to solicit approval for a new theatre building and the
latest artistic technology were turned down by the Corporation.
Furthermore, even the "fascinating nightmare" of Massachusetts
Hall did not securely belong to the workshop.

Dear Mr. Baker, There has been, as you know, some feeling that our
oldest building Massachusetts, ought not to be more exposed than is absolutely necessary to the danger of fire, and that such a danger cannot
be wholly avoided while it contains so much scenery as it does now. It
has been suggested that Gannett House – which is no longer to be used
as a dormitory – if gutted and rearranged, would give the 47 Workshop
as large a space as, and one better adapted for its purposes than, Massachusetts. Moreover, there is a growing desire to restore Massachusetts,
making it into either rooms for living or for instruction; and as the space
is very badly needed, I suppose that sometimes this demand will acquire
irresistible force.[56]

Shocked to receive this note from President Lowell in 1923, after
two decades of theatrical instruction, Baker argued that Gannett
House was thoroughly inappropriate. Nevertheless, the university's architectural plans exerted themselves with the agentless

strength of an irresistible force. "Dear Mr. Lowell, Rather dis-
quieting rumors have been coming to me this past month that
work on changing Massachusetts Hall for other uses is to begin
immediately after Commencement. From time to time, people
have dropped in here to make mysterious measurements. . . . if so,
where else [are we] expected to go?"[57] The year was 1924 when
Lowell offered an unsympathetic reply: "At present I know of no
place where the Workshop can be housed except Gannett House,
which was offered to you before, and which you thought inade-
quate. Do you see any other place where you could go?"[58] Yes,
Baker found himself replying, I can go to Yale.

Indeed, the coincidence of a job offer from Yale in the middle
of this architectural snub proved too tempting to ignore. With
an endowment from Edward Harkness, Yale would build a theatre that radically altered Baker's work environment. In many
ways, the decision to move to Yale had everything to do with
the promise of infrastructural relief. Nearly all of Baker's formal
writing on the role of academic theatre during this decade focused on "the building" and on the necessity of having one. His
inaugural article as a new "Professor of the Literature and Practice of Drama" (an endowed chair whose long title Harvard's
Corporation had earlier edited) framed the general topic of the
"Theatre and the University" most emphatically in terms of infrastructural desires. Asking rhetorically and righteously, "What
does the university owe the student to whom it has offered a
course in the writing of plays?" Invoking the needy student who
(ventriloquized as being "stirred to expression") was "owed" a
debt, Baker heralded the building as a solution, as a right, and
as a fulfillment of an educational social contract. "More than
anything else it owes him a place where plays may be seen under
fitting conditions – in other words, a theatre."[59] Baker's quest for
fitting conditions had weighed too long on his mind and body;
in moving to Yale, the prospect of getting the building seems to
have provided the utmost incentive.

Even as years passed, a significant portion of Baker's representation of his new Yale life included references to infrastructure.
To Phillip Barry, he celebrated even "temporary quarters, which
are really attractive, and what gorgeous expanse we have on York
Street where the excavating is going on."[60] He sent his article
on the proposed edifice to Harley Granville-Barker "because it

shows the exterior of our building rather well. At present we are busy with the foundations of the structure . . . Our architect has been delaying us in a maddening fashion these last six weeks."[61] Of course, the erection of infrastructural relief would never put an end to infrastructural anxiety, as any theatre department chairman knows. Both Barry and Granville-Barker would receive later correspondence on the new problems that continually presented themselves. In 1932, the indoor boy wrote more plaintively to Barry, undone by the contingencies of "the plant." "I am sorry to have been so particularly dull the other night; but I had just been through a most devastating dress rehearsal, and I was meditating a letter of resignation of my job unless I could be guaranteed better conditions. Utterly worn out and in a state of high mental tension, I haven't the remotest idea what I said."[62]

At the same time, there was a certain masochistic pleasure in technical enmeshment. And, while "technical" was a denigrated metaphor within the humanities, it could also be a legitimating one in other parts of higher education. The appeal to pragmatism and to the how-to solidified engineering environments in the industrial and agricultural wings of the academy. Theatre proponents could reverse the terms of approbation by borrowing technicality's associations of authenticity. Indeed, the history of theatre's institutionalization suggest that "the arts" have as much to do with engineering as they do with the humanities divisions of the campus. One student celebrated Baker's academic theatre in language that foregrounded its status as a technical field.

[Baker's] instruction in playwriting has been provocative not because of any infallible theories he held as to what the well written play is or ought to be, but because he made his course a laboratory, where a playwright learned to criticize his own efforts by seeing his play performed in a "workshop." . . . No artist has ever served the theatre who did not possess the unaffected humility of a workman. The theatre remains alive by remaining a workshop. The way to learn to do anything is by attempt to do it, and by keeping up the attempt steadily.[63]

In Baker's case, the technical and engineering demands of the theatre, the ill-fit inside the humanities, were nostalgically classed as a way for an "indoor boy" to access an alternatively hearty masculinity.

Exactly what it meant to run this lab, however, was still a question. The ill-fit of theatre intellectually within the humanities also meant another kind of ill-fit in terms of the organization of its labor pool. While a specialist language had earlier enabled Baker to develop his "special field," by 1925 Baker would see the need to flip terminological alignments. Baker's language by 1925 became anti-specialist because his new institutional context required it; he needed a willing generalism on the part of students and faculty in order to keep the plant functioning. In this context, more and more prescription happened as theatre professors realized that the democratic nature of "the elective system" would not always support the technical, design, and verbal elements of the theatrical event. For this democratic art form to follow through on its potential, the anti-democratic use of the "requirement" and the "pre-requisite" had to be instituted. Baker's description of this anti-specialist necessity also borrowed the workman-like language of the plant, the engineering language of the lab, and the military language of the corps in order to describe an essentially collective endeavor inside an arts and humanities field whose professional endeavors were becoming increasingly individuated. "Perhaps it is characteristic of artists in general . . . to wish to be specialists . . . They do not like to know intimately what goes on behind the curtain if it means shifting scenery or helping the chief electrician. . . . Yet as soon as a dramatist understands what all these branches may contribute to that curiously complicated result – a produced play – his writing gains in producibility. He prepares intelligently for each complementary worker to do his part."[64] Baker even used the language of youthful malingering and unhealthful balance to characterize the specialist who was not game for theatrical generalism. He wrote as if the apathetic "mind of the undergraduate" was in danger of returning unless the student became willing to engage as a member of the corps. "The arts of the theatre, if studied separately, are likely to have the importance of each so over-emphasized that when a student thus trained must share in a difficult production there is wastage, confusion, and temperament!"[65] The notion of technique – as widely used to discuss classical argumentation, philological expertise, and playwriting itself – sounded a more engineering-like tone in the technical theatre.

George Pierce Baker's trajectory has elements that are familiar to current departmental structures. At the same time, different institutional sites brought variation and, with them, alternate opportunities and problems. As an institutional predecessor, the department of architecture – rather than the department of English – provided Thomas Wood Stevens with a curricular model for theatre. Stevens's early curriculum at Carnegie Tech began with basic skills in diction, dancing, and drawing, only later integrating a lecture course on the history of the theatre and as well as other courses on the history of "painting, sculpture, architecture, furniture, and decoration." Within "drawing," the curriculum offered finer gradations such as "sketching" and "tracing."[66] "For thoroughness in preparing the curriculum," Stevens wrote, "we based many things on the parallel problems of the school of architecture."[67] Thus, the history of design served as the baseline of the Carnegie Tech curriculum, and it was that barometer, rather than the history of poetic forms, to which theatre measured and compared itself. An architectural imagination was thus part and parcel of the "origin" of theatre studies in this strain of institutional history. The relationship between architectural and performance pedagogy looked different than the relationship between literary and performance pedagogy. While students at Harvard raised their heads from the horizontal plane of a dramatic script to consider theatrical production, students at Carnegie Tech entered the visual world of production while sitting before the angled slant of a drafting board. The architectural genealogy of performance thus foregrounded visuality and spatiality more substantially than George Pierce Baker, whose lack of "visual imagination" made the incorporation of design into theatre education a cumbersome, if awe-filled, after-thought. The difference suggests that the "page to stage" description of theatrical process is also site-specific; it is less applicable to a performance curriculum that does not begin with "the page" in the first place.

These examples demonstrate that the invocation of the technical or the practical had multiple referents and provoked different types of anxiety and celebration. That variation was also dependent upon another kind of association – the technical link to the economic, to "business," and the so-called "commercial." The prospect of using performance skills to make money legitimated them in some contexts and provoked suspicion in others. Thomas

Wood Stevens remembered the pre-professional discourse that surrounded the industrial arts curriculum when he arrived. "After four years, a student could count on hearing one of the following: 'Now you're artists – go ahead and exhibit.' To a few more, 'You're a craftsmen – go ahead and do labels for tomato cans.' And to the rest, 'You have no talent' . . . The failures pay for the development of the successes." Carnegie Tech's President Hamerschlag invited drama onto campus because "he was sure there might be another way," that is, a way of adjusting a careerist determinism with a liberal arts orientation.[68] Nevertheless, this constrained set of options structured and still structures an equivalent legitimating discourse for a theatre curriculum. A few are told that they have the talent of a theatrical artist. More are told that they have no talent at all. And the rest find some place in between, counting themselves lucky if they are allowed to hold the tomato can in a TV commercial for Campbell's soup. While Carnegie Tech's attitude toward the business of art was somewhat enthusiastic or, at least, humorously tolerant, the encroachment of a commercial consciousness was decidedly unwelcome in the world of the humanities. The anxiety brings us back to the paradoxes and disavowals surrounding the professorial-managerial class and, in particular, the professional humanist. In an early university context unsure about the significance of a rising middle class, the language of economics and business challenged the autonomy of the professorial profession and of the humanities as such. As a cultural form with a partial affiliation in the domain of literature and partial affiliation in the domain of the industrial arts, theatre threatened to intensify the challenge. If proponents of liberal culture tried to install a division between their pursuits and the domain business, then "theatre" threatened to undo that shaky border. Indeed, theatrical pedagogy exposed the fervently unremembered link between the function of the professorial-managerial class and the reproduction of capitalist relations, making the paradoxes and disavowals of the career humanist discomfortingly explicit.

The employment of performance

As George Pierce Baker began to set his sights on the domain of drama – away from Kittredge-approved philology, away from Eliot-approved argumentation – he turned to his fellow drama-lover, Barrett Wendell, for support. One of his many hopes was to create a little drama reading group that included Harvard faculty, lay intellectuals, and local theatre-makers. Wendell was surprisingly, and tellingly, aghast.

I hesitate without further knowledge of this scheme, to authorize the use of my name . . . I do not wish to find myself one of two or three sane folks in a crowd of long-haired crumbs. . . . [F]rankly, if any one asks me about this matter, I shall not be disposed to speak of it with more than doubtful cordiality . . . The truth is again borne in on me that . . . I want to have nothing whatever to do with theatre people. They always manage more or less innocently to rub me the wrong way.[69]

Despite his own interest as a teacher of the drama, and despite his own unorthodox proclivities within the profession of literary studies, Wendell was somewhat hostile to the idea of sharing space with the makers of the drama. His reference to such "long-haired crumbs" paints a picture of a denigrated Bohemianism, adding another term to a long list of anti-theatrical associations. For Wendell to display such virulence, however, was also to admit the discomfort in his own identity project. To say that "they rub me the wrong way" is to mark an anxiety in the "me" as much as a problem with the "they." Indeed, such anxiety may have had as much to do with theatre people's contagious sameness as with their long-haired difference. For someone who worried about the effects of co-education, theatre heightened the sexual dangers of pedagogical inappropriateness. For someone who worried about his alignment with the "elocutionists," proximity to performers may have exacerbated the pejorative image of Wendell's feminized anti-professionalism. For someone who felt crucified by technical pedagogies, theatrical performance may have rationalized Wendell's relegation to the dumbbells and parallel bars of the gymnasium.

Anyone interested in the disciplining of performance in the twenty-first century might want to think about the fate of the pretty talker, the extra-curricular gymnast, the technical craftsman, the long-haired Bohemian and any of the other compromising figures with which performance is associated in the academy. Without calling for full-scale endorsement or unproblematic retrieval, we have an interest in considering how attributions of anti-professionalism or anti-theoreticism are made and how their persistence extends into our current disciplinary and institutional predicaments now. The charge of "rigorlessness" embodied in the performing professor still haunts our efforts to profess performance now. Rather than allowing such figures to remain an amusing foil to our current self-construction as professional, rigorous, scholarly, theoretical (inter) disciplinary, and post-modern, I think that it is worth contending with their historical occlusions and institutional effects. Doing so helps us to frame performance, not only as a heterogeneous field capable of responding to scholarly developments in the humanities (which I believe it is), but also as a form that exposes the contradictions, the *impensés*, and the untapped potentials of academic humanism itself.

Does honoring our own history allow us to lead the hottest trends? Well, yes and no, especially when our understanding of the past is productively disrupted by the puzzle of genealogy. Disciplinary genealogy is neither a celebratory search for origins nor a self-satisfied rejection of the stodgy. It is, after Foucault, a means of approaching the past to unsettle the heretofore stable. Writing such a genealogy often means revisiting categories that performance studies itself resists or de-centers – words such as "drama," "theatre," "speech," or "literature." If we think of such labels – and others such as "theory," "practice," "interdisciplinary" – less as securely referential terms than as discursive sites on which a number of agendas, alliances, and anxieties collect, then I think that the institutionalization of performance studies and the institutionalization of something like "theatre" or "speech" or "literature" turn out to have more to do with each other than current conversations let on. Such terms function inconsistently at different times and different places; they are invoked out of convenience at moments when knowledges need re-organization or when vague institutional developments require some discursive support. As such, they also sustain a network of disavowed connection and disavowed difference, an array of blindspots, synecdochic fallacies, and reinvented wheels. In such a complicated space, one scholar's experiment turns out to be another's tradition; one scholar's core comes back as another's periphery. One field finds it too expedient to cast a dominant form as marginal in order to prop up its own centrality; another finds it too expedient to cast a marginal form as dominant in order to better stage its own rebellion. Rather than wholly succumbing to the language of the new, it seems to me at least as interesting theoretically and secure institutionally for performance studies to expose the historical entanglements of the already-was and thus still-still-kind-of-is. It seems important to show how disciplinary breaks were saturated with the terms of the field that they were fleeing and to suggest that contemporary innovations sometimes derive from arenas that once de-valued that which they now celebrate. Institutional history also suggests that assumptions of the "special" status of performance studies, enticing as they are, could do with a genealogical jolt.

3   Culture and performance: structures of dramatic feeling

> The lack of communication with other disciplines gives the drama a peculiar insularity.   Robert Brustein[1]

> I learned something from analyzing drama which seemed to me effective not only as a way of seeing certain aspects of society but as a way of getting through to some of the fundamental conventions which we group as society itself. These, in their turn, make some of the problems of drama quite newly active.
>   Raymond Williams[2]

Performing cultural studies

My first epigraph is taken from an essay entitled, "Why American Plays Are Not Literature," in which Robert Brustein chastised "the drama" for not being interdisciplinary. As the title suggests, Brustein made it clear that something called "literature" was the discipline with which drama most needed contact. Not only was it, in Brustein's view, the only discipline with which the drama needed contact, but its models of value were those to which all drama should aspire. Condemning the fact that American dramatists almost never sought representation in "the literary periodicals," his 1959 use of the term interdisciplinary was thus a way of rationalizing a formula for the cultural legitimation of the drama, American and otherwise. My second epigraph is from a drama scholar who was Brustein's contemporary if also, at some level, his antithesis. Before and between renowned texts such as *Culture and Society* and *Keywords*, Williams published a series of books in the field of drama – *Drama from Ibsen to Eliot, Drama in Use, Modern Tragedy,* and a revised *Drama from Ibsen to Brecht* – a "set" that he considered a formative "critical study" of the dramatic form.[3]

Robert Brustein and Raymond Williams published some of their most widely read studies of drama in the 1950s and 1960s in two different countries and in intellectual environments that bore a vexed if interdependent connection to each other. Both began their intellectual lives as drama scholars, and both would go on to become "cultural critics" of sorts. However, while both would take up the question of whether or not "plays" were "culture," their answers differed significantly – a difference that depended on varying notions of the term "culture." For Brustein, the cultural denoted a realm of artistic preserve and artistic excellence, free from what he would later call the "sociologizing of aesthetics." Williams's name and thought, on the other hand, would become synonymous with another cultural project – the project of "cultural studies." As someone who figures prominently and repeatedly in the origin narratives of this movement, Williams thus helped to advance the theories, politics, and methodologies whose "sociology" Brustein would later condemn.[4] How "the drama" could serve as point of entry to two very different relations to the "cultural" is one of the concerns of this chapter.

It seems useful to ask such a question in light of a number of other debates currently at issue in the field(s) of drama, theatre, and performance studies. There is an efficiently satisfying way of plotting these three terms as indexes of ever widening levels of cultural analysis. The plot begins with "drama" as a discrete literary text, posits "theatre" as a larger production event, and defines "performance" as an even larger event of culture. Richard Schechner's proposed "new paradigm" for performance studies positions theatre as "a very small slice of the performance pie," one amongst many instances that could also include "rock concerts, discos, electioneering, wrestling, con games, and demonstrations, and a panoply of religious rituals."[5] Such a model aligns drama with traditional concepts of culture and performance's "restored behaviors" with newer perspectives on cultural critique. In many circles, scholars of performance studies and self-labeled progressive theatre studies claim a particular kinship with cultural studies. This means promoting an approach to performance that unsettles divisions between high and low, that advocates a radically contextual and socially grounded analysis, that takes seriously feminist, anti-racist, and intercultural critiques of identity and globalization, that deploys cutting edge interdisciplinary methodologies, and that links scholarship to modes of *praxis* outside of the academy. To claim a kinship with cultural studies and thus to assert one's "newness" in turn tends to re-cast other orientations as "old" and as antithetical to a cultural studies project. Such identifications can have the effect, for instance, of retroactively construing the scholarly project of "drama" as traditional and as metonymically aligned with all that cultural studies is not. To study drama in this caricatured light is thus to perpetuate a narrow, elite, and Eurocentric line of inquiry, one that reproduces cultural divisions between high and low, one that disavows both theatrical and materialist relations of production, and one whose "literary" mode of analysis presumes and reifies the artistic autonomy of the isolated dramatic text. Such characterizations are often peppered with supporting quotations from contemporary cultural theorists such as Stuart Hall, Paul Gilroy, Lawrence Grossberg, Angela McRobbie, as well as the luminaries from whom so many of them claim to have descended – including Raymond Williams himself. As pedagogically satisfying as these moves can be, they can severely reduce conversation about the future of and inter-relations between various components of our field. I hope to explore in this chapter a complicated and under-theorized history between drama and cultural studies, one whose disavowal paradoxically deploys the intellectual genealogy of a drama-cum-cultural theorist such as Williams to serve as ammunition for a critique of drama scholarship. Rather than conceiving of cultural studies solely as a contemporary means of revising traditional drama scholarship, I suggest that we also recognize the ways that the epistemologically-fraught "life of the drama" has propelled the development of cultural theory itself.[6] To do so is also to move from Chapter Two's analysis of the early twentieth century into a study of mid-century transformations.

As a way to focus questions about the vexed genealogies of drama, theatre, performance, and cultural studies, the argument of this chapter will also return to the concept of literature – the unproblematically valued term in Brustein's world, the ambivalently devalued term in some cultural studies arenas.

Paul Gilroy's framing of "black music" in *The Black Atlantic* is emblematic of how a scholarly turn to progressive cultural analysis often involves a repudiation of the literary. "This orientation to the specific dynamics of performance has a wider significance . . . Its strengths are evident when it is contrasted with approaches to black culture that have been premised exclusively on textuality and narrative rather than dramaturgy, enunciation, and gesture – the pre- and anti-discursive constituents of black metacommunication."[7] Recent debates in cultural theory, theatre, and humanities scholarship often revolve around the role of so-called "literary" approaches in cultural critique – as well as around adjacent notions of "textual," "discursive," or "linguistic" analyses. Indeed, arguments of legitimation and de-legitimation often pivot and twist around conflicted uses of such terms. Some performance studies scholars might associate a "literary" method with an elite, textualist, anti-materialist study of modern drama. However, when some of the same performance studies scholars engage in de-contextualized analyses of the tropes of avant-garde performance art, it is not entirely clear who is being less materialist, which analyses are more text-based, or what performance forms are actually less "high." Furthermore – Gilroy's tantalizing assertions notwithstanding – there is no absolute correspondence between an anti-textualist method and a liberatory criticism; nor is it clear that the brilliance of Gilroy's own arguments are more indebted to the rigorous study of "enunciation" and "gesture" than they are to the conventions of textualist critique. Consequently, it seems important to remind ourselves of the extraordinarily large number of associations attached to the literary. As I continue, I hope that such reminders will help to expose some blindspots in current oppositional debates amongst and within our fields and subfields.[8] To investigate such a genealogy is, after Foucault, to challenge assumptions of disciplinary singularity, even when such assumptions may be expedient for both self-labeled "traditionalist" defenses and self-labeled "counter-traditionalist" appeals. The genealogical consciousness makes it less easy to uphold divisions between "old" and "new" approaches, sometimes reversing convenient notions of who is borrowing from whom and with them the categories of intellectual precedence and descent. The conflicted referentiality of the literary is just one important arena where such binary delineations get made in drama, theatre, performance, and cultural studies; hence the investigation of literature's conflicts is also one way of de-stabilizing those delineations.

The concept of literature is also important from an institutional perspective. The profession of literature has served as the primary vehicle for establishing the cultural capital of modern English-speaking universities and hence also has served as the barometer for gauging the legitimacy of other humanistic fields. Additionally, as the professionalizing field that reluctantly housed the study of drama in the early twentieth century, as the professionalized field from which theatre's academic promoters broke free throughout the rest of the twentieth century, literary studies has long served as foil, shadow, and sometimes foundation to the emerging disciplinary identities of drama, theatre, and performance studies. Along the way, Literature and English departments have produced some of the most significant and widely circulated critical paradigms in the humanities, models and frameworks that many drama, theatre, and performance studies have adopted despite their own anti-literary rhetoric and institutional location. Furthermore, literary studies is thoroughly enmeshed in the development of cultural studies. Perhaps the most formative cultural studies critiques of literature have emerged from within the field of literature itself. The movement "from literary to cultural studies," to use Anthony Easthope's phrase, was initiated most often by professors of English who sought to enlarge literature's objects of study to include a variety of print and non-print forms as well as to expand the range of (often Marxist) questions asked of traditional literary documents.[9] Such a movement has been neither harmonious in its execution nor complete in its transformation. This chapter is thus also an attempt to install the concept of modern drama next to such disharmonies and partialities. Since it is a cultural form that has always inhabited a reluctant position inside and outside the field of literary studies, an exploration of the blindspot around drama clarifies the conflicts that inhere in the transformation from literary to cultural studies. Drama's ill-fit in both "older" literary studies and "newer" cultural studies suggests that there might be more continuity between the past and the present than contemporary paradigms admit. Finally, I hope to make connections amongst terms and sub-fields that are often too conveniently opposed as well as to defamiliarize the defensive postures and persistent ambivalences that seem to keep those oppositions in place.

Drama and literature

The term "culture" has different associations and is located in a variety of institutional contexts in which humanistic knowledges emerge, circulate, and accumulate value. The same can be said of the term "drama" in the academy. These associations vary widely and, testifying to the frustratingly flexible essentialism of performance more generally, are often not reconcilable. Drama can be both low and high, contextual or de-contextualized, commercial or avant-garde, feminized or masculinized, literary or unliterary, cultured or cultural, a text or an event, practical or impractical, more fake or more real, depending upon the legitimating or delegitimating context. Within literary studies, drama's associations have been plotted along such contradictory axes, and it is along these axes that Robert Brustein's essay also turns. The essay is perhaps most useful as an index of the kind of available metaphors and unprocessed tropes characteristic of such exegeses. He accused dramatists of being "too anxious to please," of going for "climactic emotional effects," of developing an "unsavory . . . alliance with the market place," and of having a "tainted imagination."[10] In a characteristically contradictory relationship to European legacies, he managed to accuse American dramatists of being less distinguished than European playwrights while at the same time catering to cosmopolitan influences. Brustein perhaps made a correct assessment in recognizing that detachment from the realm of literary production and its world of "literary periodicals" would threaten the status of drama as a legitimated cultural form. As John Guillory writes in his study of cultural capital in the university humanities curriculum, "an individual's judgment that a work is great does nothing in itself to preserve that work, unless that judgment is made in a certain institutional context, a setting in which it is possible to insure the reproduction of the work, its continual reintroduction to generations of readers."[11] When Brustein worried about whether drama was or was not literature, he was effectively worrying about whether drama was or was not "Culture" of a particular credible form. In so doing, he reiterated concerns about drama's illegitimate status in a process of acculturation, an illegitimacy measured by its associations with feminine artifice and commercial corruption.

Such arguments had shadowed the curricular position of drama in the academy for more than a half century. Early academic institutionalizers were both sympathetic to and embarrassed by theatre's association with the popular, a link that was the opposite of the literary. Said George Pierce Baker, "what especially marks people who pride themselves on their knowledge of the drama as literature – not on their knowledge of the theatre – is a certain haughtiness toward the mass of the public, a belief that whatever is popular, whatever the crowd likes, must be cheap, inartistic, undesirable."[12] Brander Matthews both celebrated the democratic sensibility of the ideal playwright who "must needs have an understanding of his fellow-man; he must have toleration and, above all, sympathy" while simultaneously allowing his language to erode linguistically into condescension: "he must try to find the greatest common denominator of the throng."[13] In a cultural context unsure about the significance of a rising middle class and the language of economics and business that began to enter the academy, the threat of "commercialism" easily elided with the impulse to cater to the throng. Similarly, in Robert Brustein's writing, to be pro-literature was to be anti-commercial; the equation did not need an argument. If proponents of literature tried to install a division between their pursuits and business, then "theatre" threatened to undo that shaky border as well. That possibility continues both to humiliate and to excite theatre's advocates.

As discussed in Chapter Two, the concept of "literature" consolidated as a curricular and professional category around the turn of the century. Literary credibility was determined by the degree to which a pedagogic text fulfilled the sometimes nebulous but persistent standards of a humanist liberal culture, one that sought to secure a position within a US university system increasingly preoccupied with utility, with technical knowledge, and with the paradigms of scientific inquiry. As Laurence Veysey has argued in *The Emergence of the American University*, the latter borrowed a revised version of a Germanic model in which lines of inquiry were made more rigorous by installing them within the conventions of scientific research. Some early literary scholars worked to adapt philological methods to make literature into a science and to promote an ethic of literary research whose constructed sense of "rigor" we live with in different forms today. More pernicious for the status of literature, however, were the effects of industrialization, a rising business class, and a no-nonsense distrust of intellectualism; this milieu produced a concern for practicality and "real world" sensibilities in higher education, one that dangerously positioned literature within the realm of non-utility. Reacting within and against both "the German method" and a hyper-practical emphasis that threatened to divest higher education of a "spiritual" dimension, scholars of literature joined promoters of "liberal culture" to argue for the preservation of a higher "human character, shaped 'by the deliberate choices of whatever is noble and helpful.' . . . An aesthetic, a moral and tacit social code were all to be found intermingled in the conception of culture as it existed in American academic circles in the late nineteenth century."[14] Brustein's later 1950s articulation was thus embedded in this concept of culture, chastizing the vulgar sensibility of American drama for not aspiring to Arnoldian goals. By criticizing dramatists for pandering to crowds or for sullying the theatre with the forces of economic rather than cultural capital, he resuscitated the anti-utility arguments of early cultural dissidents, condemning the effects of the "real world" ethos of American business on the products of culture.

In reserving his condemnation only for American drama, this particular Brustein essay did not incorporate the fact that drama's real worldness and manifest enmeshment in economic relations had made its academic status as "literature" (ie. as "Culture") shaky for quite some time. Indeed, the significant aspect of "drama exclusive of Shakespeare" was its equivocal status as literature that was not quite literature, a humanist form that, by virtue of its saturation with "the practical," made it not quite humanist after all. In the middle of the twentieth century, academic promoters of theatre responded to this liminality in varied and often contradictory ways. While some, such as Eric Bentley, created compensatory arguments for drama within accepted literary categories, others reversed the terms of value to characterize drama as a rugged, masculine pursuit that countered the fastidious preoccupations of the literary reading room. Indeed, Brustein's corpus can be seen as a constant ride over a disavowed ambivalence. While his 1959 essay on American plays aspired to make the cultural position of a *man of the theatre* equivalent to that of the *man of letters*, other essays and speeches would find it more expedient to emphasize the numerous ways that a manly theatre differed from the womanly conventions of lettered transmission and literary pedagogy. This vacillation is symptomatic of pervasive classed and gendered patterns in quests for cultural legitimacy. Sometimes theatre's practicality is "tainted" and "pandering"; sometimes theatre's practicality is hardy and masculine. Sometimes literature's canon is sweetness and light; sometimes literature's canon is elite and effete. While certain circumstances prompt legitimators to invoke classed cultural hierarchies unproblematically, other contexts prompt some of the same proponents to condemn such standards as feminized and/or commercial, as judgments derived from the prescriptive and peripheral tastes of a compromised imagination.

New critical ambivalences

In the 1950s, gentlemanly notions of liberal culture only vaguely represented the field of literary studies as it was being practiced and legitimated in the university at the time. By mid-twentieth century, the English methods of "practical criticism" and the American practices of "new criticism" had penetrated most English departments on both sides of the Atlantic, working to replace nebulous, belletristic notions of cultured literature with a method of rigorous "close reading" and decontextualized explication. New criticism argued for literature less as the social vehicle of liberal culture than as an object whose understanding required a formalized method of expert reading, one whose feats of interpretation matched the rigor, difficulty, and degree of specialization found in scientific research. Terry Eagleton's *Literary Theory* isolates "the brisk, bloodless" prose of I.A. Richards as the most extreme of new critical originators; "far from questioning the alienated view of science as a purely instrumental, neutrally 'referential' affair, Richards subscribes to this positivist fantasy."[15] New criticism thus served as a mid-century response to the consolidation of a so-called Germanic research university, fending off accusations of literary fuzziness by for-malizing its study. While new critical practitioners such as John Crowe Ransom, Cleanth Brooks, R.P. Blackmur, and William Empson varied in tone and perspective, they generally conceived literature – most ideally embodied in poetry – as a "self-enclosed entity" to be deciphered by "the toughest, most hard-headed techniques of critical dissection."[16] Meanwhile, as movements for coeducation and democratic legislation such as the British Education Act and the American G. I. Bill opened the doors of English and North American universities to a varied student population, humanities professors had to devise wider methods of cultural dissemination. In such a context, the text-focused, genius-tracking methods of new criticism made for easy syllabifi-cation and efficient lecturing, allowing the professing of literature to fit more comfortably within a managed university concerned that its curriculum "scale" meet the demands of an increasingly large, and presumably unlettered, clientele.[17] The trajectory of this "critical technocracy" advanced another level with the struc-turalist development of "genre criticism," most famously and for-matively embodied in the work of Northrop Frye.[18] His *Anatomy of Criticism* incorporated a circumscribed notion of literary his-tory into new critical formalism, developing an elaborate system of categories in which to place each instance of literary produc-tion. Frye's taxonomies thus were a mid-century equivalent of the genus/species laboratories of literary philology. It differed, how-ever, in that this system expelled "any history other than literary history: Literary works were made out of other literary works, not out of any material external to the literary system itself."[19] Frye's genre criticism – and the genre criticism that would fol-low – thus had the satisfying character of scientific and historical paradigms while, at the same time, severely limiting the content and character of the history it brought to bear.

Some mid-century critics – such as Cleanth Brooks and, to some extent, Eric Bentley – worked to situate the drama within the legitimating structures of new critical frameworks. Of the formative new critics, Brooks's scholarship and textbooks perhaps best exemplify new critical analyses of "the drama" and "the dramatic." A comparison of textbooks such as *Un-derstanding Poetry*, *An Approach to Literature*, and *Understanding Drama* demonstrates this constrained critical sphere, one that located drama in a relational field that measured its distance from poetry. *Understanding Drama* divides its table of contents into "Problems of the Drama," "Simpler Types," "More Mature Types," "Special Studies" whereas *Understanding Poetry* was not represented as a "problem" and divided chapters under far more secure categories such as "Narrative Poems," "Descriptive Poems," "Metrics," "Tone," and "Imagery."[20] Meanwhile, "Problems of Drama" also included extended essays that compared drama to "other literary forms" in order to recount the "vast amount of materials accessible to fiction and poetry [that] are not accessible to drama."[21] At the same time, *Understanding Poetry* included no such comparative essays and seemed not to need references to other genres to serve as illuminating counterpoint. Within such frames, the fundamentals of drama such as "place," "exposition," "tempo" and "overt action" were conceived as dilemmas – as "lacking" and "awkward" rather than as "accessible materials" on a par with the poetic materials of metrics, tone, and imagery. In its pedagogical presentation of several genres, *An Approach to Literature* also reproduced similar hierarchical comparisons.[22]

Meanwhile, Eric Bentley's widely-circulated essays and books offer a related illlustration of a mid-century dramatic discourse, one that in many ways mixed the language of cultural capital with the language of new criticism for self-legitimation. In *The Playwright as Thinker*, for example, Bentley deployed the disparaging tones of Arnoldian cultural analysis, lamenting that "drama as a high art has appeared only sporadically" and quoting Bernard Shaw's statement that "the theater is *always* at a low ebb."[23] Echoing and anticipating Robert Brustein and others, he condemned the debased contextuality of the theatre – its commercialism, its audience relations – as well as the particularly low ebb of its American forms. At the same time, Bentley could be found justifying his approach to drama by invoking new critical language. He opposed himself to those "who hold that a good play is not a thing that can be profitably examined in detail and that criticism of great drama is therefore fruitless or impossible. My own conviction is that any good thing is a very good thing and that any work of art can bear the closest scrutiny. The better, the closer."[24] Bentley's references to "detail" and to the "closest" "scrutiny" are not coincidental. They echoed the professionalist quest for minute detail in the "close reading" of new and practical criticism, even echoing the journal, *Scrutiny*, founded in England to extend the mission. Bentley's rhetorical efforts suggest how fully a formalist appeal could legitimate a mid-century critical endeavor.

Other academic promoters of drama addressed the fundamental ways that new critical methods altered the object of literature as well as the concept of cultural capital. Writing in 1952, theatre scholar John Gassner's peremptorily titled essay "There is No American Drama" exemplifies a much more suspicious if anxious response to new criticism. I will focus on it at length as a symptomatic text in an alternate genealogy between drama and cultural studies.[25] Like Brustein, Gassner used American drama's equivocal status as the basis for a lengthier meditation on cultural hierarchy. However, by exploring the disconnect between new critical models and the examples of American drama, the thrust of his argument took a very different direction. He cited, for instance, the political commitment of drama in the 1920s and 1930s, an avowed contextuality that resisted the decontextualized strategies of new critical interpretations. He continued by reciting all of the associations that clung to the drama ever since the project of literary legitimation had begun in the academy. His ardor suggested his own internalization of the dilemma, an ambivalence that would continue throughout his essay. "We were deficient in taste and intellect. We were debased by Broadway vulgarity. We were banal, blatant, and shamelessly sentimental. When we evinced sympathy with the common man, we descended to bathos. When we left plain realism, we gave ourselves up to vapid abstractions and to puerile, undergraduate metaphysics."[26] Within this provisional acceptance of a debased condition, Gassner nevertheless worked to develop a reverse snobbery as a kind of defense. He replicated contemporaneous attacks on the new criticism by invoking the threat of its "European orientation," reproducing a 1950s critique of Europeanization in much the same way that earlier scholars invoked the threat of Germanification in the study of literature. Despite the fact that new criticism was enthusiastically developed by American scholars, T.S. Eliot and other "European" critics figured prominently in Gassner's rendition. "It is a European cum Eliot-sponsored aristocratic traditionalism cum erstwhile aristocratic southern agrarianism transposed into the key of so-called New Criticism."[27]

Gassner, however, was more than simply dismissive of new criticism, but rightly anticipated a paradigmatic shift in literary studies that would not bode well for American drama. "The charges they make directly and by implication are serious and should be received seriously. They are important too because the attitude they reveal may well pervade the educated members of an entire generation upon which the fate of any signficant theatre we may have in the 1950's will largely depend."[28] Gassner, in fact, agreed with new critical objections even as he tried to argue from a different position. "The new criticism," he continued, "is often so accurate that it must be respected, but so sweeping in its condemnation of American drama that it must be refuted."[29] Gassner made the choice to refute, not by arguing for American drama within new critical paradigms, but by arguing that such paradigms could not track the significant interrelations of the American theatrical event. Indeed, he went so far as to suggest that adherence to new critical principles would compromise its Americanism. To subscribe to this dominant paradigm, an adherence embodied in the figure of Eric Bentley who Gassner called "the most Europeanized of the critics," would be to "reject everything that has been distinctly American in our playwriting."[30] Imagining over-cultivated playwrights composing "with the fastidiousness, the mental discipline, the refined or sharpened taste" of a new critical sensibility, he issued dire warnings for the future of American playwriting.

Let them make full use of the various devices of 'irony,' the various types of 'ambiguity' discussed by William Empson, the multiple levels of meaning so adeptly ferreted out in recent literary studies. . . . My suspicion, as already stated, is that the result will be rather ineffective. . . . One important reason is that an ultra-intellectual or ultra-refined kind of drama will lack any substantial basis in American manners and attitudes . . . There is no widely held tradition in America that is not democratic, and this tradition possesses no particular subtleties, cautiousness and restraint."[31]

Theatre and America were both in his view, for better and for worse, spaces of "spontaneity" of "sympathy" and of "convictions" – all of which have "a way of getting out of hand."[32]

Obviously there are many difficulties with this argument. At the starkest level, Gassner invoked a nationalist and masculinist allegiance in the service of an anti-theoretical, anti-interpretive position. The threat of Europeanization also reified a threat of feminization, couched in language that castigated subtlety, fastidiousness, and refinement in order to bolster a drama that was "masculine, buoyant, hard-driving, and uninhibited."[33] These problems notwithstanding, Gassner's defensive treatise identified different elements of drama than the "problems" iterated by Cleanth Brooks. What Gassner limitedly referred to as "American" in American drama was also a site with which to speculate on dramatic performance's relationship to the social – perhaps even to "sociology" – and to material histories other than those emphasized in contemporaneous genre criticism. As such, he promoted the analysis of drama as cultural. It was a different type of "culture" than either the Arnoldian or new critical associations, one that approached the kind of relation that Raymond Williams might have had in mind when he suggested that drama offered a key into the "fundamental conventions which we group as society itself." Gassner spoke of the dramatist's ability to reproduce "an idiom or tone of contemporary life in America," but that catching this idiom meant not "fastidiously avoiding contact with an often coarse-grained reality," something that happened when "we treat playwriting as divorced from social reality and practiced in a vacuum."[34] Gassner was aware of a theoretical turn toward a different conception of culture in the English context via T.S. Eliot's notion of the "medieval synthesis" between persons and the cultural context they mutually produced. Gassner used the reference to speculate on its limits, suggesting that appeals to the communal would remain circumscribed by elitist hesitancies.

I do not by any means ignore the fact that there has been indeed, much writing about the need for a communal or cultural context by T.S. Eliot and his associates in the field of criticism. But specifically, the 'context' to which they generally refer is non-existent in the modern world; and strictly speaking it has been non-existent since the Middle Ages. . . . I do not believe the "medieval synthesis" is actually desired for themselves even by the gentlemen who point toward it. There have been too few Thomas Mertons among them to act upon their beliefs.[35]

For Gassner, American theatre called the bluff of the literary establishment's tentative quest for communalism. To act on an alternative conception of culture, one that could not be confined to the literary object, was to risk letting things "get out of hand" and hence a hypocritical limit point in Eliot's writings. "Meanwhile," Gassner wrote, "there *is* a cultural context – a rough, bouncing and democratic one – in which to function, precariously perhaps, but vigorously."[36] The messier elements of a theatrical "contextual" aligned with the messier elements of a theatrical "communal"; both resisted the epistemological boundaries of the literary object in ways that anticipated, with intriguing if perhaps unwitting foresight, a critical redefinition of the "cultural."

Of course, saying that theatre required a democratically-inflected analysis did not necessarily mean that American theatre was democratic. And it is at this point that Gassner's enthusiasms start to ring more hollowly. Gassner was one amongst a number of American theatre historians in the 1950s who implicitly and explicitly debated just how "out of hand" they wanted their American theatre history to be. In his rough American theatre, Gassner did not actively welcome all displays of vigor and kept his analysis focused on those of white, male playwrights. Meanwhile, a handful of contemporaneous historians such as A.M. Drummond and Richard Moody wrote to open a place for the "native american rituals" and "theatres of life" in their chronicles of the American performance idiom.[37] Richard Moody published scholarship that argued for minstrelsy as a foundational and foundationally complicated American performance form. A decade earlier, Edith Isaacs had written a history of *The Negro in the Theatre*, and argued for the racially hybrid and essentially "borrowed" nature of so-called American theatre. "And that is the reason why, in music and dance, in rhythm and comedy and pantomime, we borrow so freely from the Negro Theatre."[38] Gassner's silence on such internal national hybridity appeared as formal repudiation in the work of Bernard Hewitt and Walter Meserve whose scholarship reproduced the anti-textualist appeals of American theatre history but without revising the racist exclusions of the "American" category.[39] I will return to these blindspots in the final section of this chapter. Without accepting the gendered, nationalist, and polarizing terms in which Gassner articulated his enthusiasms, however, it is still important to foreground the social phenomena and affective structures he was trying to emphasize. The study of drama thereby enabled the study of culture in a different key. The relation between that cultural and the racial, however, is another story.

Dramatic genealogies

Drama both challenged prevailing conceptions of culture and provided an all-too literal illustration of them. Hence, drama's promoters could be found defending and critiquing the same targets, expediently taking up positions in one context, expediently dropping the same positions in another. John Gassner's alternative cultural argument was still hampered by its defensive posture toward new criticism, one that homogenized the movement, equated all its thinkers, and refused to read carefully between the lines of a text like William Empson's *Seven Types of Ambiguity* for the open readings and savvy awareness of social context that others would find. Gassner's argument was also hampered by its defensive posture toward Europeanization and so-called "slavish Anglophilism." Indeed, not only was new criticism American-bred, but T.S. Eliot's "southern agrarianism" derived from an American South that was, despite Gassner's disavowals, still part of "America." Such reductions – in which available terms of de-legitimation are invoked ahistorically and without restraint – appear frequently in polemical encounters where something is at stake. The disavowals perpetuated by such rhetorical, conceptual, and nationalist moves are unfortunate for a number of reasons. Most significantly for this chapter, they would keep American academic promoters of drama in a state of constant misrecognition vis-à-vis Great Britain. The intellectual developments of literary studies characterized as English or European were neither simple nor homogeneous but actively debated and revised. Indeed, had these debates been imported sooner or differently, they might have positioned drama as a lynchpin in the transformation from the study of literature to the innovations of cultural studies. To re-read the insights, defenses, illuminations, and confusions of mid-century drama criticism is to discern the stops and starts of a drama-to-culture genealogy.

Francis Fergusson, for instance – perhaps one of the more insightful and widely-read drama critics of the period – engaged contemporaneous models of literature and culture. Fergusson adopted a more cautious and considered argument on the relation between drama and New Criticism in his widely printed *The Idea of the Theater*. He praised Ransom, Blackmur, and Empson who "have done much to make the art of letters understandable," seeing connections between "the dramatic situation" and Blackmur's "language of gesture" and Empson's studies of ambiguity and the pastoral.[40] At the same time, he forthrightly stated that, since drama was "not primarily a composition in the verbal medium," other approaches were equally necessary. Hence he decided to integrate Cambridge Anthropology into his study of the drama in order to analyze the "ritual" function of a form whose "own essence is at once more primitive, more subtle, and more direct than either word or concept," an aspect best conceived by "writers who are students of culture rather than literary critics."[41] In contrast to other drama critics, Fergusson foregrounded an anthropological notion of culture throughout his text. Positioning anthropological analysis as fundamental to his approach to the drama, he thus installed an early connection between drama and anthropology. While his approach reproduced the primitivist and structuralist reductions of such earlier anthropological models, it is still noteworthy that the contingencies of the dramatic event served as a bridge between New Criticism and classical anthropology. As such, his drama scholarship can be located on a discontinuous genealogy in literary and cultural studies, indirectly anticipating the mutual enthusiasms between literature and anthropology that would underpin the "blurred genres" and "new historicisms" of a later generation.[42] Fergusson is also obviously a figure in a discontinuous genealogy between drama and performance studies. It is thus worth remembering that "drama" could and did provide an earlier occasion for thinking about the socio-cultural dimensions of the textual artifact and for thinking about the nature of "restored behavior," something that does not always appear in the counter-traditionalist appeals.

The project of "culture" was also more complicated for many of the figures whom Gassner critiqued. While F.R. Leavis's "practical criticism" incarnated the professionalist demands of a new literary criticism, it also managed to address a number of contradictory post-war hopes and ambivalences. Eagleton elaborates:

In the face of whimsical 'taste,' they stressed the centrality of rigorous critical analysis, a disciplined attention to 'words on the page.' They urged this not simply for technical or aesthetic reasons, but because it had the closest relevance to the spiritual crisis of modern civilization. Literature was important not only in itself, but because it encapsulated creative energies which were everywhere on the defensive in modern "commercial" society.[43]

F.R. Leavis, Q.D. Leavis, and a host of colleagues and disciples saw in literature and literary reading the possibility for reacquaintance with the most vital, energetic, and authentic elements of English life. They celebrated not simply conventional texts in a high literature canon but also those that connected readers to a world of rich and authentic experience, one that would be found in the "organic societies" of pre-industrial pastures more often than in the trappings of modern "civilization" (a word that they used disparagingly). For practical critics, literary language did its best work when it evoked this world of concrete feeling. "In really 'English' writing, language 'concretely enacted' such felt experience: true English literature was verbally rich, complex, sensuous and particular, . . . one which read aloud was rather like chewing an apple. The 'health' and 'vitality' of such language . . . embodied a creative wholeness."[44] For Q.D. Leavis in *Fiction and the Reading Public* and for F.R. Leavis in texts such as *The Great Tradition*, the pursuit of culture was the pursuit of Englishness, located within the literary text and in the constitutive relation with an English reader. Whatever the political persuasion of the critics and political effects of the criticism, this language of vitality, health, wholeness, and concrete enactment set the terms for later discourses on culture. T.S. Eliot expanded, furthermore, this pursuit of a "whole life" from the domain of the strictly textual. Stimulated by his fixation on rituals of the agrarian American South, a fixation on the "communal" parodied by Gassner but that had discursive support from Leavis's concept of the organic society, Eliot developed a comparable picture for a "whole way of English life." His description of culture encompassed the self-making events of a "whole society," including "all the characteristic activities and interests of a people: Derby Day,

Henley Regatta, Cowes, the twelfth of August, a Cup Final, the pin table, the dart board, Wensleydale cheese, boiled cabbage cut into sections . . ."[45] This list, appearing in *Notes Towards the Definition of Culture*, thus moved beyond practical criticism's equation between literature and culture.[46]

With this genealogy in mind, I would like now to return to that other 1950s drama theorist, Raymond Williams, especially since the Leavisian language of the vital concrete would saturate this critic's theories of both drama and culture. As recounted in a number of histories of cultural studies, Williams is one of the declared fathers of the Birmingham School of cultural studies, a site where, along with Richard Hoggart and succeeded by Stuart Hall, literary scholars rethought their objects and methods of study in light of progressive, socialist, and Marxist ideals. These scholars would push Eliot's declared interest in the "whole society" to include not only the pastoral signifiers of wholeness but a wider range of elements within the whole of the nation. Many of them did so based upon their own histories in working-class families. Richard Hoggart expanded Q.D. Leavis's focus on the reading public to include working-class readers of popular literature. His *Uses of Literacy*, published in 1957, placed them within a personalized account that detailed the emotions and daily lives of laboring families who did not have the option of disparaging industrialization with Leavisian disdain.[47] In *Culture and Society*, Williams added to T.S. Eliot's "pleasant miscellany" other characteristic activities of the English (male) working class, "steelmaking, touring in motor-cars, mixed farming, the Stock Exchange, coalmining and London transport."[48] The creation of such lists would become a convention in the disciplinary statements of cultural studies. Indeed, Richard Schechner's list of expanded performance forms ("rock concerts, discos, electioneering . . .") can be placed in a genealogy of disciplinary gestures, expanding relevant intellectual "miscellany" in a way that some find more pleasant than others.

To position Raymond Williams as a drama theorist, however, is to emphasize aspects of his legacy that are often ignored or unknown, particularly in the US context. Connections between the principles behind cultural and theatre studies are brought to light when one remembers that Williams preceded and interspersed his foundational scholarship in cultural studies

with his less famous series in dramatic criticism between 1952
and 1968. As suggested earlier, I have found it more than intriguing to think about these early writings in light of Williams's
developing models of culture. From this angle, the transition
from literary to cultural studies can be seen to take place through
the vehicle of "drama." For instance, Williams's *Drama in Use*
attempted to place dramatic literature in a production context
by borrowing the language of utility, language that de-stabilized
the literary status of his project and thus deployed drama as a
springboard toward a materialist cultural analysis. Moreover, it
is perhaps no coincidence that a theatre-oriented scholar coined
the term "structure of feeling." Indeed, as John Higgins notes,
the development of the term "structure of feeling" coincided with
Williams's writings on drama.[49] Meanwhile, later works, notably
Culture (or what in the United States would be titled *The Sociology
of Culture*) made considerable use of theatre as a case study for
theorizing the institutional, organizational, political, and social
dimensions of aesthetic forms.[50] To emphasize this disciplinary
genealogy is thus to position drama, not only as something that
might make an alliance with cultural studies (as Jill Dolan and
others have argued), but more profoundly as a site that helped
to propel the cultural studies project.[51]

Developed through the re-writing of his drama books and into
the publication of *The Long Revolution*, the concept of "structure of feeling" was meant to give some formal ballast to his
concept of culture. As Fred Inglis writes, "'Structure of feeling' was a concept designed to catch the point of intersection
between art and historical experience as individually, and therefore as socially lived. Williams's project . . . had been to grasp
a cultural history as experience; that is to say, to interpret the
movement of change caught and held in the peculiar lenses of
art."[52] It was thus less a model of how art reflected society than
a method by which to catch emergent moments in "the active
processes of learning, imagination, creation, performance."[53]
In *Drama from Ibsen to Brecht*, Williams's definition of structure of feeling used drama to articulate realms of affective experience that matched but exceeded the conventions of literary
critique. "It is as firm and definite as 'structure' suggests, yet
it is based in the deepest and often least tangible elements of
our experience . . . Its means, its elements, are not propositions

or techniques; they are embodied, related feelings. . . . we can look at dramatic methods yet know, in detail, that what is being defined is more than technique: is indeed the practical way of describing those changes in experiences – the responses and their communication; the 'subjects' and the 'forms' – which make the drama in itself and as a history important."[54] While Williams often found such active, recursive processes in novelists such as Dickens, Hardy, and Lawrence whom he felt had listened to the voices of English culture and developed artistic conventions both to match and to advance them, he often conceived drama as the form that allowed him to "look both ways" between the aesthetic and the social. In his inaugural lecture as Professor of Drama at Cambridge University, he used dramatic form to speculate on his wider hopes for a theory and practice of a social culture. He elaborated, for instance, on the significance of Anton Chekhov's dramaturgy.

It is a way of speaking and of listening to a specific rhythm of a partic- ular consciousness; in the end a form of unfinished, transient, anxious relationship, which is there on the stage or in the text but which is also, pervasively, a structure of feeling of a precise and contemporary world . . . I don't think I could have understood these dramatic pro- cedures as methods – that is to say, as significant general modes – if I had not been looking both ways. I could have seen them perhaps as techniques . . . [but] it is where technique and method have either an identity, or as, now commonly, a significant fracture, that all the hard questions of this difficult discipline begin.[55]

Williams's discussion of structures of feeling in Chekhovian dra- matic dialogue echoed the language he used to analyze Dickens's dialogic power. Not coincidentally, Williams isolated the kind of realm that John Gassner invoked in his account of an American dramatic idiom, reinforcing the sense that Gassner's Americanist label was serving as a stand-in for an account of cultural process in general.

Hard questions about the fracture between technique and method, between consciousness and language, between feeling and world appeared throughout Williams's drama scholarship. In *Modern Tragedy*, Williams used such impulses to engage and critique a legacy of dramatic criticism. Though specifically reply- ing to George Steiner's philosophy of tragedy, he argued against a general critical strain that too easily married the systemics of structural anthropology with the systemics of literary genre criticism.[56] Such a union resulted too simply in a model of tragic form that transcended social and historical particularity. For Williams, this universalizing tendency bypassed what was most intriguing about the drama – its dynamism, its mutability, and its embedded social structures. "If, however, we think of it as a theory about a single and permanent kind of fact, we can end only with the metaphysical conclusions that are built into any such assumption . . . the assumption of a permanent, universal and essentially unchanging human nature."[57] Condemning theorists who presumed an ahistorical equation between Greek, Renaissance, and modern tragic forms, Williams went on to re-define the significance of tragedy in terms that resonated with his paradigms in cultural theory.

Tragedy is not a single and permanent kind of fact, but a series of experiences and conventions and institutions. It is not a case of interpreting this by reference to a permanent and unchanging human nature. Rather, the varieties of tragic experience are to be interpreted by reference to the changing conventions and institutions. . . . It is in any case necessary to break the theory if we are to value the art . . . [instead] to see its controlling structure of feeling, the variations within this and their connections with actual dramatic structures, and to be able to respond to them critically, in the full sense.[58]

Foregrounding the inter-relations amongst experience, convention, and institution, Williams focused on technical and social shifts in the theatrical event – upon the choral structures of Greek tragedy, upon the later secularist impulses that replotted tragic action, upon the modernizing forces that generated and isolated the psychic conventions of the tragic hero in the twentieth century. Seeking the variations within and between dramatic structure and "structures of feeling," Williams's investigation in *Modern Tragedy* thus provided the lens and the language for theorizing cultural process, anticipating and echoing the analytic paradigms of "dominant," "residual," and "emergent" for which his cultural theory would become known.[59]

Re-performing cultural studies

The "hard questions of this difficult discipline," whether that discipline be modern drama or culture in general, may have had a beginning for Raymond Williams in such structures of

feeling, but the endings of such questions are still uncertain. I
have endeavored thus far to link Williams's intellectual genealogy to the study of drama and thereby to position it as a significant precursor to the study of culture. At the same time, dramatic performance is also interesting in a Williams genealogy as
a metaphor for expressing ambivalences in progressive literary
studies, misrecognitions that persist in literature's transmutation
into cultural studies. Checkered throughout Fred Inglis's biography are constant references to the parallel ambivalences with
which Williams greeted both participation in "actual" theatrical events and participation in "actual" social relations. In fact,
Inglis tells his readers, Williams offered his inaugural speech as
Professor of Drama, despite "hardly [having] been to a theatre in
years."[60] Without recounting all of these references or overly psy-
chologizing Williams, I think that this reluctance is an intriguing
symptom, not simply of hypocrisy, but of the basic conundrums
built into our "difficult discipline." Drama seems to function
both as a springboard for extra-literary cultural engagement and
as a limit point past which literary-derived cultural analysis seems
unwilling to go. This kind of ambivalence and Eliot-like slippage
persists even in Fred Inglis's own way of treating drama as a cultural event, that is, as a form that is made analyzable and useful
in the moment it is turned back into a trope. "Drama matters
so much for Williams because, more than any other form except opera . . . it is a communal form of art. Among dramatists,
Ibsen was the first key subject, because Ibsen dramatized hero-
ism as hopefulness, even when – most of all when – the hero
or heroine was pulled down to death by desire. Ibsen prefig-
ured the essential tension between Williams's pervasive feelings
of inheritance and his unusually strong drive to break away and
keep away, keeping other people away at the same time."[61] It
is noteworthy that Inglis follows the first sentence about theatre's ensemble form with a thematic discussion of the content
of Ibsen's plays, as if one were an extension of the other. The
"communal" alliances and frictions of theatre-making of course
embody the simultaneous urges of collective inheritance and of
breaking free; however, Inglis reorients that shaky communalism
from the interactive realm of actors, writers, and designers to the
internal dynamics of the play text. That kind of move is reproduced again and again in studies of culture, drama, theatre, and
even performance, demonstrating the persistence of new critical

methods even in attempts to break free from new critical objects. Such tendencies seem to perpetuate a formalist quest for communalism, even when its "vitality" is the declared goal.

Williams's Leavisian legacies may have produced different kinds of exclusions as well, particularly in his perpetuation of a nationalist communal. Williams's expansion of the culturally relevant still kept the pursuit of Englishness as its implicit and sometimes explicit drive. In his measured reflections on Raymond Williams's contribution, Stuart Hall emphasizes this inertia. While recognizing the epistemological significance of his pursuit of "structures of feeling" and of "lived communities," Hall contends that Williams pursued a mythic wholeness.[62] The vital, concrete enactments that Williams tried to locate were derived from a nationalist "feeling" that could not always address differential "structures" of race and ethnicity. In other words, Williams's "whole way of life" had a number of unacknowledged holes. Rather than filling them, Hall's critique asks for the recognition of difference and hybridity as fundamental to a concept of culture rather than as aberrations to be resolved. Similarly, Paul Gilroy's *There Ain't No Black in the Union Jack* exposes the white, working-class, English male who operates as Williams's primary locus of authenticity. Even in Williams' explicit attempts to address race, this figure is the one who has formed his "lived identity" over "long experience." As such, Williams writes, a critic must understand if not endorse how this "English working man . . . protests at the arrival or presence of 'foreigners.' " This paradigm leaves very little room for persons of color also to have a "lived identity" or a whole way of life. As Gilroy asks, "how long is long enough to become a genuine Brit? . . . Under what conditions is national identity able to displace or dominate the equally 'lived and formed' identities which are based on age, gender, region, neighborhood or ethnicity?"[63] This kind of critique also reflects back on the status of both drama and performance in the analysis of culture. In many ways, the language of the concrete, of feeling, and of lived experience resonates strongly with historic arguments on the potential of drama as well as with contemporary arguments on the theorizing of performance. However important this emphasis in the study of performance cultures is, it is also an intensely local affect, one whose appeal and felt authenticity obscures the systems that make it appealing and that mystifies the structures that produce the feeling. In the case of both John Gassner (and fellow drama critics) and Raymond Williams (and fellow cultural critics), the quest for "culture" was also a reification of "nation," however "rough" and "bouncing" it may be. The elements that Gassner delineated as "American" were also the elements that Williams delineated as "English." In neither case did the cultural move beyond the "literary" or the "textual" actually question the racialized sphere of the national.

Different kinds of comforting reifications occur in other disciplinary debates on performance and culture, however – not only in "older" drama studies, not only in "older" cultural studies. Both contemporary performance studies and contemporary cultural studies offer illustrations of how scholars' "long experience" in certain disciplinary homes structure their assumptions of where newness and difference lie. In the middle of introducing cutting edge approaches to scholarship on black cultural expression, Paul Gilroy includes a chastening quote from Edouard Glissant. "It is nothing new to declare for us music, gesture, dance are forms of communication, just as important as the gift of speech. This is how we first managed to emerge from the plantation: aesthetic form in our cultures must be shaped from these oral structures."[64] Glissant's comment exposes the racialized hazards of disciplinary innovation. Here, a new intellectual experiment turns out to be an African diasporic tradition. What Edouard Glissant said of the "discovery" of performance culture might well have been addressed to a larger performance studies discourse that claimed to have a "new paradigm." Indeed, performance's fundamental relation to social life is a theme, not only in the realm of black folklore, but also in the explicitly philosophical texts of a black intellectual tradition. Performance studies is, from this angle, "nothing new" to those who already had read W.E.B. Du Bois and Alain Locke.

Similar kinds of reinvented traditions appear in the work of more recent cultural theorists, however. Lest I reproduce the approach that I plotted in the introduction to this chapter – one where new cultural theorists such as Hall and Gilroy are invoked to define the study of drama and theatre as "old" – let me also consider how a longer genealogy of drama and theatre scholarship can resituate perceptions of newness in cultural studies.

Consider Paul Gilroy's enthusiastic positioning of the analytic potential of "black music" in tracking the movements of the "Black Atlantic" and in understanding the nature of modernity itself. To many performance scholars, Gilroy's suggestion that such a study would require an analytic other than an "all-encompassing textuality" and a "need to make sense of musical performances where identity is fleetingly experienced in the most intensive ways" sounded quite amenable.[65] Such language has appeared in various attempts to articulate performance's exceptionalism. Perhaps less familiar, however, was Gilroy's relentless, many-paged need to position and re-position this recovery, one that would retrieve "neglected modes of signifying practice like mimesis, gesture, kinesis, and costume."[66] "At the risk of appearing rather esoteric," Gilroy wrote in 1993, "I want to suggest that the history and practice of black music points to other possibilities and generates other plausible models. This neglected history is worth reconstructing, whether or not it supplies pointers to other more general cultural processes."[67] While it is significant that a scholar of Paul Gilroy's stature recognized this need, for whom are such practices "neglected" and by whom are their analyses considered "esoteric?" A longer effort in American-American theatre and performance scholarship – one located in a related but apparently backgrounded disciplinary genealogy from that of Gilroy – had already made considerable headway in theorizing such forms. Gilroy's anti-essentialist but nevertheless adamant recognition of the "antimodernity of these forms . . . the (dis)guise of a premodernity that is both actively reimagined in the present" had been similarly framed in James Hatch's 1976 study of "neo-Africanisms."[68] When Gilroy's positioning alighted upon "call and response" and "antiphony" as the formal devices that structured diasporic feeling, he schematically invoked formal techniques that had received more specific analysis in the work of Eleanor Traylor and Eileen Southern.[69] And when Gilroy positioned such black performance as formally and philosophically necessary to the invention of dominant forms of (white) cultural production, he echoed similar arguments made by Hatch, Traylor, Southern, Errol Hill, and many more. Even Edith Isaacs' conflicted 1947 study of *The Negro in the Theatre* still noticed how "freely" white Americans "borrow . . . from the Negro Theatre" to invent an "American" theatre for themselves.[70] Despite this scholarly tradition, "long experience" and "lived and formed identities" in other disciplinary homes had given Gilroy a different picture of what was esoteric and hence "new." Gilroy's cultural studies, however, is "nothing new" (or, at least, not *as* new) to those who had already spent a lifetime teaching African-American performance.

The persistence of these disciplinary blindspots, inertias, and rediscovered "experiments" reflects back on drama's continued shaky relation to culture, an instability that appeared in Culture's early formations as a gentlemanly moral form, continued in its later formations as a rigorously studied new critical mode of cultural capital, and now reappears in culture's most recent anthropological transformations in cultural studies. That this ill-fit should continue within the socially-oriented, praxis-friendly, materially contextualized project of cultural studies seems curious. It seems curious that such cultural revisions of a literary studies project have not repositioned drama, a form whose literary status was circumspect due to its occasional vulgarity, its embedded practicality, its extra-literary aesthetics, and its hyper-contextual and relentlessly non-autonomous status as an epistemological object. Rather than lamenting this oversight, however, it might be beneficial to use its persistence to reflect back on debates about the status of "text," "language," and "the literary" in cultural studies. If the relationship between literature and society has turned into a cultural studies fascination between text and social process, then the liminal life of drama in the academy resituates and is resituated by such methodological questions. When Meagan Morris asks would-be cultural theorists to move beyond "a literary reading of the shopping mall that does not seriously engage with questions that arise in history, sociology, and economics," her argument alights on similar inertias that have produced epistemological dilemmas around drama.[71] Drama's hyper-contextuality needed "history"; its sociality invited "sociology"; and its commercialism made it difficult to avoid issues of "economics." Indeed, methodological questions about the role of "text-based" criticism in cultural studies rest upon concerns that have plagued the study of drama within and without literary studies since the turn of the century, even before Francis Fergusson's literary wariness prompted him to contact those "students of culture" in Cambridge anthropology.

The ambivalent status of drama might well be continuous with what Dorothy Hale calls a lingering "social formalism" in progressive literary and cultural studies. Hale investigates the "slippery materialism that creates a bridge between Marxist literary theory and Anglo-American literary formalism."[72] Finding this slipperiness next to contemporary scholarship in cultural studies, she cites examples of literary scholars such as Eve Kosofsky Sedgwick, Barbara Johnson, and Henry Louis Gates who use novels as the basis for wider cultural theory. Hale maintains that such work is ultimately formalist, derived from traditional new critical literary paradigms and an undertheorized belief in a tropic connection between literature and the social. Thus, the lure of new criticism's textual self-sufficiency lingers despite a rhetoric that seeks to de-stabilize the status of literature and to reach toward a progressive politics in gender, race, and queer studies. "If the novel in Sedgwick criticism is no longer a formalist world apart, it nonetheless retains much of the representational autonomy it enjoyed under the old new critical regime that Sedgwick has helped to supplant: the cultural critic who has dedicated herself to depriviliging the novel on aesthetic grounds finds herself reinstating the novel's formal privilege on the grounds of its social representativeness."[73] Intriguingly, Hale along with Catherine Gallagher traces that slippage back to scholars such as Raymond Williams, figures whose quest for materialist analysis ultimately remained mystified about how material production "dissolved" into the literary artefact.[74]

When such solid, material objects as shoes and potatoes are themselves 'read' as signifiers within complex signifying systems, the distinction between material and symbolic products breaks down. The physical object becomes a signifier, and the physical properties of conventionally recognized signifiers (eg. the aural and visual qualities of spoken and written words) are emphasized. Everything can then appear equally autonomous and dependent, determined and determining, referential and self-referential, symbolic and real.[75]

Writing from within the institutionalization of cultural studies, Lawrence Grossberg agrees about the inertias built into certain strains of literary-derived cultural studies scholarship. Despite Williams's assertions about the need to break down conceptual divisions between "culture" and "society," despite arguing that "cultural studies had to reinsert culture into the practical every-day life of people," "Williams was never able actually to escape this separation – both in his privileging of certain forms of culture (literature) and in his desire to equate culture with some sort of totality and/or ethical standard."[76] While Hale and Gallagher remain unconvinced by Williams and his descendents' attempts to foreground the materiality and embodiments of the literary text, drama's materialism and its bodies beckon for critical recognition. Nevertheless, drama's decidedly embodied bodies (not to mention its shoes and potatoes) constitute a blindspot in critical theory, inconveniencing both cultural studies principles and social formalist analysis by incarnating and exceeding them at once.

Finally, I think that this genealogy is chastening to those of us who have an announced affiliation with performance studies. As a varied intellectual and artistic movement galvanized by a cultural studies milieu, performance studies bears no singular or unfettered relationship to disciplinary traditions in literature, culture, and drama. I do not mean to suggest that we unthink-ingly embrace Raymond Williams as an intellectual predecessor nor entirely accept all critiques of formalist or "literary" cultural studies. Nevertheless, it seems important for performance studies scholars and affiliates to situate our subfields, our methods, our textualist impulses, our mystified materialisms, and our most cherished insights within a complicated institutional genealogy. I consider one of the major efforts of performance studies to be something akin to the analysis of structures of feeling in aesthetic, collective, and everyday spaces – moments when convention and emotion, technique and force, a gestural movement and a so-cial movement, collide with, rework, undo, and advance each other. Many of us imagine this project to be independent of the project of modern drama. It can be useful and humbling to rec-ognize a different genealogy, albeit a discontinuous one, amongst categories such as drama, literature, culture, and performance. Before comprehensively endorsing the connection between the disciplines of performance studies and cultural studies, it is important to step back from this equation – historically, in-stitutionally, curricularly, and methodologically. An awareness of a longer, complicated disciplinary genealogy makes opposi-tions between old literary studies and new cultural studies and between old theatre studies and new performance studies less easy to maintain or to elide. Thinking genealogically about literature's relationship to theatre before cultural studies, about Williams's theatrical relationship to literature, about cultural studies' reproduction of supposedly supplanted literary methods, and about the different types of methodological traditions perpetuated and refracted in performance and cultural studies reveals more unexpected discontinuities and disavowed connections. These various disciplinary beginnings have not always produced analytically helpful endings, but perhaps their future has yet to be imagined.

4 Practice and performance: modernist paradoxes and literalist legacies

> "Getting a show up is so gross. What feels like boredom is really panic. Everyone is exhausted, nauseous, perfectly happy."
> Deb Margolin[1]

> "Artists of the world, drop out! You have nothing to lose but your professions."
> Allan Kaprow[2]

Practice versus theory

This chapter takes the issue of practice as a central organizing concept. I begin with an epigraph from performance artist Deb Margolin in order to remind myself and my reader that the gross, boring, panicky, and exhausting process of "getting a show up" is often what people mean when they refer – generously or disparagingly – to the practical nature of performance. For some, this grossness is redemptive in its cumbersomeness. For others, it is . . . just gross. Accounts of production often use a literal language. While for some theorists and scholars, this literal mode is philosophically uninteresting, for other performance practitioners and artists, the invocation of the literal is a celebration of the concrete. Terms such as practice and the practical can also be aligned with the professional, something valued in certain contexts and repudiated – including in the declarations of Allan Kaprow. When considering the assumptions behind these and other practices, I try to remember that, following Deb Margolin, various debates about different ways of seeing, doing, and interpreting performance, practice, or anything else are often about a kind of "happiness," attempts by various persons to argue for the value of what they are good at doing and to see legitimated that which obsesses them, i.e. that which makes them nauseous and perfectly happy.

To launch my discussion of the linguistic dilemmas that fetter conversations amongst scholars and artists, theorists and practitioners, let me recall a notorious interview with Elizabeth LeCompte. LeCompte, as most students of theatre and performance know, is the central director of the Wooster Group, a New York-based performance troupe whose work has become synonymous with an American post-modern avant-garde. In productions from *Sakonnet Point* through *Nayatt School, Route 1 and 9, Brace-Up!,* and *To you, the Birdie,* LeCompte's theatre is renowned for its parodic re-using, dismantling, and re-combining of classic texts, traditions, and other "found" performance idioms. By inheriting the directorship of what started as the Performing Garage, she is also the inheritor and re-worker of an avant-garde legacy that began in the 1960s, a post-War period of cross-disciplinary innovation whose history includes figures such as John Cage, Merce Cunningham, Richard Schechner, Allan Kaprow, Yvonne Rainer, Robert Morris, Michael Kirby, and Carolee Schneeman. This period has been retroactively theorized as the beginnings of a transformation from modernism to post-modernism. This period of New York experimentation has also been retroactively posited as the disciplinary origin of East Coast performance studies. Hence, intellectual genealogies of the 1960s and 1970s will be the subject of this chapter.

Given LeCompte's aesthetic and her historical position, Nick Kaye, a scholar of "postmodernism and performance," was in an ideal position to interview her about *Brace-Up!,* a production that integrated elements of Noh Theatre with elements of Anton Chekhov's *Three Sisters.* When asked to expound upon the significance of combining Noh with Russian naturalism, LeCompte was reluctant to respond with felicitous sentences about Eastern and Western encounters, parodies, and challenges to convention. "I didn't read too much about what Noh was or what it's supposed to be," she says, ". . . I think I was probably drawn to that structure, that physical architectonic structure. How they moved, how they dealt with entrances and exits." Despite LeCompte's response, Kaye proceeds with his line of questioning, one that would seem quite logical to any theorist of post-modernism who was trying to analyze a post-modern performance. "Performances seem to comment on previous productions," he says, "images are re-used, rehearsal procedures are remember or re-presented. Were you interested in Noh's concern with its own history?" She responds, "I don't have any academic interest in Japanese theatre." Kaye tries again: "I'm just interested in what these appropriations might have to offer . . . what the juxtaposition might be doing." LeCompte responds, deadpan: "I thought we were getting to that when I said 'entrances and exits.'"[3]

Le Compte and Kaye's respective locations in this conversation are over-determined. The effort to make an artist's process available for reflection in fact produces division; the format of the interview reproduces the divisions of labor between scholar and practitioner. Where Kaye sees self-reflexive "re-use" and parodic "appropriation" of familiar elements, LeCompte characterizes her work simply as "allow[ing] them to be in the space together, without this *demand* for meaning." "Do you mean that I am demanding meaning of you?" asks Kaye, sounding like a startled therapist, "it may be that we don't have a language to talk with." LeCompte agrees: "I think it's probably very instructive . . . to be honest, just my inability to grapple with whatever it is you're telling me. It has something to do with why the work is like it is."[4] This kind of conversational stall is ubiquitous. Those who have participated in comparable interviews, in post-show discussions, and in panel presentations endure these moments, conversational misfires where the ever-sought hope for artist-scholar exchange is ever-deferred. Whether intended or not, Kaye found himself installed in the position of He-Who-Is-Preoccupied-With-Meaning. As such, he faced a moment when his interpretation was rejected, not necessarily because it was wrong, but because meaning was declared irrelevant to She-Who-Is-Preoccupied-With-Making. It is "in the piece itself," said LeCompte, "I'm not going to now make meaning separately from that piece for you."

In my department life and that of many of my colleagues in theatre and performance studies, the non-practice/practice dichotomy emerges most often to distinguish those who do not participate in the gross work of "getting a show up" from those who do, those who make meaning of a theatrical figure from those who worry about how she will exit the stage. The old, obfuscating, unhelpfully ubiquitous opposition between production and re-search typically defines how one's speech is heard and whether it will be deemed "practical" or "academic." Typically, that association in turn decides whether one will foreground the literality of performance or whether one will go through a variety of theoretical maneuvers to illustrate that performance is hardly literal at all. As we have seen, this structure is familiar in the institutional history of performance. However, with the advent of postmodern thought, the exchange came to have a different character. Many trained in "theory" would claim to know exactly how to respond to the misguided paradigms of the maker. To foreground performance practice without attention to its historical chain of signification is to remain enmeshed in an old metaphysics of presence. To focus on "exits and entrances" without "reading too much about Noh" is to disavow one's location in an appropriative series of citations. That kind of critique underwrote many of the late-twentieth century arguments that appeared in the service of pro-language, pro-discourse, pro-theory, pro-representation positions that effectively cast a Derridean rain on the realm of performance, making the literal, pro-presence, pro-itselfness language of performance almost unhearable to anyone who listened with deconstructionist ears. What seems so strange about the stall in the LeCompte/Kaye interview is that, of all performance experiments, Elizabeth LeCompte's work seems so tailor-made for deconstructionist eyes.

I think that there is a great deal that can be understood about the particular conventions and slips of this exchange between postmodern theorist and postmodern artist by going back a little earlier. To consider the historical moment of the 1960s and early 1970s is to recall the relationship between performance and something called modernism. Though the kinship between the artist and the intellectual was excavated and reconfigured throughout the twentieth century, the question of their partnership became more acute and paradoxical during this time. While it varied from place to person, the nature of the relationship was something to be discussed, contended with, and sometimes institutionalized. As Howard Singerman argues, this was one of the legacies of abstract expressionism, the modernist movement in art that lay behind the formation of residencies, art schools, and the phenomenon of the "visiting artist" on college campuses.[5]

As Sally Banes has argued, colleges and universities also became the site and implicit patron of much "avant-garde experimentation" after the mid-twentieth century.[6] In theatre, a number of doctoral programs formed with the explicit intention of integrating the scholar and the artist. And throughout the country, the number of art graduate programs (doctoral and MFA) more than doubled, making and sometimes forcing the world of the arts and the world of the university to contend with each other. When, by 1970, the MFA was declared the "terminal degree" in the professionalization of both the visual and the performing artist, the move also announced the functional role of the university in constituting the artist as a professional. These shifts were not received with either complete harmony or complete avowal. Often the versus in "the artist versus intellectual" shiboleth was reasserted more vehemently as these figures entered into institutional partnership. However, the decision of whether or not "to go to graduate school" became exactly that at this time, a self-conscious decision, a routinized choice amongst possible life paths. It is in such a context that the word "academic" could come to have specific association for someone like Elizabeth LeCompte. Whether or not artists went to graduate school, became "visitors," or founded a performance studies department, the university was something to be considered, claimed, villainized, or repudiated by this and subsequent generations of artists.

The stalls in the Kaye/LeCompte conversation can also be traced to a number of other discontinuous genealogies in modernism and performance, legacies that remain somewhat confused in current postmodern theories of performance. While her theatre has become a synonym for postmodernity, Le Compte is an avant-garde theatre practitioner who does not embrace the discourse's terms. For a theatre director who calls her pieces "constructions," attention to the deconstruction of meaning still focuses too much on meaning, something that she opposes to making. "The most important thing in all of this is that – when I go downstairs I don't have any thematic ideas – I don't even have a theme. I don't have anything except literal objects – some flowers, some images, some television sets, a chair, some costumes I like."[7] A postmodern perspective would now trouble the assumption of a "literal object" existing outside significatory operations.

And yet Le Compte places her literal object at the productive center of postmodern performance. How can this be? By looking at the critical and philosophical debates of the late 1960s and early 1970s, I think that we can gain a better sense of why confusion and misrecognition persist – and not only around the work of the Wooster Group. This means addressing the disciplines of visual art and art criticism whose self-definitions contended, not only with the professional artist, but also with the nature of the theatrical. This period is one in which the disciplines of painting, sculpture, literature, dance, performance, and theatre were working within and against each other, most often crossing in the arena of art practice and most often individuating in the arena of art scholarship. As a period of interdisciplinary artistic experimentation, it produced episodes of critical euphoria but also episodes of critical anxiety as the scholarly representatives of various fields tried to come to terms with their own professional training and this anti-professional experimentation – or, put another way, to set the terms for valuing the kind of art that they liked and the kind of criticism that they were good at doing. This was also a moment when definitions of modernism were retroactively theorized, especially in the field of art history and criticism. Consequently, a variety of artists and intellectuals found themselves at odds, and, interestingly, terms such as "performance" and "theatricality" were often deployed to celebrate or condemn the transgression of disciplinary boundaries as well as to delineate between modernist and anti-modernist imaginations. Indeed, at this point, a fixation on the literal object was aligned with rather than opposed to theatricality. This set the terms for a very different kind of anti-theatrical prejudice, one that resisted the anti-representational drives of performance a great deal more than its classically representational ones. As such, an investigation of the vexed relationship between art-making and art-theorizing at this moment in time provides a set of tools for understanding the parallels and discontinuities between more recent critical theorizing and more recent performance experiments. I will argue that the legacy of such *anti*-anti-representational theories – bearing their disavowed but always formative connection to modernist art and theory – now supports literalist accusation, something particularly apparent when post-modern critics and post-modern performers find themselves in conversation.

A genealogical consciousness also includes the philosophical context of the period, particularly the intellectual history of "deconstruction" whose modernist inclinations and post-modern derivations have confused the critical status of performance. Deconstruction was a "revival of rhetoric" that sidelined rather than affirmed the phenomenon of oral performance on which rhetoric had been defined. In violation of conventional alignments, I am going to argue that deconstruction's treatment of oral/performance supported rather than subverted modernist art criticism's suspicious treatment of the theatrical. In the next sections, I excavate these intellectual legacies. I then consider the experiments of a number of contemporaneous artists, those whose work can be seen in a genealogy with Le Compte's flowers, chairs, entrances, and exits. Finally, I conclude by reflecting on the blindspots, misrecognitions, and disavowals in this artistic and intellectual ferment, suggesting that there is a professional politics to attributions of literality and hence an opportunity to defamiliarize the postmodern theorist's modernist occupational position.

Performance and presence

As I have already discussed, one of the difficulties of articulating the significance of performance has to do with the multiple and often contradictory associations attached to the term. Such is the opportunity and hazard of performance's "flexible essentialism." The criticism of the "early late-twentieth century" exacerbated one particular pair of contradictory usages – the assumed opposition between the figural and the literal, terms that paradoxically are each as likely as the other to be attached to the theatrical. Classically, of course, the theatrical is associated with the figural. As a realm where images, actors, or pieces of dialogue stand in for things, persons, or statements, the theatrical structure is a figurative structure and, in many cases, even serves as an adjective for the condition of surrogation or allegorical signification that is meant by the notion of "figure" more generally. Though there is nothing necessarily positive or negative about being a space where one thing stands in for another, positive or negative valuations are attached to this condition depending upon the legitimating or de-legitimating context. Once again, classically, this condition receives a negative valuation. To stand in for something is to lie, to dissemble, to deceive. The debased condition of artifice receives its most damning and insidious incarnation in the theatre, laying the basis for Western intellectual history's long-standing anti-theatrical prejudice. As familiar as this association is, however, the opposite kind of attribution is also possible, and became increasingly likely in the twentieth-century context of arts and humanities criticism. Rather than philology, rather than new criticism, "Theory" began to emerge in the humanities as its own cross-disciplinary speciality. The shape of its conversations had particular consequences for the discursive place of performance and brought with it new kinds of contradictions. Theatrical conditions of embodiment, presence, duration, materiality, and audience relation were used to critique regressive metaphysics, pragmatics, vocational training, and to critique movements that destroyed good art. At the same time, and as I will show, particular kinds of literalizing moves in philosophy and art used a performance-based vocabulary in order to criticize them. Hence, while most of Western intellectual history used performance's *figurality* as the basis for its anti-theatrical prejudice, late-twentieth-century theory's valorization of the figural posited performance's *literality* as the basis for its anti-theatrical prejudice. The terms of de-legitimation changed but the de-legitimated object remained the same.

To defend this generalized intellectual history, I want to consider selected works of four major scholars of the period: Clement Greenberg, Michael Fried, Jacques Derrida, and Paul de Man. These individuals proceed from disciplinary homes that directly and indirectly affect the theorization of theatrical performance, despite the fact that the first two seem to have reality principles that differ enormously from the second two. Greenberg and Fried were major figures in the early late-twentieth century context of art criticism; Derrida and de Man are two of the most significant figures in the early development of "theory," the particular mixture of literary, rhetorical, and philosophical studies whose deconstructions would inspire and irk humanities departments for decades to follow. Fried and Derrida both wrote treatises in 1967 that would be ubiquitously translated and republished and that – however debated and revised – would alter the

critical context for understanding artistic and linguistic signification. Fried's essay "Art and Objecthood" and Derrida's *De
la Grammatologie* both would have an impact on how performance was studied or whether it was studied at all. Along the
way, the works of Clement Greenberg and Paul de Man anticipated and reinforced a similar critical genealogy. To see these art
and philosophy figures in partnership rather than in counterpoint
is somewhat unorthodox. However, they share an epistemic impact on the study of performance, at the very least structuring
the kind of from-the-hip responses that performance academics
could expect to hear about their chosen specialization in cross-
disciplinary conversations. Investigating this genealogy helps us
to unsettle attributions of the literal even as it also helps us to understand why cross-disciplinary conversations on performance
continue to break down. Hopes for inter-disciplinary harmony
need to have a better account of intra-disciplinary history.

Perhaps most significant for the theorizing of performance –
indeed the theorizing of anything – were the discursive effects
of deconstruction. Indeed, the anti-paradigmatic paradigms of
deconstruction would circulate quite forcefully in several strains
of critical theory. Derrida's critique of metaphysics begins with
the assertion that Western intellectual thought is governed by a
series of binaries that present themselves as given rather than
constructed. In 1967, he was particularly concerned with the
binary between "speech and writing" in which the former is assumed to have ontological primacy. Citing Rousseau's *Confessions*
as a case study, Derrida used the concept of orality to characterize a metaphysical search for a realm of pre-discursive being
and immediate, unmediated encounter.[8] Barbara Johnson offers
a précis. "Derrida's critique of Western metaphysics focuses on
the privileging of the spoken word over the written word. The
spoken word is given a higher value because the speaker and listener are both present to the utterance simultaneously. There is
no temporal or spatial distance between the speaker, speech, and
listener, since the speaker hears himself speak at the same moment the listener does. The immediacy seems to guarantee the
notion that in the spoken word we know what we mean . . ."[9]
Writing, by virtue of its distance between speaker and receiver, is
assumed to produce a less authentic kind of encounter. Derrida

argues against this kind of premise. He asserts that the assumption of authenticity in a non-written exchange is produced by the phenomenon of writing itself. Written representation produces the assumption of its opposite and, with it, a longing for a mode of being outside of writing, one where representational gaps between signifier and signified would be closed. As such, "presence" always bears the trace of the differential representation it would seek to transcend.

A similar thought-structure propelled Derrida's critique of Antonin Artaud, another in a list of performance-based examples that, along with orality, would be used as a foil in the development of Theory. Derrida analyzed the irreconcilable hopes embedded in Artaud's articulations for the Theatre of Cruelty. Artaud's sense of cruelty's power derived from its embodiment. Artaud's articulation asserted that the corporeality of performance produced a sense of determining necessity that, like the phenomenon of oral speech, could somehow bypass all mechanisms of representation. "Theatricality must traverse and restore 'existence' and 'flesh' in each of their aspects."[10] Derrida thus paraphrased Artaud's quest in language that foregrounded the latter's metaphysical yearnings. "The theater of cruelty is not *representation*. It is life itself, in the extent to which life is unrepresentable. Life is the nonrepresentable origin of a representation . . . Theatrical art should be the primordial and privileged site of this destruction of imitation."[11] Thus, Derrida read Artaud as advocating a theatre that closed down representational systems between signifier and signified into a state of primordial being. Rather than celebrating the figural play between signifier and signified, Derrida's Artaud emphasized an essentialist and literalist theatrical ideal. Additionally, this aspect of Derrida's critique also revolved around a temporal conundrum. While Artaud gave the Theater of Cruelty a "primal" and "implacable" characterization, he simultaneously claimed that it had "not yet begun to exist." Derrida noted the paradox: "Now a necessary affirmation can be born only by being reborn to itself." Somehow Artaud sought a mode of being that was originary despite its state of deferral. Throughout, Derrida would focus on the avowed and often disavowed implications of this improbable temporality. The Theatre of Cruelty would be "the closure of the classical representation, but also the reconstitution of a closed space of original representation, the

archi-manifestation of force or of life."[12] Furthermore, Artaud
sought a theatre that was no longer governed by speech in the
discursive sense, seeking instead a metaphysical brand of speaking. "Speech and its writing will be erased on the stage of cruelty
only in the text to which they were allegedly dictation: at once
citations or recitations and orders."[13] Artaud argued that conventional theatrical speech was "dictated" by prior representational
forms and should ideally seek an outside to this circuit – returning to a before that was before the prior, affirming the possibility
of finding, through representation, a speech that preceded representation.

It is significant that Derrida chose to turn to a theatrical figure at this period in philosophy, reviving Antonin Artaud long
enough to unsettle the Artaudian quest for revivification. In fact,
the deployment of such partial and opportunistic resuscitations
structured many of the classic arguments of deconstruction. In
"Epistemology of Metaphor," Paul de Man would revisit John
Locke's *Essay Concerning Human Understanding*, in particular
the earlier philosopher's desire to evacuate figurative language
from philosophical discourse. Locke speculated (and symptom-
ically attempted to suspend speculation) on the relationship between language and knowledge. According to de Man, Locke
was fascinated and troubled by the intimate connection, struck
by the idea that our awareness of the world depends "so much
by the intervention of words that they seemed scarce separa-
ble from our general knowledge."[14] This scarce separation led
Locke to worry whether words might "interpose" themselves between human and world and whether "their obscurity and disorder does not seldom cast a mist before our eyes and impose
upon our understandings."[15] De Man traced how Locke's concern amplified into a mistrust of figurative language and "the
art of rhetoric," an art that, quoting Locke, ultimately is "for
nothing else but to insinuate wrong *ideas*, move passions, and
thereby mislead the judgement."[16] Locke thus participated in the
anti-rhetorical prejudice that associated figuration with deception. The equation in turn propelled a longing for its opposite –
that is, the possibility of truthful, literal, and "proper" speech.
De Man critiqued Locke's articulated impulse to "speak of things
as they are," particularly when Locke imagined language to be
a "conduit" that may "'corrupt the foundations of knowledge

which are in things themselves'" and even worse "'break or stop
the pipes whereby it is distributed to public use.'" Locke's literalizing figures for the work of figuration were too much for
de Man. "This language, not of poetic 'pipes and timbrels' but
of a plumber's handyman, raises, by its all too graphic concreteness, questions of propriety."[17] The literalized imagination of the
"handyman" also structured Locke's quest for "simple ideas," a
place where he attempted to distinguish the cause of "motion"
and the cause of "light" from the idea of light and motion and
thereby to isolate these irreducible concepts. For de Man, however, there could never be such absolute simplicity: ultimately,
"the discourse of simple ideas is figural discourse or translation,
and as such, creates the fallacious illusion of definition."[18] As
the essay continued to track Locke's revisions through Condillac
and Kant, de Man would continually find that "the distinction
between a priori and symbolic judgements can only be stated by
means of metaphors that are themselves symbolic."[19] Finally, de
Man's Locke occupied a position that was similar in its impossibility to that of Derrida's Rousseau and to that of Derrida's
Artaud. As Derrida's critique of presence argued that the unmediated oral does not precede textuality but is an ever-deferred
epiphenomenon of textuality itself, so de Man's critique of literality argued that simple and irreducible knowledge does not
precede figuration but is an imagined state produced by the work
of figurative language.

This kind of *anti*-anti-representational thought-structure is
now familiar to almost any critical theorist working in the twenty-
first century. Even in venues that do not explicitly call themselves
"deconstructionist," many of us work with the assumption that
no thing, person, or experience could ever have the full irreducibility of pure presence or the self-coincidence of a simple
idea. In our working world, life is never just life; motion is never
just motion; exits are never just exits. And – in a move that be-
speaks the class privilege of Theory – many of us are quick to roll
our eyes at all the other "handymen" who don't get it.

Theatricality and literality

While in no way equivalent to deconstruction, art historian
Michael Fried can be seen participating in a brand of criticism

that incorporated and perpetuated similar critical effects. To place his work next to deconstruction is to suggest more continuity between the post-modernism Derrida inaugurated and the modernism that Fried defended. It is also to realize that Jean Jacques Rousseau and Michael Fried have very different kinds of anti-theatrical prejudices much as it may be expedient for theatre's defenders to conflate them. In his classic essay, "Art and Objecthood," Fried distinguished a strain of Minimalist art – what he called "literalist" art – from the Modernist artwork that he most valued. Minimalism was itself a complicated aesthetic category that included a number of disparate experiments; nevertheless, it was often associated with visual works that emphasized the material, sculptural, and often environmental dimensions of the art object and its receiving context. Modifying and carrying forward aesthetic paradigms and dispositions developed by Clement Greenberg, Fried focused particularly on the articulations of Donald Judd, Robert Morris, and Tony Smith. Many of Fried's sentences were packed with quotations from these sources in an amalgamated and only sporadically footnoted series of citations. He cited Donald Judd's celebration of artwork that had "a definite whole and maybe no parts," and noted how Judd criticized artwork that confined itself to the "rectangle" of a painting and to the "limit(ed) arrangements possible within it."[20] Saying that "painting is here seen as an art on the verge of exhaustion," Fried characterized as literalist Judd's notion that "actual space is intrinsically more powerful and specific than paint on the flat surface." Such a statement set off a number of warning signals for Fried. It set up a dichotomy between wholeness and "partedness" that was neither philosophically nor aesthetically sound. It also assumed that a work could and ideally should approach the condition of "actuality" and that, moreover, an "intrinsically more powerful" condition came about by extending beyond the medium of painting. Fried's critique of the desire for actuality resonated with Derrida's critique of an Artaudian quest for "life itself"; in their view, both desires naively assumed the possibility and desirability of transcending painterly (and writerly) representation. The effort was to bypass the work's status as Art in favor of its status as an Object. On the one hand, Fried preferred the "modernist painting [that] has come to find it imperative that it defeat its own objecthood . . . that it must be pictorial, not, or not merely, literal." So-called literalist art, on the other hand, "aspires not to defeat or suspend its own objecthood, but on the contrary to discover and project objecthood as such."[21] Fried's preferences for pictoriality built upon those articulated by his sometime mentor, Clement Greenberg. In an essay that elaborated on the "logical contradictions" of what he labeled "homeless representation,"[22] Greenberg critiqued a parallel tendency: "the literal three dimensionality of piled-on paint . . . [that] could be called 'furtive bas-relief.'"[23] These paintings "rely on the non-painterly use of line, and at the same time on monochromatic effects that do not need the coherence achieved through tangible representation, because they have the coherence that belongs automatically to literally three-dimensional space."[24] For both Greenberg and Fried, the emphasis on the material of the art object was an inartistic way of creating impact. Their literalist label derived from their sense that such artists were cheating by tapping the "coherence that belongs automatically" to three dimensionality rather than achieving a coherence that emerges aesthetically in pictoriality.

Interestingly and famously, Fried went on to characterize this preoccupation with objecthood as "theatrical." Without accepting his attributions of literality, or accepting the equivalence between literalism and theatricality, it is intriguing to try to understand what the associations are and why they were made. For a start, such work actively integrated the audience. "Literalist sensibility is theatrical because, to begin with, it is concerned with the actual circumstances in which the beholder encounters literalist work."[25] Fried quoted Robert Morris's statements that "The better new work takes relationships out of the work and makes them a function of space, light, and the viewer's field of vision . . . It is in some way more reflexive because one's awareness of oneself existing in the same space as the work is stronger than in previous work."[26] To Fried, however, such a goal was unaesthetically cumbersome, and sometimes, quite inconvenient. He wrote, "Things that are literal works of art must somehow confront the beholder – they must, one might almost say, be placed not just in his space but in his *way*."[27] Fried was particularly unnerved by the way that the art object and its receiving context blurred, so that "the entire situation" was integrated into the event. It was this condition that, Fried noted, "modernism finds

intolerable." "Everything counts – not as part of the object, but
as part of the situation in which its objecthood is established on
which that objecthood at least partly depends . . . including, it
seems, the beholder's *body*."[28] Fried's impulse to call this kind
of saturation between art and the receptive situation "theatrical"
thus came from a recognition of the hypercontextuality of theatre, a radical sense of situation that included embodiment and
that, in his view, contributed to its compromised status as art.[29]

In addition to the intolerable incorporation of the audience,
Fried's impulse to align theatricality with literalist art derived also
from the way that both seemed to break down divisions amongst
the arts – what, in a more generous context, would be called
their "interdisciplinarity." Here, theatre's status as an integrated
and reputedly democratic artistic mixture would be repudiated
as "the negation" of art.

Theater is the common denominator that binds together a large and
seemingly disparate variety of activities, and that distinguishes those
activities from the radically different enterprises of the modernist
arts . . . the real distinctions – between music and theater . . . and between
painting and theater . . . are displaced by the illusion that the barriers
between the arts in the process of crumbling . . . and the arts themselves
are at last sliding towards some kind of final, implosive, highly desirable
synthesis.[30]

For Fried, Greenberg, and other modernist art critics, the pursuit of aesthetic singularity was a condition of modernism itself.
"Each art," wrote Greenberg, "had to determine, through the
operations peculiar to itself, the effects peculiar and exclusive to
itself." In order to achieve modernist self-consciousness, therefore, modernist art should seek the essence of individual art forms
and "eliminate from the effects of each art any and every effect
that might conceivably be borrowed from or be the medium of
any other art."[31] Hence, to blur distinctions amongst the arts
was to be anti-modernist. Additionally, disciplinary singularity
helped to maintain, in Greenberg and Fried's view, evaluative
standards. "Concepts of quality and value . . . are meaningful,
or wholly meaningful, only within *the individual arts. What lies*
between *is theater.*"[32] The condition of theater was itself an index of anti-disciplinarity – a stand-in and label for a kind of
mixture that certain proponents of other arts resolutely stood

against. The university context of the period – one propelled by a boom economy that supported field specialization and the infrastructural autonomy of fields and departments – provided institutional support for the concept of disciplinary singularity. While the course of art experimentation would become increasingly interdisciplinary (and anticipate the university's interdisciplinary calls in leaner economic times), modernist art criticism's language of specialization dovetailed with higher education's institutional practices of the period.

The connections amongst modernist art criticism, deconstruction, and the status of theatre and performance are most clearly seen in comparing discourses of objecthood and presence. Throughout the statements of contemporaneous Minimalist artists, there was a focus on the material of the signifier and, with it, the collapse of the signified into the signifier. Robert Morris was quoted out of context as saying that the "multipart, inflected" art should be surpassed by "wholeness, singleness, and indivisibility; as much as possible, a work should be 'one thing, a single 'Specific Object.'"[33] Donald Judd further elaborated on the quest for an unelaborated art. "Materials vary greatly and are simply materials – formica, aluminum, cold-rolled steel, plexiglass, red and common brass, and so forth. They are specific. If they are used directly, they are more specific . . . There is an objectivity to the obdurate identity of a material."[34] In Fried's reading, Morris and Judd's emphasis neutralized any sense of aesthetic composition internal to the work of art, ultimately giving the art critic very little to say about it. Fried aligned such a state of objecthood with "the condition of non-art," suggesting that for such experimenters "it is as though objecthood alone can, in the present circumstances, secure something's identity."[35] Like Derrida's suspicions of "necessary affirmation," Fried objected to the notion that such a representational collapse was a condition of authenticity. Like de Man's suspicion of the purity of "simple ideas," Fried objected to Morris's invocation of "simple forms" and to Judd's assertion that materials could be "simply materials." Said Fried, "the materials do not represent, signify, or allude to anything; they are what they are and nothing more . . . The 'obdurate identity' of a specific material, like the wholeness of the shape is simply stated or given or established at the very outset, if not before the outset."[36] Akin to the Artaudian desire for the "destruction of imitation," such artists proceeded on a course that was conceptually misguided. Furthermore, such experiments faced a similar kind of improbable temporality, attempting to land upon a mode of being that derived from "before the outset" of representation. Once again, the "end of representation" was also paradoxically conceived as "original representation." Finally, Derrida, de Man, Greenberg, and Fried (and the schools of deconstruction and modernist art criticism with which they were allied) were suspicious of language that included "wholeness" or "indivisibility." While each advanced different reality principles, these critics shared a legitimating language that valued multi-partedness, division, and difference – at least in certain forms.

Such critiques perhaps sound familiar to contemporary critics. These thinkers objected to almost all of the assumptions to which a critical theorist would object now, a context where the impulse to essentialize experience and to assume indivisible identities is neither philosophically nor politically savvy. The reaction to Locke's misguided elaboration of "simple ideas" parallels the reaction many might have to Minimalism's elaboration of "specific objects." By extension, Derrida's anti-appeals to presence and Fried's discomfort with art materials that "are what they are and nothing more" parallels Kaye's startled reaction to Le Compte's literal language. For feminists, this suspicion is further compounded. Reading of Tony Smith's supposedly transformative late-night drive along a "New Jersey turnpike" – where he revels in the "reality" of an unframed environment "punctuated by stacks, towers, fumes, and colored lights" and finds himself drawn to similar "abandoned environments" such as "airstrips" and "drillgrounds" – brings to mind the trademark conventions of a decidedly masculinist quest for untrammeled authenticity. When he says, "you just have to experience it," many feminists might respond with Fried's incredulous paraphrasing. "'You just have to experience it' – as it happens as it merely is. There is no suggestion that this is problematic in any way."[37]

To review the intellectual history of this epistemic moment is not to defend the Minimalist artists or Antonin Artaud against literality per se. Rather it is to examine the discursive conditions and, more importantly, the discursive effects of coining and applying terms such as "literal." The extra move and extra effect of these thinkers was to associate such a naïve, unsuspicious consciousness with theatrical performance. Emphasizing one side of theatre's flexibly essentialist status, these works did not link theatricality to the realm of pictoriality, multiplicity, and dissimulation but emphasized instead its other assumed qualities – its condition of immediacy and temporal and spatial presentness. Fried critiqued Minimalism's brazen literality in much the same way that Derrida invoked Artaud's invitation to "implacable intention and decision."[38] Unlike Artaud, Judd, Smith, and Morris were not initially, nor primarily, artists of the theatre. However, the coincidence of an anti-metaphysical critique of a theatrical artist in terms that similarly critiqued the supposedly theatrical impulses of other artists produced a critical theory that made theatrical performance suspicious to modernist and modernist-derived theoreticians. During this period of theoretical development, the theatrical became literal at the same time that critical theory legitimated the figural. When being representational had been a bad thing in Western intellectual thought, it was theatrical. When being representational became a good thing, it was pictorial and textual – anything *but* theatrical. The critical effect on performance has been to produce a kind of template of metaphysical critique, one in which an appeal to performance can be routinely inserted and thereby dismissed as an anti-theoretical appeal to presence and to dunder-headed objecthood.

Speaking literally

It is important to acknowledge that this is an epistemic conflation to which contemporaneous artists and performers also contributed. If objecthood could "secure identity," it is interesting that "securing identity" was desirable for artists at this moment in history and, moreover, that experimental performance offered the medium of security. As Fried, Greenberg, Derrida, and de Man questioned notions of authenticity and fended off literalist appeals to presence, they were also directly and indirectly reckoning with the socio-political context of what became retroactively known as "the sixties." Derrida's 1967 *De La Grammatologie* preceded by one year the notorious student uprisings of 1968, events whose discourse would appeal to a kind of unfettered quest for presence in the effort to overthrow the highly fettered arena of educational and state politics. While Derrida tried to remain politicized despite his critique of the assumptions of activist discourse, Fried's work remained positioned against the kind of political sensibility that, in his view, eroded the quality and category of art. Additionally, a particular theatrical performance context preceded and coincided with deconstruction and with Fried's notorious essay. In 1968, Jerzy Grotowski's *Towards a Poor Theatre* appeared in English, and Joseph Chaiken's title for his 1972 book – *The Presence of the Actor* – participated in the essentializing of performance. The discursive and practical tendencies that reinforced the assumed literalism of theatrical performance characterized much of the artistic experimentation that would call itself avant-garde in the 1960s. This is the era of assemblages, constructions, environments, and happenings, the time that followed Black Mountain and the Reuben Gallery, the time of the Living Theatre, of the San Francisco Actors Workshop, of the Performing Garage, and most especially, of the Judson Dance Theater. The innovations of the 1960s were about theatre people deciding to turn the theatrical dilemma of art/process's saturation into a virtue and about artists in other forms using the theatrical dilemma to reflect on the status of their own art.

Jerzy Grotowski is a key figure in what might be conceived as the essentializing tendencies of early late-twentieth century experimental performance. To the extent that his methods have been honored and circulated in many models of actor training, the echo of his language resounds in many an actor's descriptions of their process and goal. The assumed equation between Artaud and Grotowski sets the stage for a relation between the latter and an unfettered quest for presence. While Grotowski would contest this equation, the language he used to discuss the phenomenon of the actor echoed the kind of determinist tones that Derrida heard in Artaud. Consider Grotowski's elaboration of the acting ideal as a "total act." While Grotowski critiqued Artaud for never actualizing his writings, he felt that he was right about certain things. Artaud understood, in Grotowski's view, "the very crux of the actor's art: that what the actor achieves should be (let's not be afraid of the name) a total act, that he does whatever he does with his entire being . . . The actor should not use his organism to illustrate a 'movement of the soul,' he should accomplish this movement with this organism."[39] Grotowski thus seemed to endorse

Artaud's attempt to "close representation" via the presence of the actor, advocating a performance that lived rather than "illustrated," that was itself rather than a stand-in for something other than itself. His language would take on the quality that, depending upon one's perspective, sounded inspirational or mystifying, wise or ridiculous. "When this act accomplished through theatre is total, then even if it doesn't protect us from the dark powers, at least it enables us to respond totally, that is, begin to exist."[40] Elsewhere, Grotowski described a *viva negativa* that, to some ears, would sound like the assumption of inner essence. "Neither that which touches the interior sphere, nor the profound stripping bare of the self should be regarded as evil so long as in the process of preparation or in the completed work they produce an actor creation."[41] "It is the act of laying oneself bare, of tearing off the mask of daily life, of exteriorizing oneself."[42] The actor must "give himself, sanctify his real 'incarnate' self."[43] Furthermore, Grotowski's quest for theatre in the literal sense sought to transcend theatricality in the figural sense. "We abandoned make-up, fake noses, pillow-stuffed bellies – everything that the actor puts on in the dressing room before performance . . . the mask prepared by a make-up artist is only a trick."[44]

While the figure of Grotowski in the late 1960s easily confirmed Derrida's links between theatre and naïve metaphysics, the artistic scene of New York's Greenwich Village lay behind Fried and Greenberg's associations of the theatrical with the literal. Sally Banes sums up the social and intellectual ferment of the period.

The country's postwar mood of pragmatism was reflected in the various arts, from the Happenings that made use of environments at hand to the New Realism, or Pop Art depictions of figures and object and making reference to industrial subjects and styles. The economy was expanding, and the new Kennedy administration stressed youth, art, and culture. There were few grants to individual dancers, but there was a spirit of willing participation and an interest in using inexpensive materials; one could live cheaply and make art cheaply. . . . The philosophical fascinations with Zen Buddhism, existentialism, and phenomenology fit well with certain aspects of American art in the late 1950s and early 1960s. The concreteness of existence, the interest in the everyday actions people practice, the questions of identity, both individual and collective, that were topics of these philosophical systems – at least in their popular versions – were appropriate questions for modernist artists after the middle of the twentieth century. The phenomenological exhortation "Zu den Sachen!" ("To the Things!") was echoed in the manifestoes of artists in every field. Poetry, music, theater, and dance stressed performance more than the literary aspect of their forms, aspiring to more immediacy, more 'presentness,' more concrete experience.[45]

It is hard to imagine a more eloquent description of an artistic milieu whose fundamental principles were more opposite to the principles I have described in the work of Greenberg, Fried, Derrida, and de Man. While "Things!" meant something different to each of these thinkers, their celebration was certainly circumspect to art critics who reviled "piled-on paint" and the "condition of objecthood" as well as to thinkers who critiqued phenomenology's metaphysical assumptions and for whom a fixation on "pipes" and "conduits" was all-too "graphically concrete."

Words such as "concrete," "thing," "everyday," "real," and "actual" would infuse the language used in these artistic circles – circles that often experimented in the bodied realm of action, duration, and movement. Furthermore, this context of experimentation included figures such as Richard Schechner and Michael Kirby (amongst many others) for whom such explorations would prompt a shift in a theatrical paradigm toward the formation of something called "performance studies" as a disciplinary identity. What Greenberg and Fried designated "literalist" was what Michael Kirby called "non-matrixed," a mode of presentation which tried to resist the sense that the performer "is someone other than himself or in some place other than the actual place of performance."[46] Elaborating on the possibilities of non-matrixed perfomance, Kirby listed the actions of a series of examples whose distinctive characteristics were presumably their irreducibility and self-coincidence. "The orchestra conductor walks on stage, bows to the audience, raises his baton, and the curtain falls."[47] As one of the era's most prolific chroniclers and categorizers of "The New Theatre" (and one of the first self-labeled "performance theorists"), Kirby's example was also a citation of an historical genealogy for such kinds of experimentation, specifically recalling John Cage's and Merce Cunningham's explorations and dismantlings of dance and musical presentation. From this excavation, Kirby developed a vocabulary to distinguish amongst different types of reductive performance. One of his labels – the

"Event" – echoed Cage's "Untitled Event" – the presentation at Black Mountain College that would be posited retroactively as the new beginning of avant-garde performance. Another label – the "Happening" – cited Allan Kaprow's "first" experiment in *18 Happenings in 6 Parts.*[48] Additionally, Kirby went farther back, recognizing Surrealism and Dadaism as well as Jackson Pollock's "action painting" as key inspirations.

> The Abstract Expressionist mentality which pervaded the New York art world in the late 1950's was one of the contributing factors in bringing painters into the performing arts. The *act* of painting rather than the completed composition had become the creative focus.[49]

While Greenberg and Fried would be quick to claim Jackson Pollock as an exemplary modernist artist, they would be critical of experimentation that took the notion of "action" quite this far. As I will suggest, it is one of many ways that the "New Theatre" can be seen, not so much as violating modernist attributes and principles, but as augmenting and extending them in a way that finally called their bluff.

Michael Kirby's theories of matrixed and non-matrixed performing are intriguing to place next to modernist art characterizations of "literalist art"; they are similar kinds of recognition derived from parallel critical universes. The fact that one would celebrate and the other condemn the impulse toward "objecthood" points up a key moment when a disciplinary genealogy in art criticism and a disciplinary genealogy in performance studies diverged. The historic divergence still affects the attempt to create "interdisciplinary" exchange between visual and performance studies now. Non-matrixed performance emphasized the performative – if not exactly theatrical – qualities of all levels of activity, releasing the technical arenas of performance from their backstage location in order to place the "entire situation" on view.

> If a circus were a work of art, it would be an excellent example of a Happening. Except for the clowns (and perhaps the man with lions who pretends that they are vicious), the performances are non-matrixed. The acrobats, jugglers, and animal trainers are 'merely' carrying out their activities. The grips or stagehands become performers, too, as they dismantle and rig the equipment – demonstrating that non-matrixed performing exists at all levels of difficulty.[50]

Kirby's elaboration ("if a circus were a work of Art") begged the question, celebrating a crisis of category in the arts while at the same time reinstantiating the art category itself. Nevertheless, his examples reflect the kind of pragmatic, task-based, and manual mode of performance that served as a "stand-in" for the literal. Unlike Fried's use of the term, the "merely" above was a virtuous adverb for such activities. Unlike de Man's elaboration, this was an art practice that reveled in the presumed actuality of the handyman. Kirby detailed the non-matrixed literality of Claes Oldenburg's *Washes* which took place in a swimming pool. "Four men dove into the pool and pushed sections of silver flue pipe back and forth along a red clothes line. There was no practical purpose in showing and twisting the pipes, but it was real activity . . . The men did not pretend to be anyone other than themselves, nor did they pretend that the water they were in was anything other than what it actually was."[51] The vocabulary that Kirby and others developed to characterize such forms – Situation, Environment, Activity, as well as Event and Happening – tried to evoke linguistically the sense of absolute reduction sought in such art works. Even the titles of such pieces are significant in their attempts to avoid signification – Allan Kaprow's *18 Happenings in 6 Parts* was followed by Emmett William's *Ten Arrangements for Five Performers* and Yvonne Rainer's *Dance for 3 People and 6 Arms*. Resuscitating John Locke's paradoxical maneuvers around "simple ideas," such titles attempted to isolate and to neutralize the limit point of representation. Such performances were about knowing that a broom was a broom and that a flue pipe was a flue pipe. It was about exposing rather than hiding the activity of making, placing backstage elements on view. It was about celebrating art that occurred only at a specific moment, augmenting theatre's "you had to be there" temporality and using the language of "presence" to describe it.

As numerous commentators have noted, such performances often reified a number of gendered, racist, and classed conventions in order to stage absolute reduction. The attempt to lay bare the essentials of performance often led toward a display of the primal with familiar sexual and racial codings. The number of "naked girls" who appear in the documentation and descriptions of the happenings of Allan Kaprow, Al Hansen, Richard Schechner, and others is somewhat overwhelming. Meanwhile, the spectacle of mostly white participants performing all-too familiar "rituals" of circling, drumming, and sacrificing testifies to the primitivist fascinations that propelled the search for the real. Such reifications did not go unnoticed at the time. Dance critic Jill Johnston breathed a sigh of relief when Yvonne Rainer's work appeared in Greenwich Village, thankful to see someone who was not doing a "fertility rite." Meanwhile, as Rebecca Schneider notes, Carolee Schneemann's explicit body art of the period can be read as a feminist literalization of these masculine performances of the literal.[52] And farther north in Harlem, Robert MacBeth's New Lafayette Theatre politicized the African-American practice of ritual, whether or not any of the Greenwich ritualists noticed at the time. NLT's titles, including the 1969 *Ritual To Bind Together and Strengthen Black People So That They Can Survive the Long Struggle That Is To Come*, made no effort to avoid signification even as the theatre experimented in all of the happenings' registers of space, time, and collectivity.[53] The classed sensibility of avant-garde experimentation is perhaps most complicated to critique, especially since it can exist at so many registers. On the one hand, Allan Kaprow and others experimented in performance in order to resist capitalist commodification. On the other hand, contemporaneous artists relied on the boom economy of the period, and the happenings were eventually subject to capitalist incorporation. A similar paradox held for the focus on the literality of the object. When participants in Oldenburg's *Washes* exchanged a flue pipe in the water, they cited a classed symbol of pragmatic authenticity. At the same time, this version of the pragmatic had "no practical purpose." Such gestures repeated Tony Smith's cross-class fascination with the towers and smoke stacks on the New Jersey turnpike, incorporating the symbols of the handyman's literal without knowing how to make them work and without enduring the environmental contaminations of such found "Environments." All of these examples expose the disavowed complexity in the space of the "simple," the gendered, raced, and classed work of figuration in the presumably literal. It is because of this unacknowledged appropriation that so many postmodern theorists remain suspicious of the language of reduction, of presence, and of the self-evidently literal. As such, postmodern theorists remain suspicious of a significant genealogy in postmodern performance.

A professional challenge

While I myself am similarly dubious, I think that there is also reason to be suspicious of that doubt, for postmodern theory's critiques can have their own conventionality. They also can have their own blindspots, especially when we factor in both professional and philosophical stories of disavowal and misrecognition. First, in re-assessing the legacies of modernist art criticism and minimalist art practice, it is important to consider how much the latter presented a professional challenge to the former. The experimentation of the 1960s questioned the division between the arts as well as the category of Art as such. In so doing, it also unsettled the epistemological categories on which the professionalism of the art critic stood. It challenged the kind of distinctions – between aesthetic and the utilitarian, between product and process, between the art and apparatus – that, since Panofsky, were used by the artist and the critic to distinguish themselves from other forms of labor and occupation. Furthermore, the essentialist goals of reductive art confounded the historicist and comparative practices of art criticism. The art critic's status as expert derived from an ability to set a given work in relation to other ones. Modernist art critics liked modernist art because it enabled them to exercise such skills. The significance and formal innovations of the works were not apparent "in the work themselves" but "reside[d] outside it." Thus, as Rosalind Krauss elaborated, "access to [the past and the problem] can only be achieved by a long chain of explanation that characteristically takes the form of narrative."[54] Art that received the minimalist or literalist label, on the other hand, was art that bristled against such "chains of explanation," for meaning was not to be located outside of the piece itself. To argue for the in-itself-ness of the work was thus not simply philosophically naïve but counter to professionalist practice. As Howard Singerman argues, this move flew in the face of the institutional practices consolidated in the phenomenon of "graduate school."

For graduate school depends on making visible, and making verbal, its determinations; its maker must know and insist on its contingency and its position, must always re-explain and paint over the top of the relation between past and present. In the student critique or the visiting artist's lecture, the work is always presented in the narrative that Krauss notes.

In the slide carousel, no image can be *given* because every image is framed and positioned by – is a position *on* – what is not there and on what it is not: the slide next to it on the screen, before it or behind it in the tray. Each work is linked to a past made narrative and presented to the student as part of a discourse within which they must situate themselves.[55]

Many of the interdisciplinary arts experiments of the 1960s adopted a non-contingent language that flouted the conventions of the art critic's slide projector, the this-preceded-that, that-reworked-this epistemology of art's professional historicity. If Krauss and Singerman are correct in assessing this fundamental element of university arts training and modernist arts criticism, then it is a question whether "postmodernism" has changed this occupational convention. Indeed, postmodern criticism may have replaced a "chain of explanation" with a "chain of citations," but the practice of contextualization and imagistic juxtaposition remains. Both modernist and postmodernist art criticisms are thus similarly resistant to declarations of the "*given*"; moreover, in both cases, that resistance has a professional, not simply philosophical, undercurrent. To the extent that postmodern performance theory has focused on intertextual, parodic, and appropriative re-workings, its paradigmatic analyses thus repeat rather than reject the professional habits of modernist art criticism. This partly explains why the thought-structures of Fried and Greenberg often coincide with those of Derrida and de Man, showing more continuity between the modern and the postmodern inaugurated with deconstruction. It also explains why the statements of postmodern theorists often do *not* coincide with those of postmodern performance artists, exposing *less* continuity between the professional practices of each.

This occupational undercurrent further complicates the class analysis brought to bear on the critical legacies of the 1960s. The theoretical elaborations and repudiations of particular art works were, amongst many other things, a struggle over authority and the solidification of expertise. As such, they were also an admittedly localized instance of class struggle about the professional standing of the intellectual and the professional standing of the artist.[56] In the "Education of the Un-Artist," Kaprow declared that "critics would be as irrelevant as the artists," an unsettling, if improbable, prognosis indeed.[57] Lest I give the

impression that minimalist "un-artists" and performers did not
have professional aspirations, consider also the paradoxes of their
articulations. Allan Kaprow was also professor of art history at
Rutgers University. Kaprow was one of many persons in higher
education who institutionalized avant-garde art practice, despite
the avant-garde's own anti-institutional rhetoric. Kaprow's statements can be read as attempts to reconcile his presence inside
university art departments, where professional art critics such
as Michael Fried also had to reconcile with him. Like so many
radical articulations of the period (and in anticipation of the
"liminal norm" that Jon McKenzie identifies in performance
studies), Kaprow's language of resistance coexisted surprisingly
easily next to the language of incorporation.[58] This position illustrates an artistic version of the "new class" paradox identified
by Alvin Gouldner and Andrew Ross where individuals countered the conventions of expertise while still claiming to be "in
the know" themselves.[59] In the somewhat contradictory essay
where Kaprow told artists to "drop out" and predicted their ir-
relevance, he actually anticipated a new occupational division of
labor for artists and critics. "But some critics may be willing to
un-art themselves along with their artist colleagues . . . Practitioners and commentators – the two occupations will probably
merge, one person performing inter-changeably – will need an
updated language to refer to what is going on."[60] Kaprow thus
advocated not the absence of commentary but a different kind of
commentary – one that would come from the artist's mouth. In
fact, in an earlier 1964 essay, Kaprow had already heralded the
new artist as a "man of the world" who would take up this occupational position. "Traditionally such responsibility has belonged
to critics . . . today's artists are sharing this job . . . Such artists
no longer merely represent authority-as-creator; they are going to
be urged more and more to become creator-as-authority."[61] The
presence of the artist alongside, and sometimes inside, the artwork was thus both a conceptual choice and a professional challenge, one that reversed the conventions of critical authority. In
1973, Lucy Lippard would identify the "traveling artist" as a new
phenomenon in which artists accompanied their work and stimulated interest in it.[62] In 1977, the phenomenon would receive
theoretical elaboration in Rosalind Krauss's concept of the index, characterizing the apparent excess of the artist's objects and

experiences as referential rather than actual, as doubled rather than pure and singular.[63] Krauss chose to give a figural and allegorical reading to something that Michael Fried might have considered literal. Despite Krauss' postmodern recuperation, there is still an occupational subtext to this artistic reorientation, one to which Michael Fried's "Art and Objecthood" was implicitly objecting. Most of his examples criticized the words and "commentaries" that literal artists used to describe their efforts rather than the works themselves. As such, Fried can be seen critiquing not only the content of their declarations but also the artists' assumption of the position of "creator-as-authority" in the first place. It was not only the art that "confronted" the critic; from a professional standpoint, the *artist* was also in the critic's space . . . and very much *in his way*. These artists took on the "entire situation," one that included, not only the viewing environment, but also the entire vocational context of art's enactment.

This kind of recognition in turn supports another set of questions, specifically about what it means to characterize something as literal. Is it that the artwork is literal? Or is it that an artist's ways of talking about it sound literal? Furthermore, does the deployment of literality testify to a literalist imagination? Can the technique of literality be distinguished from its effects? I ask these questions because the attribution of literalism creates a good deal of misrecognition between artists and scholars – as well as between earlier and "postmodern" generations of theatre and performance studies scholars. For one thing, the literalist dismissal bypasses the formal innovations and formal challenges that were at the heart of minimalist, "theatrical" experiments of the 1960s and 1970s. What is the effect of a literalist piece such as Activity performer George Brecht's *Recipe*? The piece consisted entirely of a list of "ingredients" . . . "cloth, paper, match, string, knife, glass, egg" – that gradually began to include activities – "Level cloth. Place paper on cloth. Light match. Extinguish. Mark paper with burning match. . . ."[64] Nouns and verbs were thus positioned on the same register, using the objecthood of the former to objectify the execution of the latter. The concept of "ingredients" foregrounded the material stuff of the art, a list that might include "ink," "canvas," or "steel" in the museum didactic of another artwork. At the same time, the linguistic representation of the ingredients doubled the presumably literal.

Ambiguous about whether the art lay in the "recipe" or in its execution, the word "cloth" could be a figural stand-in for the cloth or the reverse, the cloth a figure for the literal term. The objectified verbs also formalized – and revealed the formal consciousness in – the Activity of making an art object. The processes of leveling and marking (and occasionally burning) described the practice of making many kinds of art, even those that Greenberg and Fried would not have called literalist. Indeed, the daily reality of art-making is all about such verbs, activities that, depending upon the medium, involved stirring, stretching, dipping, pushing, and gliding brushes, bodies, paper, and cloth. The challenge of works such as Brecht's was that such activities were not located outside the artistic frame, a relocation of artistic production that unsettled the boundaries of the artistic frame itself, exposing the dependence of the frame upon the obscuring of art-making's verbs. These hypercontextual experiments gave rise to a literalized language that would permeate the experimental spaces of the performance avant-garde, even when they described complex formal and representational experiments in time and space. Whether categorized as Activity, Event, or Happening, the characteristic consciousness of this New Theatre lay in revealing the "itselfness" of objects and persons. However, the effect of that revelation was not necessarily literal, since fundamental assumptions about the art object were challenged. Certainly such experiments are inaccurately conceived as antiformalist, since formal questions drive them. It was perhaps not so much that the artwork was literal as that its critical effects were "intolerable." They were thus not so much anti-modernist as ultra-modernist, extending rather than rejecting modernism's formal preoccupations.

That formal consciousness remains in play in postmodern performance now. The effort to unsettle conventional assumptions of where the art object began and ended now makes the phenomenon of the "entrance" and the "exit" worthy of considerable attention. Similarly, a context that focused on the concreteness of a pipe, a match, and an egg would inspire related practices, making the fact of a TV, a flower, or a chair artistically generative for someone like Elizabeth Le Compte. If such experiments do not immediately enable a "chain of explanations" (or self-consciously speak their "chains of citations"), then it is worth considering the epistemological effects of that reluctance. That reluctance speaks to the formal pragmatisms that are at the heart of art-making, where a focus on meaning does not immediately enable the creation of artistic structure (or un-structure). Something about the trajectory of postmodern theory keeps it from tracking this formal innovation, positioning it philosophically, occupationally, and conversationally as literality instead. Consider again the thought-structures of deconstruction that, for the purposes of this chapter, sit in a genealogical relation with those of postmodernism. Before his disquisition on John Locke, Paul de Man had already framed the function of deconstructive reading around the uncertain relation between the literal and the figural. In *Allegories of Reading*, de Man famously offered a discussion of this differential relation through the example of Archie Bunker in conversation with his wife, Edith, characters on the television sit-com *All in the Family*.

> Asked by his wife whether he wants to have his bowling shoes laced over or laced under, Archie Bunker answers with a question: "What's the difference?" Being a reader of sublime simplicity, his wife replies by patiently explaining the difference between lacing over and lacing under, whatever this may be, but it provokes only ire. "What's the difference?" did not ask for difference . . . The same grammatical pattern engenders two meanings that are mutually exclusive: the literal meaning asks for the concept (difference) whose existence is denied by the figurative meaning. . . . Archie Bunker . . . muddles along in a world where literal and figurative meanings get in each other's way, though not without discomforts.[65]

I imagine this scenario as analogous to the artist-scholar encounters that I have described throughout this chapter. A philosopher or critic might ask a question about signification, effectively a "what's the difference" kind of question such as: What is the significance of Noh? Of the flue pipe? Of the shoe laces? In place of a desired answer, the critic receives a literalized response that mocks the assumption of difference in the first place: well, you pull the laces *under* the holes or you pull them *over* the holes. This kind of stalled, seemingly inert non-dynamic characterizes the experience of the modernist-derived art critic in confrontation with art and artists. De Man's version of this encounter does not use the word "mock" to describe Edith Bunker's gesture vis à vis the Archie/critic figure; instead, he makes her as static as the effects of her speech. Calling her a reader of "sublime simplicity," he equates her characterologically with the stall she creates discursively. However, as Barbara Johnson has suggested, a more radical and feminist relationship to deconstruction might require the much harder task of "undertaking the effort of reinflection or translation required to . . . listen with retrained ears to Edith Bunker's patient elaboration of an answer to the question."[66] One kind of retraining might focus less on the seemingly tautological content of Edith's answer than on the "ire" that tautology provokes in Archie, akin possibly to the exasperation and dread that certain statements provoked in Derrida and Fried, that certain conversations provoke in me, Nick Kaye, and other performance scholars. As Rebecca Schneider argues via Walter Benjamin, the "insistence on literal translation contains a 'direct threat to comprehensibility'" because it discomfortingly challenges neat divisions between the literal and figural. What happens instead if we let this literality stand and find something instructive in the conversational stall that it creates? There might be a "threat to comprehensibility" that actually can be made useful, forcing us to reckon with the conventions by which art forms (e.g. painting), movements (e.g. modernism), and occupations (e.g. the critical theorist) are made comprehensible.

The assumption of Edith's simplicity is akin, I think, to the assumption of the handyman's "all-too graphic concreteness," one that is paired here with a kind of feminized obliviousness. Together they testify to a classed rhetoric as well as another kind of gendered rhetoric that remained unexamined in deconstruction. The reifications in that thought-structure make practitioners in the arts of the graphic into humorous figures of theoretical naiveté, a philosophical inertia that has its effect on the classed encounter between the postmodern theorist and the postmodern artist. While there is no question that "theorists" can be associated with the effetely feminine, it also is the case that theoretical rigor can function to ward off the feminized simplicity of pragmatic embodiment. Consider the words of another postmodern performer, Trisha Brown, a figure who has inherited and expanded upon the pragmatic formalism of a 1960s avant-garde. "Pure movement is a movement that has no other

connotations," she begins, adopting a term ("pure") and a principle ("no other connotations") that counters the fundamental
tenets of a deconstructionist for whom purity is a fiction and
for whom the connotative trumps the denotative every time. She
continues.

Mechanical body actions like bending, straightening or rotating would
qualify as pure movement providing the context was neutral. I use pure
movements as a kind of breakdown of the body's capabilities . . . I may
perform an everyday gesture so that the audience doesn't know whether
I have stopped dancing or not . . . I turn phrases upside down, reverse
them or suggest an action and then not complete it, or else I overstate
it altogether. I make radical changes in a mundane way. I use weight,
balance, momentum and physical actions like falling, pushing, etc. I say
things to my company like, "Toss your knees over there," or "Start the
phrase and then on the second count start it again," or "Do it and get
off it." . . . If I am beginning to sound like a bricklayer with a sense of
humor, you are beginning to understand my work.[67]

Embedded in a statement that assumes that a context can be
"neutral" is a formal awareness of what such an approach can
yield, "a breakdown in the body's capabilities" or an uncertainty
about "whether I have stopped dancing or not." The statement
suggests the ways that an investment in the literal undoes the
conventional, whether it be conventions of bodily motion or the
boundaries (the beginning and ending, the entrance and exit)
of the art object. The momentum of Trisha Brown's statement,
however, comes from the series of verb phrases that she piles,
one after another, like a bricklayer-cum-comedian who does not
quite give us the "what's the difference" punch-line. "I turn . . .
reverse . . . overstate . . . make . . . falling . . . pushing." "Toss
your knees over there." "Start the phrase . . . start it again."
Much of art-making and performance-making gives rise to sentences like this: "enter now" "exit from there" "enter here, but
cross then." All of this so-called pragmatic work is a conscious
attention to form, albeit one that does not place "meaning," "signification," or "citation" at the creative forefront. Rather than
assuming the theoretical naiveté of this domain – an assumption
that also tacitly reproduces the slurs of modernist art criticism –
it is more sound professionally and interesting philosophically
to retrain our eyes and our ears. "You lace the shoes over,"
says Elizabeth Le Compte. "I thought we were getting to that

with 'entrances and exits,'" says Edith Bunker. Each theatrical minimalist recalls the practices of the handyman, telling us to beware of the simplicity of their "constructions," foregrounding the classed anxieties that circulate when a bricklayer decides to speak.

Re-practicing theory

There are a number of things that we can learn about the "disciplining of performance" from this network of genealogies. The relationship between the phenomenon of "performance" and a movement called "modernism" is severely tangled, largely because of the enormous number of connotations attached to each of these terms. Much of the art that visual art critics implicitly and explicitly criticized could be viewed as "modernist" depending upon which characteristic of modernism one emphasized. Jerzy Grotowski's high essentialist language of the theatre very much reproduced the value of disciplinary singularity touted by Greenberg and Fried. "We are seeking to define what is distinctively theatre, what separates this activity from other categories of performance and spectacle."[68] Grotowski's argument "that theatre has certain objective laws and that fulfillment is possible only within them"[69] sounded very much like Greenberg's call for the elimination "from the effects of each art any and every effect that might conceivably be borrowed from or be the medium of any other art."[70] The link between modernism and theatre broke down, however, as soon as Grotowski named the objective law of the theatrical medium: "our productions are detailed investigations of the actor-audience relationship."[71] This externalized sense of an actor's "deepest calling" was of course "intolerable" to Fried and Greenberg. A modernist focus on artistic essentials was undone if one of those essentials was the audience relation. Theatricality's pure nature was thus itself an impure essence, corrupted by its fundamental status as a relational encounter.

A reconsideration of these critical alignments shows the retroactive process of disciplinary formation at work. As other critics have noted, the same sense of partial fit and internal contradiction applies to modernism's relationship to sculpture, and even to Specific Objects. The "simple, self-sufficient, geometrical shapes" of sculpture, the reduction of dance to pure movement, and the objective focus on theatrical essence would seem to embody the modernist quest for self-sufficient aesthetic forms. Additionally, as I argued earlier, the focus of such forms on the "action" of making a particular artistic object was in some ways a hyper-formalist, rather than anti-formalist, move. The fact that such works induced an environmental imagination that could be called "self-conscious" might also have aligned them with modernism. Furthermore, these arts and performers were interested in "difference," however they located it "differently," that is, in the relation between art and the "entire situation" of its receiving context – a relocation and expansion of what types of multiplicity and difference were relevant. That the modernist possibilities of such experiments were discredited suggests something about the instability of modernism itself. In fact, such so-called "theatrical" responses exposed the limits of modernist critical sensibilities by, in a sense, literalizing them. It was upon seeing the effects of Greenberg's program taken to such an extreme degree that Fried's "Art and Objecthood" appeared as a kind of back-formation, extolling modernist principles as if they had been articulated in foresight rather than hindsight. The critical response to such a threat resulted in a variety of backhanded gestures of theoretical entrenchment and retrenchment, declaration and qualification. Art should pursue artistic essence, but not when that essence lies in the audience relation. Art should be singular and pure but not concrete or material. Art should be self-critical but not critical of boundaries between its "self" and the "other" arts. Art should have an internal relationality but never externalized relations. Art should be multi-parted but not multi-disciplinary, autonomous but not minimalist. Art should be self-sufficient but still rely on the art critic to illuminate its self-reliance. By unsettling all of these literalist attributions, we see more clearly the compensatory effort in such unstable critical maneuvers.

I have argued that the "New Theatre" context of avant-garde performance lay behind Michael Fried's equations between theatricality and literality. This brand of theatre – one that included audience participation, one that tried to achieve a "non-matrixed" condition – often did aspire to "close" representational structures in favor of a longed-for actuality. At the same time that we acknowledge the connection, it is important to note its partiality and contingency. Such equations made only selective use of theatricality's flexible essentialism and expose the partiality of a visual studies stance on performance. Most fourth wall theatre preceding (and following) this era could be said to deny rather than to incorporate the audience. And most fourth wall theatre preceding (and following) this era operated with stable assumptions of where it began and ended. The "New Theatre" focus troubled those conventions to associate audience awareness and temporal ambiguity with theatricality itself, thus skewing (albeit interestingly) contemporaneous art critics' notions of what theatre was in the first place. Theatricality came in to stand for the literal side of an artistic binary in which art objects apparently aspired to be, as Greenberg said, "nothing more than they really are."[72] Thus, for art criticism at this moment, a specific kind of historically-located artistic innovation came to stand in synecdochically for the theatricality *in toto*. It was as if one style of painting could stand in for pictoriality; as if one style of writing could stand in for textuality. Exemplifying the pitfalls of an interdisciplinary encounter, a unique and historically-specific genre of experimentation became an index of an entire condition.

Furthermore, the New Theatre experiments would receive the retroactive label "performance studies" and oppose themselves to theatre, an intra-disciplinary move that would confuse further what Fried meant by "theatricality" in the first place. For theorists such as Josette Féral and, later Richard Schechner, theatre came to stand for tradition and convention while "performance" was the term that did the troubling. Philip Auslander notes the different discipline-specific uses of the same terminology.

That the term 'theatre' can function as a figure for an emerging postmodernism for Fried and as a figure for a dessicated modernism for Féral is symptomatic of the medium-specificity of both arguments. In the context of the visual arts, Fried's theatricality is a postmodernism threatening to an established modernism; in the context of performance, theatricality is the modernism against which an emergent postmodernism defines itself.[73]

This apparent contradiction is only resolvable when we realize that Fried's "theatricality" and Féral's "performance" are referring to the same scene of postmodern experiment; the former condemns and the second celebrates it. Another way to say this is that postmodern anti-theatricality is the opposite of Friedian anti-theatricality.

From yet another angle, Fried's prejudices remind us of the type of "theatricality" that was explored in early genealogies of performance studies. The prejudice against a literal theatrical was a different kind of prejudice than the one that theatre has classically endured. More often, the figural theatrical has been the basis for Western intellectual history's anti-theatrical prejudice. Recognizing how often the same terms refer to such different qualities might neutralize a great deal of theoretical confusion. Furthermore, we might want to ask what we can learn about the fact that theatrical performance so often ends up on the negative side of a critical paradigm, serving as the most prominent figure of a debased figural, on the one hand, and as the most prominent figure of a debased literal, on the other. For those who appeal to anti-theatrical prejudices – whether to reinforce them or to resist them – it might be helpful for all of us to be clearer about which prejudice we mean. A cautious attitude toward critical theory's stance on theatre and performance is particularly important for scholars and students in the twenty-first century, since its precepts now shadow almost any critical gathering in the humanities and structure the terms of discussion. The rejection of experience, of unmediated access, of a just-thereness of an object is exactly the sensibility that would undergird a host of subsequent critical and social paradigms. This is simultaneously a time in which the theatrical is made into a figure of literality, a strawman against which such accusations of naïveté, essentialism, and literality can be wielded. As such, this kind of theoretical genealogy creates a discursive situation in which any appeal to what sounds like a presential term can be easily denounced as an anti-intellectual, anti-interpretive, and naïve reification of metaphysics. I do not mean to suggest that we argue against this critical vocabulary directly – indeed, as a 1990s graduate student, I became too steeped in deconstruction's paradigms ever to reject them totally – but to ask for more care and caution before knee-jerkedly going on deconstructionist autopilot. I would also suggest that we be critical of the occupational and professional structures that such vocabularies support. Howard Singerman makes a similar suggestion in his analysis of the professional context of postmodern theorizing.

But the university's demand for the production of knowledge – indeed, its takeover of the training of artists, its fashioning of art as research and art criticism as science – belongs to the specialization, administrative rationalization, and 'professionalized treatment of the cultural tradition' that is not so much postmodern as characteristically and familiarly modern.[74]

Ultimately, I suspect that contending with this entire conundrum means acknowledging the happiness issue – and asking how it might be that a variety of skills, forms, obsessions, and "things that we are good at doing" could be valued in the academy . . . with less panic.

5　History and performance: blurred genres and the particularizing of the past

> We mine what are sometimes called counterhistories that make apparent the slippages, cracks, fault lines, and surprising absences in the monumental structures that dominated a more traditional historicism.
>
> Stephen Greenblatt and Catherine Gallagher[1]

> Their idea was to show that action went on within a matrilineal sociocultural space. Somehow this device didn't work.
>
> Victor Turner on a restaging of a Ndembu female puberty ritual[2]

Local knowledges

In 1980, anthropologist and cultural critic Clifford Geertz published an essay in *The American Scholar* that projected for many the intellectual shifts that would pervade the humanities and social sciences over the course of the next decade. In "Blurred Genres," Geertz wittily surveyed a range of "new" approaches in the analysis of culture and what he called "the refiguration of social thought." By the end of the first paragraph, he had isolated three trends that, he said, were not only "true" but "true together."[3] First, echoing his title, he noted the "enormous amount of genre mixing in intellectual life." Second, he noted that such mixed genres tended to focus less on the general and more on the particular, that scholars were not quite as interested in "the sort of thing that connects planets and pendulums" as much as they were in that which "connects chrysanthemums and swords." Finally, he identified an analogical impulse in cultural analysis, an incorporation of the central metaphors of the humanities into sociological understanding. The analogies on which he focused were "game," "drama," and "text"; all three were newer interpretive concepts for the study of human behavior.

In the same decade that Geertz, the figure who came to sym-
bolize "anthropology" for a generation of non-anthropologists,
waxed eloquent about the blurring, particularizing, and analo-
gizing of social thought, the discipline of performance studies
secured an institutional hold. After creating and documenting
their own blurred genres in the theatrical avant-garde of the
1960s and 1970s, Michael Kirby, Richard Schechner, and other
New York scholars and artists gradually formalized their pursuits
in the editorship of *The (Tulane) Drama Review* and, by 1980,
the coordination of an eclectic faculty into a department of performance studies. By 1985, the oral interpretation wing of the
Speech Communication Association (later NCA) changed the
name of its central journal from *Literature and Performance* to
the more analogically expansive *Text and Performance Quarterly*.
At the same time, the Interpretation division changed its name
to Performance Studies and speech departments at Northwestern, University of North Carolina, University of Texas, and more
followed suit. These simultaneous intellectual and institutional
"refigurations" are no coincidence. The concept of the blurred
genre underwrote the concept of "interdisciplinarity," a move
that legitimized the kind of interdisciplinary genre-mixing espoused in performance studies. And certainly, the deployment
of "analogy" as a basis for intellectual engagement rationalized the deployment of "performance" as a principle for cross-
disciplinary binding. While analogical terminology in both the
humanities and social sciences was often accused of "jargonism"
or of instituting a variety of synecdochic fallacies in cultural analysis, such terms enabled scholars to push the boundaries of their
respective fields. The appropriation, redefinition, and expansion
of borrowed analogy provided the rationale behind the institutionalization of performance studies. Perhaps less explicitly, but
no less importantly, Geertz's second identified trend – the focus
on the particular – also legitimated performance as a domain,
a method, and a mode of attention. In an intellectual climate
that resisted large-scale abstraction in favor of case study, that
addressed the minute movements of the everyday in "thickly
described" local contexts, the imaginative life of performance
was an appropriate match.[4] Scholars and artists of performance
brought their ways of perceiving gesture, image, space, voice, facial expression, corporeal motion, and collective gathering to a

scholarly arena that valued the most "local" of local knowledges. This transition was made easier in that avant-garde performers of the 1960s and 1970s had already been tuning performance knowledge to "blur" the boundary between "art" and "the everyday," facilitating (though never resolving) the exchange between the professional worlds of the scholar and the artist.

The less explicit domain of "the particular" actually will figure quite prominently as the rest of this chapter analyzes the nature and impact of selected intellectual formations that consolidated in the 1980s. The focus on what Geertz called "case studies and interpretations" rather than grand theories manifested itself in a number of new key terms. The particular meant valuing rather than discrediting symbolic forms of knowledge such as "stories," "narratives," and "anecdotes." It also meant searching for the symbolic in other realms, indeed, defining realms of knowledge like the "background," the "contextual," the "marginal," and the "periphery" *as* symbolic and dynamic rather than as stable and inert. The particular could refer to size, emphasizing the "micro," the "detail," and the "minute." It gleaned interpretive utility from the fleetingness of "ephemera" and found nothing trivial in the randomness of "trivia." The particular also characterized a performance of normality, focusing attention on "common sense" and on the "ordinary," the "everyday," and the "routine" as keys to cultural understanding. This highly focused and specific mode of attention influenced the discourse and practice of a number of disciplines in the humanities and social sciences, especially the subfields within these schools that sought cross-disciplinary interaction. It also testified to the influence, not only of Geertzian anthropology, but also of poststructuralist historians and theorists such as Michel Foucault. Foucault's anti-foundationalist histories homed in on minutiae and on what he called the "capillary" process of institutional authority. His influential work encouraged critics of the 1980s to read the particular not only as the connective tissue of the benignly cultural but also as the insidious operation of the not-so benignly powerful. Not everyone greeted these intellectual developments with enthusiasm. Conservatives in all fields worried that the rise of disciplinary blurring would entail the loss of disciplinary standards. Meanwhile, Marxists and other progressive critics found the Geertz-validated, Foucault-inspired focus on the local to be a signal of the left's capitulation. As student activists of the late 1960s pursued their research in the conservative climate of the Reagan/Thatcher 1980s, the utopic ideal of large-scale revolution was supplanted by an "always already" embedded model of the intellectual, a figure who could no longer position herself outside of the institutions that she critiqued and who could no longer turn to grand narratives of domination and rebellion. For better and for worse, the focus on local instances of power and culture seemed to offer a way of maintaining Left suspicion without having very high expectations of where that suspicion would go.

In what follows, I return to these themes and genealogies to consider their relevance to the study of theatre and performance. To do so is to return to many of the historical developments presented in Chapter One, especially as issues of interdisciplinary exchange and the "culture wars" became more explicit. It also means addressing this period's engagement with "culture" and "cultural studies" as anticipated, and resituated, by the earlier genealogies of Chapter Three. For the purposes of this chapter, however, I will also consider how shifts in cultural analysis affected the discourses and practices of history, historicism, and historiography. Within different wings of the academy, historical practice altered and, depending upon the field, increased under banners such as the New Historicism, the New Cultural History, meta-history, and "the linguistic turn." In Europe, the French *annalistes* composed vast histories of micro-practices and local beliefs while members of the Radical History movement in England developed an historiographical practice that interpreted political economy "from below," that is, through the everyday experiences of laboring peoples. These and related historiographical movements blurred interdisciplinary genres and attended to the anecdotes, localities, and tropic representational practices of historical events and of historical writing itself. While they all promiscuously borrowed and developed interpretive analogies across a variety of fields, such experiments also varied depending upon period, politics, and the disciplinary homes of respective practitioners. A focus on "historicism" looked somewhat different depending upon whether a scholar derived from the field of literature, anthropology, or history itself. The cultural turn prompted reflection on the practice of theatre and performance history as well. In their collection-cum-textbook, *Critical Theory and Performance*, Joseph Roach and Janelle Reinelt's survey of the era's most important intellectual transformations included sections on both "Cultural Studies" and "Theater History and Historiography." It is no coincidence that the terms, principles, and references in both of these entries overlapped significantly.[5] As the next sections argue, similar intellectual influences can be traced to the work of many "cultural" and "historical" works of groundbreaking scholarship. That intellectual confluence also spurred the methodological interest in the particular. Using debates around New Historicism as an illustration and counterpoint, I consider the connections between such historical practices and the precedents and innovations of theatre and performance historiography. In later sections, I consider some of the effects, specifically gendered effects, of these cross-disciplinary borrowings. I suggest that a focus on the detail, the local, and the particular has a gendered history, one that is more apparent in feminist critiques of anthropology as well as in feminist critiques of Foucault. Hence, if "anthropology" and "Foucault" can serve as markers for intellectual paradigms that galvanized interdisciplinary scholarship in history and culture, scholars of theatre and performance would do well to investigate the gendered consequences of applying such paradigms.

New historicism, cultural anthropology, and performance

To consider New Historicism, and especially New Historicism's relationship to theatre and performance history, requires a review of an older historicism, one that affected the study of drama, theatre, and literature in the historicist paradigms of philology. While American theatre scholars such as Brander Matthews and George Pierce Baker often expressed resistance to the "German" philological trend, they most often borrowed its methods. In addition to adapting its genus/species models of genre development, theatre scholars also employed its methodological preoccupation with minute details, elsewhere referred to as "facts." As argued in Chapter Two, such theatre scholars took philology's emphasis on historical research and on the conventions of literary transmission to rationalize the investigation of such "extra-literary" realms as street lay-outs, building configurations, set designs, managerial structures, actors, and audiences. To a philological method acutely preoccupied with the accumulation of facts, the hyper-contextual circumstances of the performed event offered an endless supply of discoverable data, even if they were not always the kind of data that literary philologists were interested in or skilled in discovering. Such acts of accumulation were more enthusiastically systematized in Germany under the label *Theatrewissenschaft*. As Michael Quinn and Marvin Carlson have argued, the once-ambivalently embraced methods of the Germans founded and eventually routinized the field of "theatre history" as a distinct disciplinary speciality throughout the US and Europe.[6] Even when mid-century literary scholars broke from the "old historicism" of philology in favor of the de-contextualizing analysis of New Criticism, the practice of philology persisted in its theatrical guise. Societies, journals, and hirings professionalized the practice of theatre history and consolidated the identity of the theatre historian. The avid study of the detail, the minute, and the contextual galvanized and maintained the professional profile of theatre in higher education. It will be important to remember the "historicism" in this performance genealogy as we consider a new historicism's focus on the detail, the minute, and the contextual at a later period.

In 1980, literary scholar Stephen Greenblatt published *Renaissance Self-Fashioning.*[7] It was one of several texts, along with Catherine Gallagher's *The Industrial Reformation of English Fiction*, Walter Benn Michael's *The Gold Standard the Logic of Naturalism*, D.A. Miller's *The Novel and the Police*, and subsequent texts of colleagues and students that signaled a new movement in the analysis of culture.[8] Initially clustered in Berkeley's intellectual community, what would occasionally be called "cultural poetics" and more often receive the label "New Historicism" began as an interdisciplinary reading group whose shared authors included Lacan, Althusser, Foucault, Geertz, and other authors of works of "theory" emanating principally from Paris, Konstanz, Berlin, Frankfurt, Budapest, Tartu, and Moscow.[9] Searching for a term that could unite the disparate backgrounds and interests, they founded a journal under the title *Representations* to include historians and social scientists who took the idea of representation seriously; it also included art and literary historians who were expanding their analytic domain beyond canonical works. Greenblatt's study of "self-fashioning" showed the legacy of such cross-disciplinary reading. In particular, it deployed a Foucauldian model of power to argue that an emerging concept of an individuated "self" functioned as a vehicle for the exercise of larger structures of authority. Thus, rather than exerting a repressive power from on high, the Renaissance's discourse of selfhood simultaneously advanced a practice of "self-regulation" such that individual subjects could be counted on to subject themselves to regulatory operation even as they adopted a language of self-constitution. That classic Foucauldian structure was the springboard for other types of analysis. In what is perhaps Greenblatt's most famous subsequent essay, "Invisible Bullets," he studied "subversive" voices next to religious texts and institutions, ultimately focusing on how such apparent instances of resistance were actually produced and, furthermore, "contained" by the orthodoxies that they seemed to contest.[10] In diffusing larger and grander models of power, Foucault's model also multiplied its objects of analysis. That is, by showing the co-saturation of authority and resistance across a wide spectrum of practices, his paradigms also rationalized a methodological expansion into a range of previously neglected arenas. "[T]his new historicism projects a vision of history as an endless skein of cloth smocked in a complex, overall pattern by the needle and thread of Power. You need only pull the thread at one place to find it connected to another," Carolyn Porter summarized.[11] For literary scholars such as Greenblatt, this expansion was happily two-fold. It meant that the literary canon expanded to include tracts, pamphlets, letters, and popular writing; at the same time, it could also mean that the domain of the literary, often seen as extraneous to politics, could be positioned as a charged and relevant site for the analysis of social processes.

That renewed sense of relevance also came from another significant set of intertexts for New Historicist work: Clifford Geertz and cultural anthropology. Geertz's anthropological embrace of what he called humanist metaphors and methods spurred humanists in turn to speculate on the utility of parallel concerns in anthropology and the social sciences. Reflecting back on their initial readings of Geertz's "Thick Description" in his landmark book, *The Interpretation of Cultures*, Greenblatt and Catherine

Gallagher recalled the thrill of hearing a social scientist call the analysis of culture the "sorting out of structures of significa-tion . . . and determining their social ground and import," an enterprise that, Geertz said, was "much more like that of a literary critic."[12]

[I]t made sense of something we were already doing, returning our own professional skills to us as more important, more vital and illuminating, than we had ourselves grasped . . . we were excited to find a sophisticated, intellectually powerful, and wonderfully eloquent anthropologist who could make use of the tools in our disciplinary kit and in so doing renew in us a sense of their value.[13]

Emboldened by this endorsement, *Representations* writers began to adapt their skills to the task of "thick description," a term that Geertz developed from the work of philosopher Gilbert Ryle. Ryle had distinguished "thin" from "thick" description by the latter's ability to place accounts of behavior within a net-work of affective and symbolic structures that gave them co-herence. In his famous examples of the difference between a "twitch" and a "wink," or between a sequential description of "pumping a bike" and an interpretation of the reason one might pump at all, Ryle argued for the importance of the symbolic in the analysis of human behavior, an argument that Geertz adapted to argue for the analytic power of the "cultural" in cul-tural anthropology. That emphasis on the symbolic and cultural further supported the adaptation and expansion of the literary and humanist disciplinary kit. This pivotal instance of scholarly "blurring" would end up marking New Historicism as a key force in the "cultural turn" of the 1980s. The recognition of its sig-nificance showed up everywhere. Theatre scholars Roach and Reinelt selected Greenblatt and New Historicism as key overlap-ping figures and terms in the accounts of culture and historiog-raphy. Meanwhile, James Clifford, the historian of social science who in the 1980s supplied influential interpretive histories of ethnography and anthropology, incorporated Greenblatt into his fold. Clifford's chapter on "Ethnographic Self-Fashioning" in *Predicament of Culture* placed Greenblatt on a par with ethnogra-phy's much-touted fieldworker, calling the former a "participant-analyst."[14]

As numerous scholars have noted, New Historicism ended up diminishing and augmenting the significance of the literary at once. Literary critics privileged what had been heretofore peripheral to their training while simultaneously positing literary training's centrality in the analysis of culture. One of many later twentieth-century developments that reacted against the mid-century New Criticism, New Historicism revisited the once-discredited contextuality of literature and interrogated accepted notions of what came under the category of literature altogether. While New Historicism claimed not to be New Criticism, it also claimed not to be "old" historicism, or what Michael Warner called "the somewhat dreary and encyclopedic historical work that the philologists used to do."[15] Such reductive, if expedient, characterizations effectively positioned philological historicism as the domain of "thin description," a transparent litany of facts in which history functioned "as a stable point of reference, beyond contingency, to which literary interpretation can securely refer."[16] While New Historicism had a kind of neither/nor relationship to both New Criticism and philology, in other ways it could be seen as integrating them. Its scholars made use of new critical methods – conducting close reading, deploying explication to illuminate textual ambiguity and contradiction – and applied them to the "non-literary" realm of the historical, now illuminating ambiguity and contradiction in what was once considered securely referential.

New Historicism is an exemplary illustration of an interdisciplinary site. As such, it also exemplifies some of its hazards, including the disavowals, synecdochic fallacies, and reinvented wheels that I have addressed throughout this book. As argued in Chapter One, disciplinary breaks often carry more disciplinary continuity than they initially acknowledge. Often such continuities more easily appear to the outsider; outsiders see the reproduction of codes and conventions that the reproducers cannot see themselves. Hence, New Historicism's break with literary studies still seemed quite "literary" to those outside literature departments even if they seemed incredibly un-literary to many New Critics. The kinds of arguments generated did not look "historical" to many historians, who found any "analogy" between what Donald Kelley parodied as "The New Anecdotalism" and their own ways of analyzing the past impossible to fathom.[17] Similar kinds of skeptical responses appeared not only in debates about New Historicism but also in parallel moves to

unsettle relations between literature and history. Historian Joan
Wallach Scott was one who found herself defending a "linguistic
turn" in the field of history and arguing that the use of discursive analysis was not necessarily an "unhistorical" capitulation to
the literary.[18] Eventually, critics within literary studies began to
reckon with the reproduction of literary codes and conventions
within New Historicism's announced rejection. Brook Thomas's
"The New Historicism and Other Old-Fashioned Topics" first
appeared as an essay and then turned into a book describing its
links to traditional literary methods and concepts. Despite its important provocations, New Historicism was for Thomas a classic
case of a reinvented wheel. Carolyn Porter specifically named and
elaborated the effects of several of those "old-fashioned" concepts, particularly the "formalist" methods of New Criticism.
She argued that the quest to unsettle literary studies had disin-
genuously augmented the status of its methods. "[It] serves to
legitimate a suspect formalism which seems to treat the social
text in much the same way it has been accustomed to treating
the literary one. As if you could say, in response to the question
of how you relate text to reality, reality *is* a text, and then proceed to read it, like a New Critic, for its paradoxes, tensions, and
ambiguities."[19] While the phrase "everything is a text" was also
a defensive one used to fend off as much as to embrace the idea
to which it referred, for Porter and others it was deservedly suspect. In the compendium of interdisciplinary hazards, textuality's
analogical expansion could rationalize an "everything is just like
me" attitude in literary scholars, positioning the domains and
objects of other fields as patiently awaiting illumination by their
own methods of explication. Porter called this dangerous attitude "colonialist formalism," and her argument suggested that it
had institutional effects.[20] Given that "formalism has remained
institutionally inscribed, despite the fact that we ritualistically
denounce it at every opportunity," its insidious re-use was a way
of maintaining the academic authority of literary studies despite
an announced scholarly interest in institutional critique.[21]

The relationship of theatre and performance to this interdisciplinary convergence is complex, unsystematic, and ongoing.
Scholarship in these fields certainly bore the traces and influences of apparently newer historical models of culture. Often the

"cultural turn" was used to rationalize an expansion of interest beyond theatre to a wider network of performance forms. While this is a heuristic move, it had the effect of ignoring the ways that theatre itself can be richly theorized as an exemplary site for cultural analysis. Bruce McConachie and Tom Postlewait's edited collection *Interpreting the Theatrical Past* compiled essays that demonstrated an array of approaches, methods, and genre-bending analyses.[22] In performance studies, Brooks McNamara emerged as one of the leading historians of popular performance, offering detailed histories of the vaudevilles, burlesques, amusement parks, and other extra-canonical performance venues. To map New Historicism to theatre/performance, however, is at once a match, a mis-match, and a curious redundancy. As argued in Chapters Two and Three, theatre already had an uncertain canonical status from many perspectives in literary studies. In a sense, then, to study theatre was already to enact the New Historicist search for the "extra-canonical." A familiar redundancy also surfaced in the deployment of Clifford Geertz's paradigms, for to tell theatre scholars to "blur" their "genres" seemed both appropriate and much-delayed in its directive. Theatre scholars had spent a great deal of time addressing performance as a site of artistic mixture and integration long before it was trendy to be "interdisciplinary." The relationship between these intellectual markers and theatre and performance thus changes depending upon where one locates such forms and disciplines in a longer intellectual history. Similarly, the use of New Historicist principles to transform theatre scholarship can seem both compelling and misplaced. Roach, Reinelt, and Bruce Mc-Conachie made calls for theatre scholars to take New Historicist principles to heart, particularly the conception of historical context as itself symbolic, dynamic, and subject to determination.[23] That kind of critique is directed from a specific place to a specific audience, however. It addresses the philological legacies of theatre history, at least in their "thinly described" forms. To the extent that some fact-preoccupied, "monological" theatre scholars had not made use of the cultural potential of theatrical culture, their critique is appropriate. However, one might also map a New Historical connection to theatre and performance from a different place and in a different direction. As reformed New Critics touted a return to historicism, it is worth remembering that theatre scholars never fully left it behind. The interest in the contextual remained in theatre even when mid-century literature scholars repudiated it. A consideration of that genealogy not only positions New Historicism as a corrective to theatre scholarship but also as an unacknowledged re-discovery of theatre's disciplinary tradition.

I will try to illustrate the complications of these different types of mappings by focusing on one example, specifically another use of a theatrical analogy inside a New Historicist debate. One of the central tenets of the New Historicist approach revolved around text and context, particularly the goal of unsettling the distinction. The New Historicism's turn to the contextual distinguished itself from old historicism by positioning the contextual as contingent and interpretable. Rather than being the stable and referential background behind a text's interpretive instabilities, context too was actually textual. This kind of principle gave rise to a number of unsettling assertions around fundamental epistemological constructs; with the text/context division, other divisions such as that between foreground and background, between center and periphery, between figure and ground, unsettled as well. Interestingly, Carolyn Porter used a theatrical analogy to characterize this shift.

As we all know by now, the relation between the literary and the historical has been radically reproblematized. To put it far too simply, in trying to approach literature as a historically situated cultural phenomenon, we no longer regard 'history' as given backdrop against which to see the literary text. It is neither something that springs forth from that back drop, spotlighted by its transcendent expression of the 'human spirit,' nor is it the result of the fellow working the lights, exposing a fixed, historically 'set' scene. Neither lamps nor mirrors will do anymore. Further, the stage metaphor breaks down . . . According to Frederic Jameson, the entire range of conceptual models dependent on depth (essence/appearance, latent/manifest, authenticity/inauthenticity, signifier/signified) has given way to a 'new kind of flatness or depthlessness' which he finds characteristic not only of postmodern art but of contemporary theory as well. No longer on, or behind, or in front of the stage, we instead inhabit a discursive field.[24]

Porter's statement would thus seem to position theatre – the stage – as an index of an older historicism, one that needed to believe in divisions of texts and contexts in a mode analogous to the belief in frontstages and backstages. Provocative as her illustration is, however, Porter's theoretical use of the stage metaphor is not a helpful disciplinary use. It does not factor in the specific disciplinary history of literary studies' relationship to drama, one characterized by a break in which theatre analysts wanted – some years ago – to study more than the play itself and to conceive backdrops and the fellow running the lights as themselves objects of study. An interest in conceiving such aspects and persons as being something other than "context" has been a fundamental principle of theatre history. In theatre studies, the backdrop has not been part of the background for quite some time. Of course, while theatre scholars have placed such realms at the interpretive center of their analyses, this does not mean that they have always treated these domains with the same tools as the writers of *Representations*. If they had, Roach, Reinelt, McConachie, and others would not have felt the need to call attention to New Historicism's "flourish" of critical paradigms.[25] However, it does mean that the study of theatre had already implicitly exploded a number of epistemological constructs, even when its scholars had little interest in claiming that explosion. Now that historical and cultural innovations in the humanities and social sciences have unsettled the boundaries between text and context, it seems only appropriate to highlight the disciplinary utility of a performance form whose hypercontextuality has always confounded such distinctions. Such highlighting would not necessarily come from within literary studies, however, where the use of a theatrical theoretical vocabulary did not always translate into an interest in the form and discipline of theatre itself. New Historicism's relativizing frame was not enough to undo scholarly habits based in earlier cultural hierarchies. Its provocative anecdotalism did not itself ensure that theatre's anecdotes would make their way into the foreground.

New Historicism was one important instance of a "cultural turn" that pervaded the humanities and social sciences and that sought to create an interdisciplinary bridge. In this discussion, I have focused more attention on connection and disconnects to something that called itself "theatre," largely because the disciplinary identity of theatre history is entrenched enough to argue for

possible links. The discipline of "performance history," while
practiced by many earlier and recent historians, did not emerge
as a labeled and consolidated area of inquiry until the last decade
of the twentieth century when project proposals and job descriptions began to add to or amend their titles. I will consider an
example of such historiographical work later in this chapter. At
this juncture, however, I want to track another set of connections
to the particularized study of culture, one that more explicitly affected the domain of "performance" and "performance studies."
Working from my introductory suggestion that the turn to culture
and the turn to performance studies were propelled by the same
"blurred" intellectual climate, let me briefly survey some of its incarnations. Clifford Geertz discussed three humanist analogies
that, in 1980, were "refiguring social thought": game, drama,
and text. While the above discussion of New Historicism is an
example of the third term in action, the first two terms identified
conceptual paradigms that would become fundamental to the
epistemology of performance studies. Indeed, the scholars listed
under Geertz's analogies would appear on many performance
studies syllabi over the next two decades.

   The work of Erving Goffman was Geertz's dominant example of "gamelike conceptions of social life."[26] While Goffman
often used dramaturgical metaphors, Geertz argued that his "to
and fro" models of social interaction ("ping-pong in masks")
were best positioned as game theory.[27] Whatever the preferred
analogy, Erving Goffman would be appropriated in performance
studies as the founding architect of a subfield called "the performance of everyday life." In truth, this founding was performance studies' re-discovery of a longer sociological tradition, one
stretching back at least to the work of Chicago School sociology.
Nevertheless, Goffman's engaging examples and performance-
based vocabularies were particularly resonant to performance
scholars who were trying to see the theatrical in places other than
the proscenium stage. Goffman spoke of the co-dependence of
frontstages and backstages, seeing their operations of display and
secrecy in homes, offices, classrooms, and other everyday sites.
He spoke of social actors who played "parts" and had "routines,"
what he defined as "pre-established patterns of action" that structured situational encounters.[28] Goffman sounded a conundrum

familiar to "New theatre" practitioners when he discussed the issue of whether or not actors "believed" in the realities that they were creating, noting that no one should underestimate "the strength of a little self-delusion."[29] His model of the individual encounter was one where a person "projects a definition of the situation" and then enjoys and endures subsequent interactions that may affirm or discredit that projection.[30] Just as projections depended upon the performance of certain affirming behaviors, so the identity of everyday spaces depended upon and altered with the nature of the actions performed. "There are many regions," wrote Goffman, "which function at one time and in one sense as a front region and at another time and in another sense as a back region."[31]

[O]f a Sunday morning, a whole household can use the wall around its domestic establishment to conceal a relaxing slovenliness in dress and civil endeavor, extending to all rooms the informality that is usually restricted to the kitchen and bedrooms. So, too, in American middle-class neighborhoods, on afternoons the line between the children's playground and home may be defined as backstage by mothers, who pass along it wearing jeans, loafers, and a minimum of make-up, a cigarette dangling from their lips as they push their baby carriages.[32]

In *Presentation of the Self in Everyday Life*, and later in texts such as *Interaction Ritual* and *Frame Analysis*, Goffman portrayed a world where the highly local and detailed aspects of individual performance – demeanor, dress, facial expression, linguistic codes, and more – were central to the analysis of social process.[33] While his perspectives were not themselves post-structuralist, they suited post-structuralism's intellectual climate. In addition to the blurring and appropriation of humanist analogy, Goffman's insights could be patched to a post-structuralist conception of power. By the time he wrote *Gender Advertisements* – to some, his best work – the connection between the performance of everyday life and disciplinary docility was readily apparent.[34] If human subjects behaved within and against imputed projections, supported by the "strength of a little self-delusion," then there was a great deal of resonance between Goffman's "encounters" and Foucault's paradoxical world of agentless self-regulation.

In explicating the "drama" analogy, another familiar scholar figured centrally for Geertz – Victor Turner. Turner's ritual

theory, in particular the concept of the "social drama," brought
out the "temporal and collective dimensions" of social action as
well as the capacity of such performances "to transmute not just
opinions but . . . also . . . the people who hold them."[35] While
Geertz appropriately found there to be a formulaic quality to
Turner's theory – "a form for all seasons" – there was no denying its epistemological impact. In performance studies, Turner
would be chronicled as one of the two "men who gave birth"
in performance studies' origin narrative. Performance scholars
would find instances of social drama's *breach, crisis, redressive action,* and *reintegration* in all domains of social and artistic life.[36]
Richard Schechner, the other forebear, would cite Turner's theories extensively in his own definitional scholarship on performance. Schechner's "restoration of behavior" not only made use
of the social drama but also of Turner's concept of "liminality,"
an in-between state within ritual structures in which individuals
and groups temporarily lacked definition and inscription. While
Turner ultimately argued that such liminal states "reintegrated"
into socially conventional ones, Schechner and other performance anthropologists such as Dwight Conquergood argued for
their peculiar productivity.[37] For Conquergood, the liminal was
intriguingly theorized as an illuminating break, an aporia within
accepted patterns of behavior that exposed their vulnerability.
This kind of theoretical development around the concept of performance matched and carried forward contemporaneous concerns with power and resistance. As New Historicists and their
critics wondered and worried about relations of mobility and
constraint, as other kinds of Foucauldian disciples speculated
upon the interaction between subversion and containment, performance discourse also carried the opportunity and burden of
this double bind. Sometimes, performance was the mechanism of
social constraint, and sometimes performance was the vehicle
of social mobility. Sometimes performance was about making
community, and sometimes it was about breaking it. In either
instance, the vocabulary of performance propelled the analysis
of culture. While performance studies' initial incarnations more
often took the scholarly form of "ethnography" – writings based
on fieldwork conducted with co-present participants – eventually
such theories and concepts found their way into the analysis of
"performance history."

Gendered genres

Throughout my examples thus far, the "particular," the "detail," and the "local" have appeared prominently in various forms as the methodological basis for a new cultural analytics. So, too, texts and contexts, foregrounds and backgrounds, frontstages and backstages, have been invoked, analyzed, and reconfigured by the phenomenon of performance. The examples have attended to the ordinary and to the everyday. In all cases, analysts are encouraged to see the presence of big things in small things, to make use of the humanist capacity for "close reading" and the assessment of the minute and marginal. "We live in an age when the detail enjoys a rare prominence," wrote Naomi Schor in 1987 in *Reading in Detail*, a book that excavated contemporary social theory (Foucault, Freud, Barthes) as well as eighteenth-century aesthetics. Schor reminded readers just how unusual such prominence actually was, for, "until very recently, the detail has been viewed in the West with suspicion if not downright hostility."[38] Such hostility and "censure of the particular" took two forms under neo-classical aesthetics and subsequent reinscriptions. It is "bounded on the one side by the *ornamental*, with its traditional connotations of effeminacy and decadence, and on the other, by the *everyday*, whose 'prosiness' is rooted in the domestic sphere of social life presided over by women."[39] Thus, the detail is historically associated with different types of femininity, an equation that has been the basis for their mutually defined negativity. What then is the significance of the rare prominence of the detail given this gendered history? Does it "signify a triumph of the feminine with which it has so long been linked?" asked Schor, or does the detail "cease to be connoted as feminine at the very moment when it is taken up for the male dominated cultural establishment?" I would like to use Schor's line of questioning to consider the tacit gender politics of cultural paradigms as they have been adapted and developed in theatre and performance studies.

In the same period that humanists and performance scholars began to become enamored of all things "anthropological," an internal critique of anthropology's basic paradigms appeared in the work of feminist social scientists. Sherry Ortner published her widely circulated essay, "Is Female to Male as Nature is to

Culture?" in 1974, contributing to a burgeoning field of inter-disciplinary feminist critique. Ortner summarized the gendered bifurcations that structured anthropological analysis. Women "represent lower-level, socially fragmenting, particularistic sorts of concerns"; furthermore, female/male distinctions are often made across an axis of "relative concreteness vs. relative abstract-ness: the feminine personality tends to be involved with concrete feelings, things, people, rather than with abstract entities."[40] A whole generation of feminist anthropologists subsequently un-settled the "naturalized" associations attached to terms. While some worked to show women's participation in abstract domains outside of the domestic, others demonstrated that there was nothing "natural" about the domain of the particular. To attend to "concrete feelings, things, and people" was to participate in the production of culture at the most intimate level. For Naomi Schor, a similar set of associations appears in the history of aes-thetic theory. "Viewed as congenitally (rather than culturally) particularistic, the woman artist is doubly condemned to pro-duce inferior works of art: because of her close association with nature, she cannot but replicate it."[41] Similarly, the feminine fo-cus on the detail confounded Idealist aesthetics. In both literary and visual theories, a particularist consciousness distracted the artist from achieving the sublime. Schor argued further that the anti-feminine prejudice against the detail derived from a more pointed threat. "The irreconcilability of details and the sublime and the concomitant affinity of details for the effete and effemi-nate ornamental style point to what is perhaps most threatening about the detail: its tendency to subvert an internal hierarchic ordering of the work of art which clearly subordinates the pe-riphery to the center, the accessory to the principal, the fore-ground to the background."[42] Consequently, to give attention – especially feminist attention – to the particular was potentially to subvert an internal hierarchic ordering in the arts and anthropol-ogy. Within the social sciences, it was to expose the contingency of the heretofore natural, showing the dependency of the cul-tural on the supposedly "trivial" activities of the domestic and, furthermore, exposing the domestic as itself a product of skilled, if devalued, labor. In aesthetics, it was not only to distract from the achievement of artistic excellence but also to disrupt the per-spectival conventions with which that excellence was defined, dismantling the precarious balance and precarious dependency of the centralized foreground on the peripheral background.

Given this gendered intellectual history and an available feminist critique, one might think that the prominence of the particular in "the cultural turn" would have explicitly incorporated feminist theorization. Interestingly, for all of Geertz's focus on "local knowledges" instead of abstractions, on "cases" instead of "laws," the feminist implications of this methodological revaluing went unannounced. Instead, he and other colleagues analyzed many of the same public rituals, but did so by using a thickly described mode of analysis that would have been called "excessive" and overly "concrete" in the rhetoric of the anti-feminine idealist. Similarly, the reciprocal humanist enthusiasm for anthropology did not highlight the gendered implications of a social analysis of the detail. For those in the humanities, including theatre and performance, the engagement with anthropology was more often a way to gain a kind of masculine legitimation, "a touch of the real," the relevant, and "the efficacious" that redeemed the effete realms of arts and literature. Nevertheless, the feminist connections are unmistakable. An article such as Geertz's "Common Sense is a Cultural System" pointed up the constituted character of the presumably given, a move that had its parallel in feminist critiques of the ordinary, the mundane, and the natural. Furthermore, if the disciples of Erving Goffman found the notion of the "performance of everyday life" provocative enough to found a subfield, they did so by covertly incorporating a feminist epistemology. That the personal is political, that the private is performed, that the everyday is made – all were variations on a feminist critique that foregrounded the cultural constitution of the heretofore "natural." That "everyday life is performed" is more apparent to the women most responsible for maintaining the conditions of its production. That details and particulars constitute the connective tissue of the cultural is an insight apparent to anyone saddled with the task of making a laundry list.

The gendered history of the particular has another less benign trajectory, however, one that returns us to Foucault's poststructuralist model of power. As I argued above, Foucault and his followers dispensed with centralized models of authority in favor of dispersed ones, operating in the minute behaviors of bodies and selves, indirectly exerting its productivity on docile participants. As it happened, a number of critics found an exemplary site for such dispersal in the domain of domesticity. Victorian New Historicists especially found Foucauldian critique and domestic performance to be an all-too perfect match. The concept of domesticity had considerable currency in the nineteenth century as female writers worked to give the domain of women some discursive specificity. Catharine Beecher, a protegée of British reformer Hannah More, published *Treatise on Domestic Economy*, emerging as the leading voice of domesticity in the United States. As numerous scholars have demonstrated, this circumscribed arena gave women a means to exercise a degree of power and indirect influence over their otherwise circumscribed lives. Saying that female education was too preoccupied with cultivating female appearance rather than female competence, More and Beecher turned to a conveniently theatrical metaphor: the life of the young lady "too much resembles that of an actress; the morning is all rehearsal, and the evening is all performance."[43] To More and Beecher, women's confinement and lack of substantive training made them ultimately ill-equipped to run a household, ignorant of domestic skills, and unable to face the compendium of minute, repetitive, constant, and simultaneous tasks that constituted household labor. Beecher advocated another type of female performance, one that sought a balance of mind and body, exterior and interior, abstraction and absorption, confinement and mobility in an orderly domestic sphere. By moving from the position of "actress" to stage manager, women would be in a better position to maintain the healthy environments that produced healthy citizens. Such discourses of domesticity theorized bodily comportment, the relation between bodies and material culture, the processes by which spatial habits developed, the efficient coordination of multiple actions, the dynamics of interpersonal sociality, the emotional ruptures of displacement, and the environmental creation of kinship.

Domesticity was an intensely productive discourse in the nineteenth century. It offered a domain and a set of mechanisms that women of a variety of race and class positions unevenly appropriated to secure a modicum of legitimacy. As Claudia Tate argues, African-American women deployed this discourse on behalf of abolitionism in order to install themselves as the life-giving force in a movement for social justice. The sinister edge

to domesticity's program appeared when Beecher and her disciples positioned it as the locus of female authority, as a way of
"extending over the world those blessed influences, which are to
renovate degraded man."[44] To the ears of contemporary critics,
of course, such language is circumspect, partaking in a bloated
vision of American citizenship and its sense of superior entitlement. Furthermore, and more pointedly for this chapter, the
exercise of women's knowledge is characterized not as a privilege that she holds but as an "influence" that she wields. This
is the formal problem of domesticity and, by extension, of feminized authority. It is a power secured indirectly, less a thing
possessed than a force exerted. As Lora Romero writes, "It represents a way of figuring citizenship for a population imagined
as too mired in personal, affective, and local bonds to participate in an abstract national identity."[45] Not surprisingly, the
domestic woman's formal ambivalence has also produced ambivalence amongst her critics. She is simultaneously criticized for
not achieving a position of direct power as well as for enabling
indirectly the power of others. As it happens, this insidiously indirect formal structure also makes it a match for Foucauldian
critique. In the British context, Nancy Armstrong argued that
domestic ideology signaled a "cultural change from an earlier
form of power based on sumptuary display to a modern form that
works through the production of subjectivity."[46] From thence, it
was quite logical to interpret domesticity as the primary example
and vehicle of disciplinary power. Similarly, D.A. Miller's *Novel
and the Police* exposed a nineteenth-century "field of power relations" masquerading as a "domesticating pedagogy."[47] Such
works positioned middle-class femininity – sometimes figured as
a generalized maternal, sometimes figured as the service worker
of the feminized "helping professions," sometimes figured as an
identificatory position within a text – as the efficient vehicle of
a tacit power structure. Such a model found and critiqued domesticity's localized focus on "people, things, and the concrete"
in the nooks and crannies of social life, seeing it not simply as
the connective tissue of culture but also as the capillary exertion
of power.

In *Homefronts: Domesticity and Its Critics*, Lora Romero takes a
critical look at the coincidence of a Foucauldian critique of power
and the exercise of female authority. Without defending the

latter unproblematically, she suggests that feminists should reconsider a critical paradigm that inadvertently positions women as an insidious force in an otherwise agentless mode of power. The fact that many subsequent critics end up feminizing microdisciplinary operations suggests the presence of a latent gender politics.

More recently, New Historicist criticism of the Foucauldian variety has encouraged us to regard the feminization of culture as a symptom of a larger feminization of power. Yet, the novelty of New Historicism does not reside in its emphasis on power. Earlier, cultural analysis also equated feminization with normalization. . . . Neither the poststructuralist upheaval that divides the cultural analysis of the 1960s and 1970s from that of the 1980s and 1990s nor the feminist critiques to which these analyses have been subjected have altered the basic narrative: normalization is women's work. Even if exposing the rhetorical work of Foucauldian history does not *in and of itself* undermine the facticity of New Historicist claims (all facts require human interpreters and so all truth is necessarily rhetorical), still its practitioners cannot possibly hope to direct their own rhetoric toward progressive ends without first inquiring into the gender and race politics perpetuated by their use of Foucauldian knowledge."[48]

Romero finds this positioning all-too familiar, apparent in the earlier scholarship of Christopher Lasch and in Ann Douglas whose *Feminization of American Culture* unapologetically aligned female power with "devious social control."[49] Such alignments are pervasive in "Americanist" and American feminist literary scholarship. They move from Nathaniel Hawthorne's castigation of "scribbling women" to modernist poets such as Hart Crane who invoke domesticity as a stand-in for both a suffocating, micro-managing maternalism *and* the unthinking conformities of an ornamental, feminized mass culture. Whether conceived as insidious stage management or as superficial display – as trivial "prosiness" or as excessive ornamentation – domesticity became equated with capitulation, with normalization, and with unself-conscious conformism. For avant-garde artists, it was and has been conceived as an arena to be transcended. It was by defining this gendered populist sphere as conservative that they could define the high cultural arena of the avant-garde as subversive. For Romero, post-structuralist literary history has done little to unsettle this equation. Whatever its theoretical aspirations, applications of Foucault to this domain have reinforced a long-standing anti-feminine prejudice.

These tacit prejudices and conceptual blindspots have been reproduced in cultural and performance theory with varied and discontinuous effects. It is no coincidence that Carolyn Porter's critique characterized New Historicist power models as a "skein of cloth" woven by "the needle and thread of Power." Her domestic metaphor obliquely invoked the equation between insidious diffusion and female authority. Erving Goffman's amused readings of the performance of everyday life can now be read as a parodic replay of Catharine Beecher's rules for domestic balance, deploying her focus on ordinary minutiae in order to expose the dependence (and sometimes subversion of) the private on the operations of performance. Furthermore, examples such as Goffman's cigarette-toting stroller pusher – described in tones that are at once fascinated and condescending – implicitly invoke without explicitly analyzing the gendered consequences of disruptions in frontstage and backstage. Not only did Goffman's mothers extend the backstage to the street and the park, they also unsettled the image of the backstage, the home, and the interior as stable and secure. Neither the location nor the character of domesticity is fixed, given, or natural in his depiction. The partial and unsystematic invocation of gendered examples appeared in other domains of cultural performance theory. Schechner's "restoration of behavior" analogized the generative stages of the performance process to "the mother-baby relationship," using D.W. Winnicott's theory of transitional objects to characterize "workshop/rehearsal" as a liminal "not not me" period between immersion and self-differentiation. "These same operations of dissolving ordinary hierarchies, of treasuring things beyond their ordinary worth, of setting aside certain times and places for the manipulation of special things in a world defined non-ordinarily: this is also the definition of the workshop-rehearsal process, the ritual process, the performative process."[50] Interestingly, having theorized performance next to an archetypal process in the maternal domain, Schechner says that "those who are masters at attaining and prolonging this balance are artists, shamans, conmen, acrobats."[51] While such a conclusion is understandable given the discipline-specific goals of Schechner's argument, it has the familiar effect of excluding women or other maternal figures from such forms of mastery. The argument positions the female as an environment, as the place in which ritual occurs, rather than as a ritual subject herself. While her presence provides an enabling metaphor for the performance theorist, the metaphor does not enable her own transformation.

For feminist critics of the male avant-garde, the location of women as the enabling background is all-too conventional. While, as suggested above, some artists characterized that back-grounded position as insidious maternal control, others merely naturalized the position, characterizing it as the surrounding material for staging their own self-development. Rebecca Schneider argues that the "bad-boy art" of the performance avant-garde consistently used women's bodies as markers of nature and as the line to be crossed in often violent rituals of self-differentiation.[52] Laura Levin argues that such violence partakes of a longer tradition of masculinist primitivism reaching back to the Surrealists.[53] Richard Schechner himself seems to fuel a feminist critique when he writes that "the imagination of the adolescent boy is the core of theater. It is the celebration of his achieving the status of manhood that is the subject of theatre."[54] Such an incriminating formulation transposes the early liminal dramas of the "mother-baby relationship" to the hyperbolic liminal dramas of the teenager, staged by a male performer who alternately returns to and rejects the protections and constraints of the maternal. It is in such a structure that Schechner finds the dramatic, something made clear when he speculates on the effect of women attempting to occupy the position of ritual participant. "Women's ceremonies, though often ribald, joyous, enthusiastic, lack the intensity, brutality, aggression and storylike structure of man's ceremonies. In a word, women's ceremonies are less dramatic. With few exceptions, the heroes of drama are young men, or old men who dream and scheme of becoming young again."[55] The lack of "intensity" can be ascribed to the formal difficulty of women's position. If women are historically ascribed to the realm of the supporting prosaic and the tacitly mundane, then they are not easily installed in the explicit and cathartic structures of the most vivid ritual processes. If "normalization is women's work" – as confirmed by Schechner and critiqued by Romero – then women's work can never be made "dramatic."

Thus, to answer Naomi Schor's questions for theatre and performance studies, it is not necessarily the case that the analytic rise of the detail coincided with a conceptual valorization of the feminine. The effects have been multifarious if not exactly feminist. Sometimes the focus on the particular sidelined the feminine, happily interpreting local knowledge without reference to the gender politics of locality. Sometimes the feminine appeared in performance analysis, but then as a naturalized index of the backstage, as the site for rather than the subject of activist transformation. And sometimes the feminine factored prominently, but then as a marker of the role of the detail in perpetuating insidious regimes of power. In all cases, it seems that the feminized domestic is something to be transcended in order to enter the analysis of an "efficacious" performance culture.

This intellectual tendency can have its effect on the application of cultural performance theory to the domain of the historical. It explains, for instance, what some have found to be a gendered occlusion in what is on the whole an exemplary and brilliant instance of performance history, Joseph Roach's *Cities of the Dead*. Along with Geertz and Foucault, the body of performance theory outlined above is a significant set of intertexts for Roach's project, where the concept of restored behavior provides a way to position bodily practices as a central means of historical transmission. Roach deftly maps these performance paradigms to the work of other social critics – annales historians such Pierre Nora and Jacques Le Goff, social theorist Paul Connerton, and critical race historian Paul Gilroy. Combining an analysis of African ritual practices, British theatrical traditions, and the performance conventions of the American South (specifically Louisiana), Roach integrates his theorists and archival research to dramatize the often violently embodied operations of what he calls a "kinaesthetic imagination" in a circum-Atlantic world. Upon investigation of Roach's models, it is possible to discern a gendered blindspot similar to the ones I have been describing above. Pierre Nora makes an important distinction for Roach between different types of memorial transmission, distinguishing the alienated, bicameral structures of modern memorial (*lieu de memoire*, or places of memory) from the unalienated, ritually latent, and tacit structures of pre-modern memorial (*milieu de memoire*, or environments of memory).[56] Such a distinction mapped provocatively to Paul Connerton's division between "inscribed" and "incorporated" practices, opposing the former's textual and intentional methods of remembering to the latter's bodily enactments of habitual behavior.[57] With a barely concealed nostalgia, Nora's provocative discussion of environments of memory privileged performance's embodied focus on memorial practice. However, the historical association between the environmental creation of restored behavior and "women's work" went unacknowledged by both Nora and Roach. Similarly, Connerton appropriately cited a longer intellectual tradition for the analysis of such latent realms – in hermeneutics, phenomenology, and pragmatism. Once again, however, the gendered implications of valuing such realms went unannounced. Connerton neither considered the maternal sphere as a conventional site of bodily incorporation nor tracked the feminist implications of highlighting this particularized domain of intimate practices. Without investigation of the gendered blindspots in such paradigms, performance historiography is at risk of reproducing them.

Other elements in Roach's appropriated theoretical models make it difficult for women to appear in *Cities of the Dead*. In addition to a gendered occlusion in theories of bodily performance, the project is also at risk of maintaining a gender prejudice about what qualifies as vivid and illuminating in cultural analysis, that is, what qualifies as "dramatic." In a study whose central system of bodily transmission is the circum-Atlantic slave trade, Roach's study appropriately foregrounds the violent conventions embedded in performance processes and the forceful instances of literal and metaphoric mutilation that structure them. The prominence of crisis and violence as key processes in the foundation of culture develops the paradigms theorized in Paul Gilroy's *The Black Atlantic*, where "the complicity of civilization and brutality" rationalizes a "turn towards death" for the descendants of African slaves.[58] Gilroy's theories of circum-Atlantic culture thus dovetail with Richard Schechner's theories of performance – where "violent," "turbulent," "bloody," and "perilous" activities constitute the dramatic heart of ritual process.[59] Necessary as such a model is for *Cities of the Dead*, it runs the risk of bypassing other kinds of "kineasthetic" performance processes and, moreover, of excluding or over-determining the position of women in the analysis of performance history.

That risk is perhaps more easily seen by considering an example and testing my arguments next to an episode where a female figure *does* make a prominent appearance. One such place is in Roach's analysis of a mid-nineteenth century performance of Dion Boucicault's *The Octoroon* where Zoe, the adored offspring of the master of Terrebonne Plantation and a slave, submits to the auction block in order to save her late father's estate from bankruptcy. The moment of crisis occurs when Zoe stands atop "a table in the mansion she once graced" and offers her husband a wrenching inventory of her body: "Of the blood that feeds my heart, one drop in eight is black . . . for I'm an unclean thing."[60] In Roach's provocative analysis, Boucicault's dramaturgical decision to place Zoe atop a table is a significant bodily recalling. "This action represents onstage the restored behavior of the slave auctions of the New Orleans Exchange, the transformation of cash into flesh and of flesh into property."[61] Roach's consideration of gender in this analysis thus focuses on the sexualized violence routinized in the performance conventions of the auction block. What this insightful analysis does not consider, however, is the specific, entrenched, and affectively binding domestic performance that is bodily recalled and potentially overturned when the young woman of the house stands on a table. Can the gesture be read as a way of performing her thwarted claim to the environment that she "once graced?" Is her step upon the table then a hyperbolic and self-inflicted enactment of the disorder and racial inversion of domestic stability? Indeed, a great deal of the dialogue heretofore has focused on the fact that Zoe's mixed-raced status will prohibit her from "gracing" the house with full entitlement. Despite the fact that one could never meet a "lady more beautiful in person, or more polished in manners, than that girl," despite the fact that all heirs and would-be purchasers of the estate have fallen in love with her, Zoe's claims to Terrebonne and its contents will be forever partial.[62] Of course, to ask whether the table top is a reflection of a crisis in Zoe's domestic identity would mean valuing domesticity as a source of identity in the first place. By characterizing Boucicault's transposition of the slave auction to the domestic sphere only as a "surefire appeal to bourgeois anxieties of displacement," Roach leaves little room for such an analysis, allowing the "gracing" of the home to remain a trivial and ornamental activity rather than a fundamental basis for Zoe's potential authority and thus compromised subjectivity.[63] Whether or not Zoe's moment on the table top can be more heuristically interpreted, it is still significant that a female figure makes her most prominent appearance by "restoring" violent and "perilous" behavior. The moment may have as much to do with the influence of Gilroy on Roach's analysis as with the conventions of cultural performance theory. To Claudia Tate, this kind of over-determined position derives from the centrality of "violence" in the analytic paradigms most often used to interpret African-American culture. Such an interpretive tendency bypasses the local, life-coordinating performances of domesticity in the production of national culture.

African American women gain entrance into Gilroy's cultural history only by forsaking domesticity, which is to say by forsaking a discourse about the management and maximization of life. . . . The quotidian responsibilities of nation building [however] involve processes of nurturing, education, and social reproduction; therefore, they speak the language of life. Nationalism organizes itself around a gendered division of labor between the task of founding the nation and the task of guaranteeing its posterity – even if these activities are never wholly distinct or necessarily diachronic in their performance. The privilege of the nationalist idiom of violence suggests an unevenness in the recognition of nationalism's different chores.[64]

Women thus appear only when they participate in the performance of cultural violence rather than in the everyday activities of cultural maintenance. For all of the emphasis on local knowledge and kinesthetic imagination in cultural performance theory, the gendered inertia of contemporary analysis still cannot find a way to make such performances "dramatic."

Gender and performance history

Finally, the impact of a "blurred" intellectual climate on the study of theatre and performance was enabling in many ways, though its effects and influences were varied and contradictory. Newer "cultural turns" in the humanities and social sciences contributed to the discursive rise of performance in the sociological and anthropological strains of performance studies. At the same time, they occasionally produced a reductive consciousness with regard to the discipline of theatre, ahistorically casting theatre studies as an "unblurred," canonical field that awaited dispersal from the interdisciplinary intervention of performance studies. Furthermore, the analogical diffusion of the p-word did not in itself transform the methodological habits and predispositions of the disciplines that deployed the term. Nonetheless and despite their disconnections from each other, various versions of the cultural turn in social theory, literary studies, and theatre and performance studies reckoned not only with the interdisciplinary impact of cultural anthropology but also with post-structuralist models of power. As such, their analyses explicitly and implicitly grappled with the political ambivalence of those models. From scholar to scholar, from project to project, their interpretations waivered over issues of domination and resistance, accepting power's pervasiveness but still hoping to find places of subversion. In performance theory, the unprocessed traces of that ambivalence appear in the varied array of associations that were appropriated for its umbrella, theorizing the habitually implicit, on the one hand, and repeatedly celebrating the dramatically explicit, on the other. While performance was touted as a means of making community, it became far more interesting politically and theoretically when it ended up breaking it. As other critics have noted, this ambivalence only suggests that the institutional consolidation of performance studies in the 1980s was a product of its time, sharing the attributes of other former activists-turned-professional-intellectuals who "dreamed of being young again."

I have argued, however, that that ambivalence also participates in and derives from gendered prejudices and occlusions. It is important to note, moreover, that such occlusions can persist in feminist analyses where domesticity has not fared well as an analytic paradigm. The self-deferential nature of domestic discourse – coupled with its practices of enactment on behalf of persons other than women themselves – did not lend itself well to a feminist movement that stressed self-activation and self-advancement. The figure of the maternal was simultaneously too weak and too suffocating to feminist daughters who inherited a few of those male modernist preoccupations. It was similarly too weak and too suffocating to many feminist theatre critics who allied their hopes instead to a feminist performance practice within the sphere of the avant-garde. This conceptual blindspot now contributes to a schism between the

study of historical and the study of contemporary feminist performance or – what often amounts to the same thing – between
"historical" and "theoretical" feminist performance scholarship.
Indeed, to the extent that much feminist performance theory is
also quite focused on finding instances of resistance, subversion,
and transgression, other types of gender performances remain in
the theoretical background. The transgression framework makes
the implicit, domestic, everyday, life-producing performances of
women in earlier periods particularly difficult to track, casting
such historical examples as the regressive foil to present-day progressivism. With different valences, those prejudices have also
limited the theorizing of activism and the nature of the dramatic in variously gendered and racialized arenas, especially arenas of the past. "Critics' tendency to regard domesticity as the
quintessential marker of mindless capitulation rather than as a
symbolic system compatible with a range of political positions has
prevented them from reading the relation between black women's
domestic fiction and black activism," writes Claudia Tate.[65] The
same can be said for a variety of historical cultural production
produced by female performers of color.

Finally, by locating a gendered blindspot in the cultural analysis of the detail, I do not mean to suggest that there have not
been intriguing and important applications of particularistic performance paradigms to women's lives. I would suggest, however,
that such applications can have a kind of redundancy – "look
how local these women's knowledges are" – that perpetuates
rather than exposes that blindspot. The point is not simply to
say that women (like men) perform their private lives but that
the knowledge that even "private" life is performed has an historical (if not congenital) association with the feminine. While
the genderedness of social life has been fundamental to another
strain of theatre and performance studies derived from feminist
theatre and speech act theory (the subject of the next chapter),
that recognition has not been a focal point in the anthropological
strains of performance studies whose fundamental concepts still
only reluctantly incorporate gender critique.

6 Identity and performance: racial
performativity and anti-racist theatre

The orientals have no vital drama because they are fatalists,
because they do not believe in that free will without which the
drama cannot exist . . . A belief in free will is always favorable
to the drama, whereas a belief in foreordination may be not
be unfavorable to the novel, the chief figures of which are not
required always to know their own minds.   Brander Matthews[1]

I can't let you get away with thinking you know what I mean.
Ntozake Shange[2]

Professional passing

One of the most well-circulated essays by an artist of color in the
1990s begins with a description of a university gathering. It is a
"new graduate student reception," and the artist in question is
also an entering student in Harvard's doctoral program in philosophy. This would-be philosopher is thrilled to be there, proud
and giddy to be surrounded by the men whose work she has read
and heard lauded for many years.

As often happens in such situations, I went on automatic pilot. I don't
remember what I said; I suppose I managed not to make a fool of myself.
The most famous and highly respected member of the faculty observed
me for awhile from a distance and then came forward. Without introduction or preamble he said to me with a triumphant smirk, "Miss Piper,
you're about as black as I am."[3]

Adrian Piper uses this anecdote to open "Passing for White,
Passing for Black," a meditation, analysis, and indictment of the
interpersonal structures that reproduce and entrench the larger
structures of American racism. By 1991, when she first composed the essay, Piper had produced a large body of artwork that

176

took the dismantling of racism as its central goal. While more properly positioned as a conceptual artist rather than a performance artist per se, her use of the mechanisms of performance and her incorporation of her own body in her works drew the attention of theatre and performance circles. As a light-skinned African-American woman, Piper's social embodiment proved an all-too appropriate staging ground for interrogating the dynamics of everyday racism. Through a variety of media and through the management of various locutionary situations, her work deployed what she elsewhere called "the indexical present" – the "concrete, immediate, here and now" – to expose the racist dynamics of situations such as those she described in graduate school.[4] "Artwork that draws a relationship with the other in the indexical present trades easy classification – and hence xenophobia – for a direct and immediate experience of the complexity of the other and of one's own responses to her. Experiencing the other in the indexical present teaches one how to see."[5] By 1991, Adrian Piper had also begun to enjoy and endure a notoriety that she had not previously experienced in her professional life as an artist. Having begun working as a conceptual artist in the late 1960s, having watched the audience for her work diminish between 1974 and 1987, she noted that it was not until "the late 1980s, when the topic of gender, race, and difference became fashionable in critical circles that I was rehabilitated."[6] While characterizing a new interest in gender and race as "fashionable," Piper wryly identifies a historical juncture in art and academic circles of the late 1980s and 1990s, a time when issues of "identity" and "multiculturalism" were alternately celebrated and condemned, a time that – whatever its fashionable limits – altered the political terms of artistic and intellectual legitimation.

I want to use aspects of Adrian Piper's work in conjunction with other examples to consider how performance – as both a theatrical object and as a mode of analysis – responds to issues of racial identity. By locating this excavation at the millennial shift between the twentieth and twenty-first centuries, this chapter is also an excavation of performance's relation to what has often been labeled "identity politics." Throughout, I will be engaging a larger theoretical concern about the epistemological and disciplinary connections between theatre studies and contemporary theories of performativity. Because the language of "performativity" has produced both a disciplinary crisis and a disciplinary opportunity for theatre and performance, it seems important to include a chapter that brings the frames of performativity in dialogue with theatrical performance. For many reasons and in different ways, asking these questions returns my study to a rhetorical genealogy in theatre and performance studies. I see the theatre/performativity conundrum as embedded in a larger set of genealogical tensions and obfuscations between the fields of drama and rhetoric. At the same time, I also want to argue that such tensions and obfuscations in theatricality/performativity debates parallel the tensions and obfuscations in debates about racial identification and racial injury, a parallel that makes each serve as a vehicle for illuminating the other. Adrian Piper's work offers a starting point for thinking through this connection. If, as I suggested in the opening to this book, the conceptual opposition between theatre and performativity is also one that exacerbates an occupational division between the artist and the academic, then Piper's status also resonates uncannily. The management of two careers as both a professional artist and a professional philosopher – while incidentally also being a committed yoga practitioner – has been a running source of tension in Piper's life.

Each field demands my full energy, attention, and commitment; each resents my involvement with the other; each suspects such involvement when I am absent; each feels personally betrayed when this suspicion is confirmed; and each is absolutely and unconditionally unwilling to concede any legitimacy to that involvement, much less make any accommodation to it.[7]

Thus, in addition to the conflicted performance of racial identity, Piper has felt compelled to develop various "maneuvers" for "partitioning" her professional identities, finding polite ways to respond to fellow artists' "pointed remarks about not needing a Ph.D. in philosophy to make good art," making sure to hide her commitments to yoga when an analytic philosophy professor berated "fuzzy-headed Eastern mysticism" during a course lecture, and learning not to "take the bait" when philosophical colleagues raise eyebrows at her art-making.[8] The institutional tensions that underwrite theatrical and philosophical explorations of identity – not only racial but also professional – thus serve as a subtext to my analysis.

As it happens, the philosophical question of identity and subjectivity has been at the heart of theoretical speculation on performance for quite some time. It has also contributed to theatre's racialization. Several decades before Piper's philosophy professor disparaged Asian and Buddhist characterizations of identity and action, Brander Matthews argued that "free will" could be both a racial and a theatrical guarantor. With his generalized characterization of "orientals," he tried to delineate the anti-fatalist structure of the dramatic event and to align it with a national (and implicitly American) temperament. Revisionist histories and theories have dismantled the fundamental assumptions of such a statement (even if their effects persist in the offhand repudiations of "Eastern mysticism"). Not only does Matthews' racist categorization appear ludicrous, many question the possibility much less actuality of something like "free will." In concert with such revisions, I want to trace how the theatre, far from assuming reductive conceptions of the self-sufficient subject, actually foregrounds its contingency. Anti-racist theatres in particular expose the difficulty of "knowing one's own mind." As it turns out, unsettling the equation between "drama" and "free will" goes a long way toward unsettling disciplinary and theoretical debates between theatre and performativity as well.

Performance, performativity, and racial identity

Recalling an American intellectual climate at the end of the twentieth century, it is no coincidence that issues of identity and issues of performativity simultaneously came to the fore. As described in Chapter One, the university context at this time responded to feminist and multicultural critiques of curricular and institutional exclusion. Heralded and repudiated as "identity politics," students and scholars grappled with the historic effects of sexism and racism and with the after-effects of a series of legal and political struggles that belatedly and circuitously changed the content and character of higher education. While the term "identity" served as a placeholder with which to argue for inclusion, in fact the nature and stability of something like coherent identity was also under question. Feminists of color did some of the most important work in troubling essentialist identity claims, even as they simultaneously theorized their political importance. As persons with multiple affiliations who endured different forms of prejudice, women of color were particularly attuned to the limits of homogeneous identity labels. Kimberlé Crenshaw's concept of "intersectionality," Gloria Anzaldua's theorizing of the "mestiza," Deborah King's discussion of "multiple jeopardy," and Norma Alarcon's complex surveys of scholarship by feminists of color are examples of such identity critiques. At the same time, a post-structuralist critique of the subject both advanced and aggravated these political explorations of identity. The social theory of Michel Foucault argued that relations of power were constitutive of identity, rather than simplistically "oppressive," and hence questioned the possibility of locating agency outside of power at all. Psychoanalytic revisions of Jacques Lacan theorized the subject as relational, as processual, and as fundamentally unknowable either to itself or to others. Such poststructuralist theorizing often appeared antagonistic to the identity claims of identity politics, and many wondered aloud why something like "free will" had become theoretically impossible just as disenfranchised people tried to exercise it. Others, however, made careful deployments of identity critiques within politicized writing. In fields such as subaltern, post-colonial, and critical race studies, such deployments were especially innovative. Gayatri Chakravorty Spivak's notion of "strategic essentialism" managed a both/and approach to identity politics, offering essentialism less as a referential term than as a necessary rhetorical gesture. Patricia Williams's *Alchemy of Race and Rights*, a key text in what would become the field of critical race studies, placed personal autobiography in conversation with legal theory's deconstructive dissections to expose the processes by which some identities secure the fiction of wholeness.

Indeed, the political utility of post-structuralist arguments was (and is) perhaps easier to see when applied to identities that were privileged by forces of race, gender, sex, and class. Rather than undermining essentialist claims in marginalized sites of struggle, it was more useful to undermine the assumed integrity of dominant sites of normalcy. Those who most needed to hear a critique of free will were those who thought that they had it.

Those who most needed to hear a critique of self-knowledge were those who thought that they knew their own minds. Several scholars in post-colonial studies took this tack, focusing not only on the experience of colonized peoples but also on the anxieties, self-divisions, and what Homi Bhabha called the "ambivalence" of colonizing subjectivity. Critical race theorists similarly sought to particularize whiteness, a move that countered the assumption that race was something that only non-white people had. Limited discussions of racial others presumed the centrality and normalcy of an unexamined white self, one whose particularity needed to be underscored, one whose sense of personal normalcy and naturalness needed to be de-normalized and de-naturalized. Post-structuralist arguments about power and the psyche provided paradigms for theorizing this secret complexity. Critical race theorists argued that it was precisely by not seeming to be about race that whiteness secured its racializing power. Naturalness was not a pre-given component of identity but an effect of historical and rhetorical operations; an absent normalcy was less a thing possessed than an obliviousness produced by one's location in a racializing structure. The dilemma of representing racism lay precisely in this simultaneous thereness and not-thereness, advanced every time a person of color's hyper-visibility translated into social invisibility, amplified every time the particularity of white identity braced against its resilient sense of its own generality. Thus, this exposure of the unacknowledged, normalizing operations of racism helped to undermine the fictional wholeness of dominant identities. As such, post-structuralist theorizing uncovered the mechanisms and effects of what civil rights activists had earlier called "institutionalized racism" and "internalized oppression," offering a critique of the subject and a critique of power that understood racism's insidious ordinariness.

How does this genealogy in theories of race bear on the vexed relationship between the act of theatre-making and the analytic framework of performativity? As it happens, the debate about identity and subjectivity in race studies had its parallel in performativity's critique as well, one that had a retroactive theoretical relationship on theories of the theatre. Before elaborating, I want to back up to recall this book's introductory remarks and to map performativity's theoretical derivations. As noted earlier, the term derives from speech-act theory, a subfield of ordinary language philosophy where J.L. Austin and his colleagues analyzed the world-making power of certain speech acts. To emphasize language's constitutive function was indeed to unsettle a classical opposition between rhetoric and philosophy, sidelining the question of language's truth or falsity by placing efficacy and force (what rhetoricians called "persuasion") in the analytical forefront. Austin's landmark book, *How to Do Things With Words*, delineated language's reflective or constative function from its performative function. His project, however, became more renowned for exceptions and qualifications, for the ways he got himself into his own rhetorical conundrums by examining failed speech acts. By distinguishing a locution's illocutionary goal (the intention of the speaker's doing) from its perlocutionary effects (its "taking up" in a receptive context), he opened the door to a wide field of linguistic complexity. Austin often portrayed a world of miscommunication, of infelicitous misfires, of "unhappy" performatives that bypassed their targeted interlocutors, that were vulnerable to "infelicitous" uptaking, or that seemed too precipitously dependent upon the conventions of particular discursive spheres. Problems of misfires and contextuality surfaced in speech that tried to pass itself off as constantive; meanwhile, performatives did many things but not always the doing that their speakers intended. Perlocutionary effects did not always match illocutionary intents. Several critics alighted upon the exceptions in Austin's own theory, on what Shoshana Felman called the "implicit performatives" of supposedly constantive speech.[9] The "original distinction between performative and constantive was weakened, indeed, dislocated," not only for Felman but also for Jacques Derrida who recast the issue as one of implicit citationality.[10] Derrida argued that no speech could pass itself off as autonomous given its saturation in a context of conventions, values, labels, and protocol that it is always already "citing."[11] A kind of self-division and internal difference emerged as the very condition of speech. Thus, alongside the metaphysical critique of presence outlined in Chapter Four, revisions of performativity functioned as both target of and vehicle for much of what became known as deconstruction. As such, deconstruction heralded itself as a revival of the rhetorical in new form, deciding to see the operations of the figurative and performative in unexpected places and to theorize the structuring traces implicit in all that called itself ordinary.

Such theorizing laid the groundwork for performativity's contribution to the larger issues of identity outlined above. In particular, this intellectual genealogy fundamentally altered the course of sex/gender theorizing. Consider, for instance, the writings of Judith Butler and Eve Kosofsky Sedgwick. In their work, the not altogether improbable assertion that we "perform our gender" is actually complicated by the performative operations of those performances. Butler questioned the heterosexism of the sex/gender concept, one that allows delineations of male and female to have a kind of constantive foundation in the realm of sex. In addition to such a critique, Butler also emphasized that the citationalities of sexual and gendered operations are actually obscured from the view of their performers. For Butler, the thorny difficulty of this citational performativity is that it "consists in a reiteration of norms which precede, constrain, and exceed the performer and in that sense cannot be taken as the fabrication of the performer's will or choice."[12] Eve Sedgwick took sex/gender and performativity in a slightly different direction in her elaboration of "queer performativity." Extending Austinian and Derridean analysis next to Butler's revisions, Sedgwick explored other knotty locutions – silence, secrecy, disavowal – and their relationship to attendant structures of shame, paranoia, and narcissism that persistently shadow and undergird queer experience – even, and most especially, the queer experience of heterosexuality.

Theories of performativity have important implications for understanding not only sex/gender identity but also racialized subjectivity, including the racist experience of non-raciality. Butler and Sedgwick's discussions of the recursive performativity of a sex/gender structure echo earlier ways of talking about institutionalized racism – that it maintains itself by being unregistered, that its performers (both dominant and marginalized) are less aware of the ways its production depends upon their own repetitions. Performativity names the iterative processes that do the "institutionalizing" in institutional racism and that do the "internalizing" in internalized oppression. Racism is thus the ultimate performative. In such a model, however, the question of resistance is harder to fathom. To the extent that performativity imagines institutional power as diffuse and internal self-knowledge as deferred, alteration in racist performativity poses an epistemological conundrum. "Resistance" requires a quite complicated and formally obtuse act of "disidentification" from/within normative citational processes. Such a formally impacted model of institutional racism thus sheds light on the dilemmas of individuals working within racist and even anti-racist institutions, including the institutions of the theatre and of the university.

In *Excitable Speech*, Judith Butler has developed her reflections on performative speech next to issues of race by focusing on the phenomenon of hate speech. I plan to take these thoughts in another direction by attending to environments of liberal and even anti-racist intention. In addition to tracking the unacknowledged processes of racial convention, performativity's speech-act theory brings a more specific mode of discursive analysis to the encounter between performer and receiver. Furthermore, I find it helpful to analogize this interactional space of performance next to the dynamics of inter and intra-racial sociality in contemporary American public spheres more generally. This means remembering how saturated with Austinian "misfires" is that most ubiquitous of encounters, the cross-racial dialogue – or to adapt Eve Sedgwick, how resiliently threatening is the possibility of being shamed by them. It also means examining the dynamics of intra-racial locutionary spaces, where speech activates a circuit of reciprocity that props up racial identity. In such spaces, one sees and hears persons doing many things with their words, managing culpability, shame, self-censorship, secrecy, and paranoia. Certainly, such structures activate many kinds of public interactions, including those of the university classrooms that try to grapple with the impact of identity politics. It seems to me that the position of the theatrical performer can illuminate such dynamics. Sensitized to the vagaries of performative speech, persons in such a position are always at risk of infelicity, constantly enduring the threat of not being "taken up" by an audience of targeted interlocutors. Theatrical performers try to instantiate a sociability that always threatens to withdraw itself. In the next sections, the work of Adrian Piper, Cherrié Moraga, Diana Son, Ntozake Shange, and Anna Deavere Smith provide different opportunities for analyzing the performative contingencies of theatrical speech.

Adrian Piper is an artist who specializes in the complicated dynamics of racial identification and its dialogic infelicities. In her famous piece, *Cornered*, this light-skinned, African-American woman addressed an unspecific audience from a video screen, asking viewers to reconcile her apparent lightness with her stated racial identity. Her questions increasingly targeted the apparent lightness of white viewers, asking them to consider the possibility that they too were black. What would they do with this information? Piper asked. Would they keep it a secret? Tell some people, but not others? Piper created an interactional space in which interlocutors had to decide how to "take-up" her proffered questions and, in the process, recognize that the capacity *to decide* varied with racial privilege. Another notable performance piece, the "calling card," consists of a business card that Piper passes out at key moments in everyday exchange.

Dear Friend:
I am black.
I am sure that you did not realize this when you made/laughed at/agreed with that racist remark. In the past, I have attempted to alert white people to my racial identity in advance. Unfortunately, this invariably causes them to react to me as pushy, manipulative, or socially inappropriate. Therefore, my policy is to assume that white people do not make these remarks, even when they believe there are no black people present, and to distribute the card when they do.

I regret any discomfort my presence is causing you, just as I am sure you regret the discomfort your racism is causing me.

In "calling card," Piper deploys a subtle performance mode – one that might be located in a series of avant-garde performance and invisible theatre experiments – to intervene inside racism's everyday performativities.

In a recent *Lingua Franca* article, "Black Like Me," Adam Shatz surveys Piper's significant body of work. He writes, "Piper's aesthetic program . . . is mainly concerned with patterns of cognition . . . Piper believed that shock tactics could force her interlocutors into rational reflection on their own racism."[13] While this might seem a reasonable assessment of the work, it is interesting to note Piper's response to the article. Her qualifications illustrate the dilemmas of anti-racist performance as one produced by performativity's operations. Piper responds: "I do not try to 'force' viewers of my work to do anything. I do not believe in 'racial shock treatment' or 'shock tactics,' and I do not have an 'aesthetic program.'" She concludes that she is simply "depicting the truth as I see it."[14] What exactly should be made of these repudiations? Piper's reaction could be construed as an artist's anti-intellectual resistance to being interpreted. Before immediately assuming this all-too familiar stance, it is worth lingering on her act of disidentification and considering how her amplification rests upon an awareness of unhappy addressive structures.

Many white viewers of my work are shocked by it because it confronts them with circumstances, images, and ideas with which they are unfamiliar and uncomfortable. However, the truths I try to depict are not news and not sources of discomfort to most members of the black audience. . . . [B]ecause many whites often feel themselves to be not in control of their reactions to my work, they often shut down cognitively and emotionally and panic. They automatically assume that I am controlling them; they then infer that I must have intended to "shock" them: and they conclude that I have "forced" them into having those strong reactions as part of my "aesthetic program."[15]

Within the well-intentioned, even progressive-minded orientation of a *Lingua Franca* article, Piper still finds herself caught within a network of what Austin would have called illocutionary and perlocutionary effects. A work of art that provokes identification and self-recognition in one audience member elicits "shock" and "discomfort" in another. But she is isolating more than a difference in interpretation. White audience members' consequent "panic," she notes, is simultaneously posited as an *intended* effect, a positing that locates and circumscribes Piper as a strategizing subject. Rather than remaining cognizant of how their panic is produced in the moment of their own receptive uptake, white interlocutors instead construe Piper as the sovereign and willful originator of their discomfort, disorientation, and shock. This kind of dynamic is exactly the one that Piper tries to counter with the strategy of the calling card. Having found that an anticipatory notification of her racial identity ("by the way, I am black") was labeled "pushy, manipulative, or inappropriate," Piper realized that the act of racial self-identification was immediately received as a racially directed accusation by her interlocutors.

The difficulties of coming to terms with Piper's anti-racist performance thus make explicit the locutionary politics of performative speech. Intriguingly, Piper's dilemma speaks to Judith Butler's elaborations of performativity in *Excitable Speech*. To locate and specify the mechanisms of homophobic speech acts, Butler develops a concept of paranoia. Her goal here is to understand how naming one's sexual identity ("I am a homosexual") can be interpreted by the non-homosexual as seduction; "a statement is construed as solicitation . . . a self-ascription taken as an address." What Butler argues of homophobic reaction applies to the racial encounter. While the declaration of sexual identity is received as seduction, the declaration of racial identity is received as accusation. Butler describes a complicated and paranoid process of psychic displacement. "The slights and injuries experienced within what is called paranoia are the psychic traces of existing social regulations, even as those traces have become estranged from the regulations from which they are derived."[16] In paranoia, the residue of a subject's estranged desire becomes conflated with an externalized social (presumably judgemental) encounter. "The coincidence of the judgment of Others and a turning back upon oneself," registers "psychically as the imagined slights and injuries performed by Others."[17] Piper's work elicits such coincidences, moments when an audience member "turns back upon herself" registering that turning as "a slight or injury performed by" Adrian Piper. As I will discuss throughout this chapter, a partial, attenuated, non-identificatory, or simplistically identificatory relation to a racial performance can cause an interlocutor to position herself as the performance's "target." Piper may not intend to shock in an absolute sense; however, her performances are deployments of this kind of rhetorical complexity and involve complicated networks of illocutionary and perlocutionary force. Thus, her urge not to be assigned absolute intention does not eliminate the fact that the projection and deflection of intention and culpability are pervasive in both racist and anti-racist encounters, including the encounters of her performance and installation work. In such forums, everyone seems to have a "program," at least to everyone else. Whether the culpable subject is the racist or the figure who claims racial injury, participants sort through with more and less complexity the formal dilemmas of being tagged an intentional subject and, by extension, a willful injurer. As persons accused and accused of doing the accusing, Piper and her audience members find themselves being injurious by claiming injury and feel themselves injured upon being labeled injurious.

My discussion thus far offers one way of mapping a theoretical relationship between performativity and theatrical performance – and to use that relationship to understand the complexities of liberal racist and anti-racist exchange. I argue for a connection between theatrical exchange and the (in)felicities of performative speech, further adapting the deconstructive critique to suggest that the uncertainty of a performer's intention is part of the complexity of cross-racial exchange. To align theatrical performance and performativity, however, is to flout Austinian disalignments as well as to modify some of the more recent elaborations of their relationship. J.L. Austin famously called the "utterance" of the stage actor "hollow or void," characterizing such locutions as "parasitic" upon and derivative of primary linguistic use.[18] Such a stance would make Adrian Piper's theatrical speech irrelevant to serious or substantial philosophical analysis, a prejudice that also supports the professional divides between artist and philosopher that Piper knows all-too well. Intriguingly, a number of contemporary critics have roundly criticized Austin's neo-Platonic description of theatrical language as "etiolated" ("lacking in vigor or natural exuberance"[19]). Indeed, Derrida's concept of "citationality" makes derivativeness a rule rather than an exception and suggests that there is nothing uniquely "etiolated" about the theatre. As William Worthen has argued, however, the theoretical counter to Austin's anti-theatricalism has not necessarily resolved other persistent anti-theatricalisms.[20] Dramatic theatre still does not appear as a favored object of analysis in critical theory.

Indeed, scholarly debates about and between terms such as drama, performance, and performativity contain much disavowal and a great deal of misrecognition. Theorists from different disciplinary homes use a variety of unstable oppositions (drama versus performance, performance versus performativity) to delineate their own interests, to target others, and to stake new claims. The disciplinary conversation around these terms is itself an instance of unhappy uptakes, of imputed slights, and of unintended effects in which theoretical paradigms (e.g. performativity and textuality) are erroneously conflated and aesthetic forms (e.g. drama and performance art) are opportunistically aligned and opposed. Whether performance is characterized as drama, dance, theatre, or performance art, however, there is a certain line of theoretical thinking that distinguishes all of these forms from the registers of performativity. In the aftermath of her provocative book of 1990, *Gender Trouble*, Judith Butler worried that readers mistakenly assumed that the performance of gender was voluntary, and that alteration in gender performance occurred through the intention or politicized will of the performer. In "Critically Queer" (reprinted in 1993 in *Bodies That Matter*), she felt compelled to specify *performativity* as a "reiteration of norms which precede, constrain, and exceed the performer" and characterized *performance* as a realm that assumed "will" or "choice." She concluded her clarification by asserting infelicitously that "the reduction of performativity to performance would be a mistake."[21] I call the assertion infelicitous because of how very unhappily it could be taken up by scholars of theatre, dance, and performance. While it was not Butler's "intention," these and similar kinds of assertions were displaced onto and taken up within performance's disciplinary spheres, unwittingly "citing" a longer history of institutional exclusion. The use of the word "reduce" in reference to performance sounded too familiar to its academic proponents, reinforcing rather than rectifying an equivocal academic history. For Jill Dolan, such a theoretical move appeared to rationalize disciplinary oversight. "As much as performativity captures the political field, theatrical performances, as located historical sites for interventionist work in social identity, are rarely considered across the disciplines, methods, and politics that borrow [theatre's] terms."[22] That "performativity" appeared to Dolan to be "borrowed" from theatre studies rather than from speech act theory demonstrated the term's unwitting enmeshment in several chains of citation. Even when the speech-act genealogy was acknowledged, however, performance scholars still speculated on its disciplinary effects. "Though 'performativity' is not an 'act' but a 'reiteration' or 'citation,'" wrote Elin Diamond, "why should we restrict its iterative sites to theory and to the theorists act of seeing? Theatre, too is theory."[23] In forum after forum, theatre and performance scholars meditated on the irony that performativity theory undermined rather than enhanced the theoretical potential of their favorite objects of study.

If the main point of Judith Butler's clarification was to assign intentional self-consciousness to performance, then she certainly had a point. Brander Matthews' alignment of drama and free will anticipated such an equation. Indeed, late twentieth-century identity-based performance reproduced Matthews' formulation even as it sought to counter the generalization of its racism. In feminist, anti-racist, and anti-homophobic theatre – in the collections of its plays, in the program notes that introduced productions, in the syllabi that disseminated the playwrights – the presence or absence of self-conscious intention became equated with the presence or absence of political relevance. As such, performance was repeatedly invoked as the vehicle by which fragmented identities were made whole, the silent given voice, the invisible made visible, and the injurer targeted by the injured. While often factoring an anti-essentialist stance on the nature of identity, theatres of identity still seemed to emphasize essentialist notions of power, the psyche, and the theatrical form. Theatre would delineate the powerless from the powerful and move marginalized subjects from a state of unknowingness to the more enlightened state of knowing one's own mind. When Dolan elaborated on how theatre scholars might "borrow back" the theory of performativity, she wrote that we "might put Butler's provocative performative metaphor to use in theatre spaces, in which the intentional performance of gender acts might be examined, disrupted, and reconfigured."[24] Elin Diamond too had theorized feminist theatre as a site where "the gender lexicon become[s] so many illusionist trappings to be put on or shed at will."[25] For Butler, however, it was precisely the "*intentional* performance of gender" – the "at will" – that was under question.

Several scholars attempted to craft a relationship between performance and performativity, including Judith Butler herself. For Butler, theatre emerges as a necessary type of hyperbolic gesture, a spectacle that might expose habituated citational scripts. Later, in *Excitable Speech*, she developed this assertion in a way that sounded less "reductive" to the proponents of performance. The "aesthetic reenactment *uses* the word, but also *displays* it, points to it, outlines it as the arbitrary material instance of language that is exploited to produce certain kinds of effects."[26] To theatre and performance scholars and practitioners, this characterizaton of the aesthetic enactment is familiar. The language of overt display, of pointing, of exposing the arbitrary, echoed Brecht's language of defamiliarization. This is how theatre theorists such as Elin Diamond and William Worthen have reconciled theatre and performativity, lodging Brechtian defamiliarization inside Butlerian resignification. José Muñoz's elaboration of "disidentification" utilizes a similar strategy in its analysis of queer performers of color who cite conventions of race, gender, and sex with a parodic difference.[27] Such ironic performances repeat normalized stereotypes not to reify them but in order to expose them and, after Butler, "calling attention to it as a citation, situating that use within a citational legacy."[28] This is an intensely productive move and one that I would not argue against. However, I am not sure whether it always resolves the issue of intentionality. The defamiliarization paradigm still might assume the self-consciousness of a subject who does the displaying, the pointing, and the outlining – that is, the subject who has a "program." I think that it is particularly important to refine this model of ironic defamiliarization when it comes to anti-racist theatre in the United States. If there is ever a time when the tolerance for ambiguous address is low and the quest for literal representation high, it is in instances of explicitly racialized performance. In anti-racist performance, audience members often forget whatever they once knew about theatrical irony.

Most theories of the theatre develop aspects of its ocularcentric etymological root: "a place for viewing." As a hyperbolic place of display, theatre requires the seeability of its object. Such a space has also been historically conceived as a space of performer agency; as Matthews asserted, "free will is always favorable to the drama." Finally, the idea of "drama" is formally bound up in a dyadic interaction; the thrill of an exchange between protagonists and antagonists creates the drama in the dramatic. Performativity, on the other hand, emphasizes radically different elements, especially in its deconstructive mode. It identifies conventions that are unregistered and unintended rather than fully visible and willed; it also questions the possibility of locating a discrete antagonist outside of the subject who is injured. Performativity thus seems to question the foundations of the theatrical. Now, if I add to this impossible mix my contention that racism is the ultimate performative, I think that it becomes easier to understand why the effort to theatricalize racism has been so difficult. It also makes its theorizing somewhat tricky. Peggy Phelan's 1993 book, *Unmarked: The Ontology of Performance*, is significant in this regard, particularly for the way that it theorizes performance as an ephemeral site of invisibility and disappearance rather than unproblematic visibility and presence. Eve Sedgwick's own theorizing on "Queer Performativity" initially opposed these deconstructive and theatrical legacies outlined above, particularly their respective introversion and extroversion, but offered the operation of shame – its doing and undoing of the subject, its rituals of exposure, its averted head and downcast eyes – as a kind of pivot on which both trajectories could meet.[29] Meanwhile, Anne Cheng's *The Melancholy of Race* took seriously the fundamental impossibility of complete self-knowledge; toward the end of the book, she offered the concept of "immersion" as a risky but necessary practice in politicized encounters where the "successful" identification of racial subjectivity can never be fully assumed.[30]

In the next sections, I take seriously the formal difficulty of reconciling racism's tacit performativity with theatricality's explicit visibility. In other words, I use a discussion of theatricality and performativity to understand the formal dilemmas of antiracist performance. My attempts to connect race, performance, and performativity will suggest that the vexed relationship of one pairing can help us to understand the difficulties of the other. Thus, I will argue not only that critical race and feminist discourses can be adapted to drama and performance but also find an alternative sense of their own possibilities in them. In such experiments, theatre's high extroversion meets the habituated introversion of race privilege. Such theatres attempt to perform racism within and despite the secreted, normalizing, and unregistered operations of racism's performativity. They attempt to narrate injury and, in doing so, stage the difficulty of locating the injurer. In the case of white privilege, they attempt to use the extraordinariness of public space to make character from an experience of characterlessness, to make theatre of an experience whose distinctive attribute is the feeling that nothing dramatic is happening. Theatrical performances of racism thus offer a particularly illuminating laboratory for exploring the possibilities of integrating theatrical and deconstructive genealogies of performance. They are also a good place to think about what it means to create a pedagogical public sphere that investigates race privilege and racial injury. Such an arena might reveal that the difficulties of creating such a sphere are often formal problems and limited by the operational, gestural, spectatorial, and verbal conventions of publicity, especially when they meet the unnoticed, fleeting, and mired dynamics of normalcy.

Anti-racist theatre and rhetorical infelicity

A look at other theatrical public spheres dramatizes more connections amongst performative speech, theatre, and racialization. As a co-editor of *This Bridge Called My Back*, Cherríe Moraga is a particularly significant figure as both a critic and an artist. *This Bridge*, published by Kitchen Table Press, countered essentialist identity claims within racial, cultural, and feminist movements by exposing what Kimberlé Crenshaw would call the "intersectionality" of multiple claims of affiliation. At the same time, this anti-essentialist work sat uneasily, and productively, next to the radical language of revolution, love, hope, and healing. Moraga sought, with other women of color, persons "who you can sit down to a meal with, who you can cry with."[31] There is nothing "essentialist" about being able to engage the felicitous conventions of the kitchen table; however, they could feel essentialist when an unfamiliar person sat down. In the response to texts such as *This Bridge*, essentialism became a placeholder for imputed sovereignty, the projection of an intentionally bounded, autonomous, and exclusive identity. Whether *Bridge's* reader felt addressed or ignored, included or accused, often dictated whether such a text was labeled essentialist or anti-essentialist – and whether that label received a positive or negative valuation. For Moraga, an appeal to the experiential could expand rather than reduce the array of possible identifications. She recalled that addressing race became necessary *in order* to address her sexuality. "I wanted/needed to deal with racism because I couldn't stand being separated from other women. Because I took my lesbianism that seriously."[32] Furthermore, she became better able to understand the mechanisms of racism after facing the injuries of homophobia. "The joys of looking like a white girl ain't so great since I realized I could be beaten on the street for being a dyke."[33] Moraga's statement figures intersectional identity not simply as an addictive mixture of racial and sexual elements but as a network of identifications that mutually and sometimes backhandedly construct and disavow the other. Consequently,

Moraga's playwriting has self-consciously addressed themes of race, culture, gender, and sexuality. As such, her plays have also endured the homophobic reaction of imputed solicitation as well as the racist reaction of imputed accusation. In *Giving Up the Ghost*, she specifically addressed intra-cultural and cross-cultural lesbian love. In *Shadow of a Man*, a story of lesbian sexual recognition was perhaps less volatile than her dramatization of Chicano male homosociality as simultaneously erotic and misogynist. Writing plays that address a variety of cultural, sexual, and political contexts, Moraga's audiences can find different ways of being accused, injured, or left out. In such theatres, being ignored and being targeted are surprisingly compatible forms of uptake.

The fraught dynamics of performative speech are blatantly illuminated by another element of identity-based theatre in a US context: that is, the use of languages other than standard English. Debates over the construction of Latino/a, Mexican-American, and Chicano/a identity most explicitly engage the issue of speech. In heated discussions over English proficiency and bi-lingual education, in theorizing and counter-theorizing on the indexical authenticity of Spanish, Spanglish, and English-Spanish code-switching, speech emerges as a powerful and strangely threatening mode of instantiating identity. As such, these discussions also make explicit the constitutive relation of linguistic forms. In analyzing Moraga's *Shadow of a Man* at Brava's center for performing arts in San Francisco, for example, Yvonne Yarbro-Bejarano noted the dynamics of its reception.

The bilingual voice of the play was a source of discomfort for non-Latino spectators. Some white male critics . . . spoke of the bilingual dialogue as a 'drawback' or of the play's 'frequent excursions into Spanish.' This perspective is shared by the interviewer . . . who referred to the 'novelty' of the script's mixing of Spanish and English. This novelty has a twenty-five year history in Chicano theater.[34]

Non-Spanish speaking reviewers thus illustrated a range of different responses or modes of "taking up" this play. Casting Spanish as an "excursion" reified the presumption of English as a standard convention, a naturalized assumption maintained when a second critic cast it negatively as an aesthetic "drawback" and

when a third cast it positively as a theatrical "novelty." Yarbro-
Bejarano appeals to the simultaneous normalcy of another set of
conventions, however, when she refers to the "twenty-five year
history" of Chicano theatre that the script implicitly cites. In
the public sphere created by Moraga's *Shadow*, there exists more
than one set of linguistic and aesthetic conventions. The critics'
reception – an Austinian "uptake" – occurs within that contingent sphere, even if the unqualified use of terms such as drawback, excursion, and novelty disavow it. Of course, the capacity
to effect such performative disavowals is itself a racial privilege;
racial privilege means being able to hold the world accountable
to one's projections.

There is another aspect to this addressive moment that is also
worth exploring, for the disavowal can be construed more precisely as a response to *not being addressed*. An audience's response
is thus an attempt to secure, through speech, a way out of critical disorientation. The non-Spanish speaking audience does not
have the skills to inhabit the interlocutionary positions that the
play provides. To call Moraga's technique a "drawback" or, more
well-intentioned, a "novelty" is an attempt to assume a position
that the interlocutor cannot find for herself in the play. However,
if the assumption that one is always addressed is a consequence
of privilege, it is also an everyday principle that often goes unrecognized by those who hold it. Thus, if a privileged person enters
a space whose language is unfamiliar and *still* assumes that s/he is,
as usual, being addressed, then such a person might not always
capitulate to disorientation. Instead, she may decide that there
is addressive intent in the non-address, that s/he is being intentionally left out, that being left out *is* her position. This scenario
exemplifies the deeper narcissism of interpreting a lack of address as a personal assault, in this case a "slight" to the centrality
of the non-Spanish speaker. S/he thereby generates the psychic
fantasy of being "injured" by an Other, "shocked," "forced" –
the "target" of an Other's "program."

If the predicaments of Piper and Moraga illustrate two different versions of addressive and receptive entanglements, Diana
Son's *R.A.W. ('Cause I'm a Woman)* shows yet a third theatrical encounter with performative speech as well as an attempt to
diminish the risk of infelicity. Son's play consists of four female

Asian-American actors as well as a slide projector that creates a fifth type of speaking position. Throughout the production, the slide projects different kinds of racial locutions, ranging from a list of stereotypic adjectives ("Exotic," "Submissive," "Chic," "Obedient") to condescending dialogue that instantiates racial and gender identity ("I love your eyes" . . . "I love Oriental women"). Around the display of each screen, actors work to disengage from this performative positioning. Responding to the comment about her/their eyes, each actor takes on a different part of a first-person response, ending in a literalization that short-circuits her/their exoticization.

2: My eyes.
3: That they have given earnest love to men.
4: And complex love to women.
3: That through them he feels the grace that God has lent me.
1: That they're slanted.

After the slide "asks" the questions, "Where are you from?" and later "I mean what *country* are you from?" the four female actors speculate on the spectral speaker's illocutionary fascinations. "Because he wants to hear: /I'm from a fishing village off the Yangtze river/ Where my mother was a shaman who taught me shiatsu/ Where my father made musical instruments out of fish bones and moss. . . ."[35] Both of these moments re-perform and, in so doing, de-familiarize a chain of racist citations. Son's text uses the word "slanted" in order to "outline" and "display" its erotic and prejudiced effects as well as to foreground the complexity and "grace" that it occludes. *R.A.W.*'s rendering of the longer interior monologue also exposes a particular brand of racial differentiation experienced by children of immigrant-Americans from China, India, Japan, Korea, and other Asian countries. Even third-generation Americans find themselves positioned as inhabitants of an elsewhere; racial identification as Asian thus seems to stall national identification as American, a process de-naturalized in the play.

The paradigm of defamiliarization tracks only part of what is going on in Son's dramaturgy, however. Son's discussion of her decision to use the slides shows her negotiation of audience "uptake." The slides not only de-familiarize but also attempt to mollify the theatrical event's paranoid structure.

I didn't want lines like 'I've never been with an Oriental woman before' to be delivered with exaggeration or mockery. Slides are non-judgmental. I am not trying to condemn men who say lines like this. The words express themselves; no commentary is necessary. But I want people to know that Asian American women have to hear these comments all the time.[36]

However one interprets the assertions that slides are non-judgmental or that words express themselves, Son at the very least can be seen facing the issue of performative address – that the reflective attempt to let "people know" can be interpreted as the active attempt to "condemn." Indeed, rather than assuming the disingenuousness or political weakness of Son's claim that she is "not trying to condemn," her play might be appropriately read as a navigation of the performative complexity of racial injury. *R.A.W.* theatricalizes racism by unsettling rather than specifying its source. By matching the complexity of racial performativity to an alternative theatrical rhetoric, her stage directions say, "the audience can give the man whatever voice they hear internally."[37] In some ways, the slides diminish rather than heighten the effect of parody – or more accurately, the risk of an interlocutor feeling parodied – and so the perception of accusation. Of course, it could be argued that audiences are always receiving theatrical speech through "whatever voice they hear internally," placed as they are in a theatrical structure where the "judgment of others" coincides with their own "turned back desires." Son's rhetorical technique, however, offers a space to modulate that coincidence. By receiving the words of explicit and liberal racism onstage, an audience member can take up a position as its target, listener, or speaker. Some may find themselves addressed and addressing. Hearing the speech of another couched as her own, the comfort of listening might simultaneously return as the echo of an all-too familiar speaking. It is through such techniques, however, that *R.A.W.* alights upon the secret, psychically deferred character of racial performativity via racialized theatricality.

These questions about the convolutions and formal dilemmas of racialized addressive structures provide an interesting way to rethink past instances of identity-based theatre in the United States. Indeed, that longer history is filled with instances of racial accusation that occasionally miss their target; meanwhile, other attempts to portray racial experience are perceived to do more "targeting" than they intend. Such deflections and projections in identity-based theatre require artists and critics to address the diffuse, obtuse, but no less impactful operations of power and the psyche. Anne Cheng argues that the mid-century civil rights struggle asked US citizens to take such dimensions seriously. By arguing that racism exerted psychic damage that warranted retribution, Brown v. Board in particular "may be said to be an unprecedented judgment about the necessity of examining the invisible but tenacious aspects of racism – of allowing racial grief to have its say even if it cannot definitively speak in the language of material grievance."[38] In many ways, late-twentieth-century playwrights have been galvanized by the discursive milieu marked and advanced by the Board ruling. As such, they have also endured what Cheng identifies as its potentially conservative effect, the "beginnings of the slip from *recognizing* to *naturalizing* injury."[39] Turning from grief to grievance, that is, narrating and formalizing the injuries of race, can have the effect of fixing that which it seeks to undo. In many ways, Ntozake Shange's plays exemplify this kind of movement in anti-racist performatives. Shange is a playwright who has made a habit and a political project out of exorcising the damage to which Board referred. In both academic and theatrical contexts, Shange's work also figured centrally in critiques of the theatrical canon, occupying a pivotal space in syllabi, anthologies, and production seasons that sought to expand the representation of female artists and artists of color. *For colored girls who have considered suicide when the rainbow is enuf* voiced the intangibles of internalized oppression ("I can't stand being sorry and colored") and of racial injury. To the extent that her play also portrayed the deleterious intersectional experience of race and gender in the lives of both black men and women, however, *for colored girls* also received cross-racial and intra-racial approbation. Whether white audience members felt accused or excluded or black men felt accused and berated, Shange's play also seemed to risk naturalizing the injuries that it sought to recognize.[40]

The subtle difference between recognition and naturalization, however, might well be a matter of uptake. Shange followed *for colored girls* with *Spell #7*. I want to linger on this text in order to foreground its rhetorical choices and to consider how they reflect on the dilemma and opportunity of performing racism.

Written in the mid-1970s, *Spell* takes place within the imaginative space of Eli's bar, a space where female and male African-American actors gather routinely after rehearsals, auditions, and day jobs to reminisce and to imagine possible lives. Actors named Alec, Dahlia, Lily, Maxine, and Natalie initiate fantasy scenes in the middle of the bar, propelled by fellow actors who alternately perform roles as characters, co-narrators, and audience members. Meanwhile, another character named Lou serves as the show's primary narrator in the role of Mr. Interlocutor, taking on the role of magician, trickster and story-teller as he guides the action as well as the audience's relationship to that action. As a traditional African-American figure of trickery and dialogic interaction, Mr. Interlocutor is a reminder that performativity and counter-performativity have racialized histories and that locutionary conventions such as testifying, witnessing, the dozens, and signifyin' cite a long-running counter-tradition of disidentificatory speech. When audience members take their seats at a production of *Spell #7*, they are confronted by a "huge black-face mask hanging from the ceiling of the theatre." Shange's stage directions are explicit – "the audience must integrate this grotesque, larger-than-life misrepresentation of life into their pre-show chatter" – thus simultaneously expanding the circumference of performance to incorporate and aggravate the conventional behaviors of theatrical spectators. Many have discussed this play's use, or re-use, of the minstrel mask and other racist imagery. Within the context of speech-act theory, the decision to incorporate rather than to eradicate the racist grotesque exemplifies Judith Butler's call for a resignification of hate speech; once again, this theatre *uses* the word, *displays* it, points to it, and "outlines it as the arbitrary material instance of language that is exploited to produce certain kinds of effects."[41]

Spell #7 coordinates several levels of story-telling at once, an integration of different narratorial modes. I call these techniques rhetorical for specific as well as general reasons. Not only do they have performative effects, but they secure those effects by manipulating registers of narration and realigning the conventions of self and other along the way. The critique of such formal manipulations in narrative and performance has a specific disciplinary history, having received sustained critical attention in the rhetorical genealogy of performance studies. Indeed, the ways and means of performed narration – diffused, split, deferred, and re-routed – has been the historic domain of that gently mocked field known as "oral interpretation." Oral interpretation's formal rather than thematic approach to literature finds an especially productive intersection in identity-based performance. *Spell #7* interlaces and overlays several narratorial frames at once. Stories such as the tale of Sue-Jean, a woman who gives birth to and later kills her longed-for child whom she calls "myself," are embedded within the actors' conversations about employment, the racist stereotypes of casting, and other stories about their lives. The story-telling at the bar is itself framed by Lou's direct addresses to the audience and actors. Shange's stage directions have a meta-theatrical awareness of performative speech. The inhabitants understand that this space is reciprocal, where interlocutors know how to uptake so as to allow the relatively safe exploration of unsafe things. Meanwhile, the levels of story-telling are fluid and occasionally subvert the authority of a primary narrator. New narratives begin with an actor's enunciation and occasionally another actor may join in. The narratorial authority constantly shifts between initial locutions and uptakes, careful to maintain a felicitous context. Sometimes the primary character of a story may narrate herself in the first person. Sometimes another figure serves as primary narrator. Often self-narration occurs in third-person and past tense. In the latter use, the implied first-person of the actor's body rests in counterpoint with the third-person pronoun; similarly, the action's past-tense articulation unsettles the present-tense incarnation. Thus, rather than deploying a monologic form to reify theatrically a sovereign, self-originating speaking subject, there is a deferred and deflected quality to these enunciations. Speech is exposed as an "act," as alterable and contingent, by presenting language alongside a contrasting and variable bodily enactment. Channeling the discontinuous possibilities of the theatrical medium, of pronoun and gesture, of speech and image, of intonation and focus, *Spell*'s speaking subjects perform their difference from themselves by presenting conventions of speech and body in unconventional combinations.

I also want to consider the position of spectators toward such stories and their many-pronouned locations and locutions. Lou and other characters often employ the word "you" throughout the play, asking audience members "why don't you go on & integrate a german-american school in st. louis missouri" or, continuing to invoke Brown v. Board, "why don't ya go on & be a red niggah in a blk school in 1954."[42] At such moments, spectators must decide 1) whether they will try to engage in a form of racial identification or 2) whether they are outside the theatre's addressive structure. Both positions are different types of ill-fits for white spectators. The first is a "see what it feels like" positioning that will be partial and lacking as white spectators imagine "integrating a school in arkansas" and know that they never had to. Since, as Eve Sedgwick suggests, such interruptions of identification are shame's way of making identity, it is often in this structure that white audience members will complain about being made to feel guilty. In the second, white spectators endure the feeling of not being addressed, witnessing from a distance a circuit of reciprocity amongst the actors and other non-white audience members. Such moments expose how habituated to being addressed white spectators often are, usually and by definition, without knowing it. Without such tacit locutionary comforts, the white would-be interlocutor is at sea. Missing the normalizing foundation of racial reciprocity, it is often within this structure that white audience members will complain about being left out.

While non-white audience members may find different ways of felicitously taking up Lou's address – whether recalling a specific African-American history or adapting its stories to another Latino or Asian racial history – it would be reductive to call such uptaking "happy." As Lou's address continues, he moves through a tale of his magician father who "put all them rassamatazz hocus pocus" away the day that "a friend of mine/from 3rd grade/asked to be made white on the spot." Speculating that "colored chirren believin in magic/waz becomin politically dangerous for the race," Lou sets different terms for *Spell #7* and closes his opening with the phrases that will be this play's most memorable refrain.

> all things are possible
> but aint no colored magician in his right mind
> gonna make you white
> i mean
> this is blk magic
> you lookin at

> & i'm fixin you up good/fixin you up good & colored
> & you gonna be colored all yr life
> & you gonna love it/ bein colored/ all yr life/
> colored & love it
> love it/bein colored.[43]

As Lou finishes these lines, the stage directions call the rest of the cast onto the stage wearing "tattered fieldhand garb, blackface, and the countenance of stepan fetchit when he waz frightened. their presence belies the magician's promise." This series of images, gestures, and words sustains a functional ambivalence. Like Shange's earlier *for colored girls*, the play represents the dilemmas of systemic inequality and internalized racism. In the earlier play, the sensibility evoked by the condition of "bein sorry and colored " eventually gave way to a final "layin on of hands" in which the damage was provisionally healed through a shared ritual. The black magic of *Spell #7* also represents the legacy of this psychological and structural redundancy and the urge toward recovery and pride. Moments such as Mr. Interlocutor's introduction, however, position African-American audience members somewhat differently by representing the legacy and the urge at once. Channelling the simultaneity of the theatrical medium, shame and pride compete in the juxtaposition of the minstrel smile with Mr. Interlocutor's welcome; the comforting tones of storytelling brace against references to the self-hating desire to "be white." The repeated phrase – "yr goin to be colored an love it" – is both inspirational and prescriptive, evoking a "lovin it" that could also be a command to be colored and take it. The play gestures to the possibility of cross-racial identification and then, cognizant of its pain and its dangers, adjusts its own magic to the limits of a more constraining social imagination. Even as Mr. Interlocutor offers particular intra-racial identifications, the play manifestly performs their aggression. Finally, his repeated "why doncha" is an invitation that some do not have the option of taking – even as it is also an offer of racial identification that others do not have the option of refusing.

Issues of racial identification and reception become more explicit toward the end of the play. Lily, a bi-racial actress, has just finished a frustrated story involving a casting director who tells her that she is "too light to play blck" but that casting her as a white girl "wdn't be ethical." After Lily elaborates on the social limits of the theatrical imaginary, Natalie, another actress, responds to her story by initiating a new scene "as a red-blooded white woman/ i cant allow you all to go on like that" declaring that, "today, i'm gonna be a white girl."[44] Natalie decides to play a white girl for a day, creating a send-up of stereotypic white femininity. She meditates on hair (and on how white girls "fling" it) on beauty treatments (where "I sit under the sunlamp to get more color back" after all "beauty can be bought"), on 'lil black and caribbean boys (who "notice how beautiful i am . . . they love to look at me") on valium (since "i am a protestant suburbanite with 2 valiums slugged awready"), on ignorance ("like if i do anything/anything at all i'm extending myself as white girl"), and on dependence upon housekeepers ("im still waiting for my cleaning lady") – all expose the particularity and contingency of white female identity. Natalie thus performs the magical desire to be white that had earlier been deemed "dangerous for the race"; however, she does so on different ground, attempting to recognize its damage while maintaining her distance. Reaching for the metaphoric pivot "as," she declares herself to be (like) a white woman with red blood, thus slyly parodying the color fetishism of racialization along the way. The simile-making preposition is one that typically sets up unabashed equivalences in the forums of identity politics, where self-nomination ("Speaking as a . . .") precedes any statement or conversation. However, the statement in a theatrical frame shows up the tenuous condition of the simile; Natalie will fragilely alight on an "as" instead of an "am" throughout her speech. In the next line, for instance, the tenuousness emerges through an alteration in tense, "cuz today im gonna be white girl" juxtaposing a present-tense simile with a future conditional ontology. This discontinuous enunciation creates a built-in self-deferral, for the actress commits to the indicative fullness of immediate, vocal embodiment next to the deferred grammatical articulation of a prospective identity. The white girl comes into representation via a self-conscious metaphor that is perpetually "gonna be."

Despite this internal discontinuity and despite the fact that Shange's stage directions link its performance directly to "Natalie's pain," the monologue has provoked notoriously virulent responses from white critics and audience members. While some simply noted their disapproval by saying that the monologue "doesn't work," is "fuzzy" or is "too long," others called it "savage."[45] Most who have taught this play in a mixed-race context know how often white students feel themselves "accused." I think that there is something interesting in the unhappy (and sometimes even the happy) reception of this hyperbolic gesture. More than being simply an instance of misinterpretation, it highlights the formal complexity and formal difficulties of eliciting consciousness about racial privilege, a project that is often at risk of infelicity. As Peggy Phelan writes, "using visibility to rectify invisibility often misfires."[46] Phelan's statement holds true not only for the social invisibility of racial marginality but also for the secreted invisibility of racial privilege. Consider how Shange packs the lines of this monologue, exposing the recalcitrant dilemma of theatricalizing white performativity. "i'll retroactively wake myself up," Natalie says next, casting the difficulty of particularizing the normal in temporal terms, as a realization that is always and by definition "retroactive," "ah low & behold/a white girl in my bed." Shange manipulates pronouns here, introducing what will be a recurring ambiguity between the monologue's first and third referents. Is the "i" the same as the girl she wakes up? The white girl – who may or may not declare that the bed is "mine" – is paradoxically within view of the speaker, one who simultaneously claims to be the one sleeping. The conflation of third and first person positionings continues at yet another register in the next line: "but first i'll haveta call a white girl i know to have some accurate information." This line has the potential to make explicit use of the built-in addressive structure of the theatrical event. Self-identified white girls in the audience might decide at such a moment whether or not they are its "target," especially as Natalie continues. "what's the first thing white girls think in the morning/ do they get up bein glad they aint niggahs?" The pointed question risks infelicitousness for what might seem a number of reasons, but I am most interested in the ways that the line parallels the difficulty of "retroactive self-waking." Can such a subject outline the contours of white privilege when they contour her? Can she watch herself sleeping? At the same time, the self-righteous denial to the thought that one would wake up bein glad – "no!" – cannot successfully disengage from the question. For it is the privilege of not being either glad or sad, not waking to an awareness – hyperbolic, willed, intentional, theatrical, and seeable – of what one is not that is precisely the point. However, it is also for this reason that Shange's project often seems to misfire, get called fuzzy, too long, and savage. The self-consciousness that would make these phrases about "being" glad seem felicitous, one that achieves the work it seeks to do, is not a condition of the targeted interlocutor. The overt intentionality of "bein glad" is at odds with the unhyperbolic state of conditioned obliviousness.

Of course, even the focus on this moment in the play risks reproducing a particular way of taking it up. For critic Sandra Richards, Shange's play walks a constant tightrope, "depict[ing] truths painful to Blacks" while running the risk of "confirming existing negative stereotypes."[47] Sue-Jean's story of unwanted pregnancy and Maxine's mourning acknowledgment of intra-racial conflict precede and follow Natalie's monologue. If Shange's challenge is to *recognize* racial injury without *naturalizing* it, Richards argues that Natalie's monologue is strategically positioned, functioning to quell the disturbances that are and will be engendered by Sue-Jean and Maxine, respectively. To Deborah Geis, one of the critics who originally called the monologue savage and extreme, Natalie's monologue seems to be the moment that *most* provokes disturbance, a marked difference in uptake. While Richards reads this monologue inside a larger effort to represent internalized racism, Geis finds this displaced dramatization of psychic damage itself to be injurious. Even attempts to disengage from the accusatory structure can sometimes miss their mark. Geis specifically comments on the interlocutionary position of the "white girls in the audience" who "may feel too angry at Natalie's speech to find it funny. Or they may laugh to distance themselves from the reality of her words."[48] Both laughter squelched and laughter forthcoming emerge as different types of audience self-distancing. The first manifests itself in stony silence, creating the theatrical version of a misfire. Such moments are often the ones that theatre practitioners will say are "not working" or that theatrical reviewers will call "fuzzy." The second kind of position – laughter forthcoming – allows the audience a means of uptaking – and thus the chance for a felicitous exchange, a theatrical moment that "works." However, the uptaking simultaneously involves a deflection of self, a "white unlike me" strategy of white spectatorship. Such moments of reception inspire a fine-tuning of Brechtian defamiliarization as well as of Judith Butler and José Muñoz's concepts of disidentification.

These paradigms need specific analyses of the different kinds of strategies that may call themselves "dis-identification" from a racialized "normative." If much white liberalism is fueled by the desire not to look bad, then there is a kind of will to disidentification already built in to its discourse about itself. The question remains, however, whether such linguistic and comic modes of self-distanciation – a Butlerian or Brechtian means – function to Butlerian or Brechtian effect. If white privilege operates as a thing that is often unregistered and is, at this historical moment, also the thing that no one wants to be caught having, then some types of self-distancing might reproduce rather than resist the motivations that underpin white racialization in the first place. Given that white liberal disidentification is already too happy a performative, perhaps a more proximate positioning of the racialized self is called for.

Theatricality's racial performativity

To "perform" racism thus appears in these moments to be theoretically redundant, theatrically impossible, and hence productively volatile. The representation of grief risks essentializing the figure who endures it. Meanwhile, the narration of pain is received as accusation by the one who does not feel it. In the first case, the intangibility of psychic damage wrestles against the conventions of representation, showing up in non-continuous uses of pronominal, narrative, and bodily identity markers. In the second case, the limits of avowal in white audience members lie in the manifest difference between the reception of hyperbole and the operation of obliviousness, the intentionality of theatricality and the intentionlessness of white privilege. The redundancy of performing racism in the deconstructive sense thus produces the apparent impossibility of performing racism in the theatrical sense.

> Because the panic was so high
> that, oh my God,
> I was almost thinking:
> "Did I deserve this,
> do I, do I deserve it?"
> I thought me, personally – no,
> me, generically,
> maybe so.[49]

These phrases belong to an "Anonymous Man #2 (Hollywood Agent)," one of dozens of characters in Anna Deavere Smith's *Twilight: Los Angeles 1992* who is called upon to narrate the experience of the 1992 L.A. uprisings. Most characters in the play such as Mrs. Young-Soon Han, Elvira Evers, and Josie Morales are named and often stand in for some kind of group identity – Asian American, African-American, Latino. The Anonymous Agent is one of a handful whose names are kept secret; other anonymous characters in the play are, as the script says, "a former gang member" and "a Simi Valley juror," inviting the question of whether there could be similarity between the stakes of their respective positions as speaking subjects. The Anonymous Agent's speech (both as theatrical monologue and as linguistic arrangement) constantly displays and works to recover from panic, embarrassment, and humiliation. It also approaches the issue of a kind of culpability – "do I deserve it? – an approach that is simultaneously deflected by phrasing it as a question, by saying that he was "almost" thinking it, by delineating "personal" versus "generic" categories, and by concluding the thought with an ambivalent "maybe."

I want now to resituate the problematics of this chapter through the vehicle of Anna Deavere Smith's *Twilight*. From one perspective, Smith's language-based method of research and performance is tailor-made for Austinian musings and deconstructive revisionings. Indeed, her theatrical process provides a comeback to Austin's notorious dismissal of the theatre. Acutely preoccupied with how to do things with words in speech, Smith begins by casting herself as a kind of Ms. Interlocutor, seeking out sites of struggle and the enunciations that emerge in the midst of such personal and social trauma. After the uprising in Los Angeles, Smith interviewed people at liminal moments when they had just begun to place words around the crisis, saying that she finds herself most artistically moved and enabled as a performer during the point in an interview when "language breaks down." The stops and starts, the slips, the run-on sentences – such linguistic punctures provide a workable point of entry.

I'm mostly interested in when people fail to say something, like when they maybe say the wrong word or get caught in stutters, because I think character really exists in the struggle to say something . . . I'm more interested in their *pursuit* of the perfect sound bite. When language doesn't work, when it fails, when it falls apart, it usually ends up being a moment or a time, once I try to re-enact it, that brings me closer to what I would think of as the feeling of that person.[50]

Rehearsing with a constant, almost Skinneresque repetition of their words, pacings, and intonations – rewinding her ever-present headphones – Smith's replaying of this struggle to speak is the key, she says, to "character." The process thus joins a certain kind of deconstructive fixation on linguistic failure with a theatrical understanding of linguistic productivity. The undo-ingness of deconstructive performativity here activates the doing of theatrical performance.

There have been many different kinds of responses to the pub-lic spheres Smith created in performances of *Twilight*. Among them is a recurring preoccupation with the presence or absence of sympathetic white characters, a fixation that suggests some-thing about racial felicities in the Broadway-bound performance. In a more laudatory piece on Anna Deavere Smith, John Lahr chose to devote some time to this concern, publishing a quota-tion from one of Anna Deavere Smith's notes to her dramaturgs. "It's crucial that white people in the audience find points of iden-tification . . . points of empathy *with themselves*."[51]

To create a situation where they merely empathize with those less fortu-nate than themselves is another kind of theatre. . . . My political prob-lem is this: Privilege is often masked, hidden, guarded. This guarded, fortressed privilege is exactly what has led us to the catastrophe of non-dialogue in which we find ourselves . . . I'm talking about the basic privilege of white skin which is the foundation of our race vocabulary.[52]

Smith's active attempt to perform white privilege, to theatricalize the "masked, hidden, guarded" dimensions of racial performa-tivity, thus provides a useful case study in the investigation of a theoretical redundancy and a theatrical impossibility. First, the response to Smith's effort is heterogeneous, even and especially amongst self-identified white audience members. Some review-ers focused on the representation of Daryl Gates in a way that suggested success in creating "points of identification." "Former police chief Daryl Gates comes across as more human than some may suppose," wrote Christopher Meeks, "a man whose weak-ness is his inability to see himself or his actions in context."[53]

Meanwhile, Jack Kroll felt that "Smith transmits Chief Daryl Gates . . . without caricature."[54] Robert Brustein, however, took up the representation of white privileged characters quite differently, saying that such characters came off as "the patsies of the piece," asserting Smith's culpability in the creation of culpable subjects. The most spectacularly explicit white person in the show is Elaine Young, a Beverly Hills real estate executive and self-nominated "victim of silicone" who made an infamous news appearance by discussing her retreat to the safety of the Beverly Hills Hotel during the uprisings. By spectacular, I mean that she is seeable as white and wealthy; it might be such social and, therefore, dramaturgical markings that produce a lack of identification. Young discourses freely about being a "victim of silicone," about having a date canceled the day of the riots: "Now mind you I'm only three weeks separated and I didn't want to be/alone . . . and my housekeeper goes off for the weekend." She made television history when she unabashedly told a reporter about the relief of finding safety in the Beverly Hills Hotel. As she explained to Smith, "So then you say, 'Well let me put this out of my mind for now and/go on.' So that was the mood at the Polo Lounge . . . 'Here we are and we're still alive, and you know, we hope there'll be people alive when we come out.'"[55] Young wears her obliviousness like a banner. And the Beverly Hills Hotel is the ultimate place of dubiously secured sanctuary. From the insulated house of Shange's white girl and now to the Beverly Hills Hotel, this is the space of paralyzing exclusivity and privileged enclosure – "safety in numbers." Elaine is all extroversion. She is not discrete.

Smith's performance of Elaine Young is usefully located in a longer genealogy of anti-racist theatre, one that includes Shange's representation of Natalie's "white girl." The deployment of such white female figures is a common strategy and a necessary one within the context of feminism. It marks as racially specific the concerns that many white feminists earlier claimed applied to all women. Nevertheless, for many white (and female) audience members, this figure provoked an all-too familiar reaction. For critic Tania Modleski, Elaine Young confirmed Smith's anti-feminism and provoked an uncharacteristically polarized response from Modleski: "If Smith was not prepared to acknowledge my oppression as a woman, I felt, I would not recognize her as an African-American."[56] While I strongly take issue with Modleski's so-thereism, I do wonder whether Smith's marking of whiteness might be in danger of another kind of regressive re-marking. The representation of Elaine Young prompts the question of whether whiteness is made more seeable when it rides atop the seeability of feminine excess. By thus de-naturalizing white privilege, the technique might be in danger of re-naturalizing female stereotype, exposing white performativity by reifying feminine theatricality. My concern comes from an awareness of how such hyperbolic figures encourage the "white unlike me" operation alluded to above. This mode of uptake illustrates the importance of refining a Butlerian concept of disidentification, of theatrical hyperbole, and of Brechtian distancing. Elaine Young receives the loudest of self-disidentifying laughs from *Twilight*'s audience. The moment that Smith's jaw drops and her eyes widen into the familiar expression of unsubstantiated self-righteousness, the moment her voice launches in to the high-pitched, unyielding tones of unjustified entitlement, the audience can disengage from any threat of identification or intra-racial reciprocity. The long misfire that is Young's monologue, however, is simultaneously a successful theatrical moment; its felicity as a theatrical performative rests on her infelicity as a speaking subject. If hyper-femininity is deployed as de-familiarization, then it seems important to ask whether this mode is *itself* estranged or whether it is only used *to* estrange. The performance of Elaine Young is a defamiliarization of racism that actually runs the risk of naturalization: "she is not me." Racial distancing in this theatrical space can translate into racist disavowal, allowing a liberal uptaking that *displays* racism by safely locating it elsewhere.

It may be that by placing Elaine Young as the object of total self-distancing that *Twilight* frees the audience to develop more complicated relationships with other characters. Like Richards's contextualization of Natalie's "white girl" monologue, Elaine Young needs to be interpreted within a longer series of performative disturbances. The Anonymous Agent to whom I referred earlier is one of the most compelling for the questions of this chapter. His speech comes closest to outlining the theoretically obtuse contours of racial performativity in performance. First, his linguistic dilemma is a formal problem of location. How does such a person narrate his experience of the uprising?

There was still the uneasiness that was growing
when the fuse was still burning,
but
it was
business as usual.
Basically,
you got
such-and-so on line one,
such-and-so on line two.
Traffic,
Wilshire
Santa Monica.
Bunch of us hadda go to lunch at the
the Grill
in Beverly Hills.
Um,
gain major
show business dead center business restaurant,
kinda loud but genteel.[57]

As the Anonymous Agent speaks, his monologue dances near
and around several kinds of rhetorical seductions and obstacles.
Throughout, he tries to come to terms with the tension between
the high drama of the uprising and simultaneous un-drama of
the spaces he occupies. In many ways, the agent's position as a
less dramatic white person in the riots is a metaphor for the non-
experience of white racialization supported by class privilege.
Certainly, his lack of spectacularity illustrates the perniciousness
of white performativity with more precision than did the non-
voluntary theatricality of Reginald Denny, the white man whose
assault during the uprising was nationally broadcast. The first
lines of broken sentences articulate the situation: there is an un-
easinesss growing even though it is business as usual. The vacillation between a perceived "unease" and an unperceived "usual"
will recur, as will the tendency toward a passive metaphorizing of
the situation. Turning to the second-person pronoun, the agent
then proceeds to elaborate on the usual normalcy, "you got such
and so on line one." He offers what are to him the conventional
tropes of everyday existence, articulated by a generalized "you"
and in the rhythmic sing-song that enacts their predictability.
The sing-song invites its interlocutor into a shared acknowledgment of the predictability, asking for a rhythmic nod that would

complete the circuit of reciprocity and thereby recursively instantiate the experience as ordinary and unmarked. He continues, "Bunch of us had to go to lunch at the/the Grill/ in Beverly Hills." The article "the" would, in an ideal reciprocal encounter, slip by unnoticed and in that unnoticing performatively insure a capital "T." But with Anna Deavere Smith as visiting interlocutor, the "t" comes back small, requiring him to double the article – "the/the" – and needing not only repetition but more qualification – "in Beverly Hills." The agent then stalls with his "um" and enmeshes himself in a sentence that has almost two predicates and no subject: "um / gain major / show business dead center business restaurant, kinda loud but genteel." Reaching for the subjectless verb – one that does not name the "who" who is doing the gaining – he deflects the focus away from the "us/I" and onto the restaurant. In this series of speech acts, language teeters. The speaker stumbles over an "um," stutters twice on an article, tries again on "Beverly Hills," and finally recovers the capacity to change the subject after a fitful ride on a non-grammatical string of words. Such precarious speech reveals the performative mechanisms that create identity positions. The struggle constitutes and breaks an interlocutionary circuit, a puncture in an ideal reciprocity, thereby exposing language's tenuous and contingent support system. Additionally, such ruptures illumine the difficulty of speaking of normalcy. The "ya's" and sing-song accompany the description of an L.A. agent's routine, but such speech always risks missing its target, failing in its quest to describe the speaker's feeling of non-particularity. Sometimes such a linguistic act comes boomeranging back, the particularity of the speaker all the more scandalously revealed because it contrasts sharply with the act's normalizing discursive intent. This all occurs in a few seconds, a fleeting and recoverable revelation of the contextuality of his sense of normalcy. But within that limited time and before it passes into the realm of the unrecorded, *Twilight*'s speaker stumbles.

And he changes the subject. He does it by returning to the opening topic of "uneasiness . . . burning," an experience that is more linguistically available than "business as usual." Within "business as usual" there is an "incipient panic . . . palpable, it was tangible, you could cut it with a knife." His description of

The Grill's atmosphere gestures to its circle of intra-class and intra-racial reciprocity.

> All anyone was talking/
> about, you could hear little bits/
> of information – /
> did ya hear?/
> did ya hear?/
> It's like we were transmitting/
> thoughts/
> to each other/
> all across the restaurant . . .
> We were just
> getting ourselves into a frenzy . . .[58]

Recursively propelling and propelled by the performative structure of a self-activating paranoia, The Grill is in a theatrical, seeable frenzy. The "did ya hear's" were perhaps less significant for the "bits of information" they contained, than for the way the interrogative multiplied itself, creating a structure in which participants amplified their anxiety and constituted themselves as a group. At the same time, this is a type of group consolidation that happens within the habitual protocols of everyday life. Over the clinking of forks, with backs of chairs remaining opposed to each other, the room filled with the steady hum of "information" that heads cocked sidewise to hear. His later descriptions of "people *running* around" or "the vision of all these yuppies . . . fleeing like/ wild-eyed/ All you needed was Godzilla behind them" are followed with the paradoxical assertion of un-drama – "I don't mean that somebody in the restaurant had a fight" or "still,/still,/ nothing had happened – I don't mean to tell you that bombs were exploding." The juxtaposition creates a psychoanalytically rich portrait of a raced and classed paranoia, where panic and anxiety spring most exuberantly from the perpetually deferred arrival of a still unspecific threat. Reminding Smith that "nothin' happened" in one moment – "nothing, just/ ya know/ Caesar salad/da-de-da/ ya know" – he then elaborates on the need for "protection," vacillating between a willingess to inhabit and urge to retreat from a positioning inside the scene he narrates.

> When we drove back,
> and it's about a ten-minute drive,
> talking about the need for guns
> to protect ourselves . . .[59]

Between the prepositional phrase beginning with "when" and the modifying gerund beginning with "talking," the grammatical subject of the sentence remains absent. A string of dependent clauses introduce and modify an unfilled position. The sentence evokes the action while avoiding the discomfort of first-person articulation, bypassing the entanglements of active (and culpable) grammaticality. Finally, this monologue sustains – in stutters, in hystericized imagery, in sing-songy da-de-da's, in the spectre of Godzilla, in passive-voiced constructions, and subjectless predicates – the simultaneity of white performativity and white theatricality. It navigates unregistered citationality and highly dramatized spectacularity, evoking the internalized ordinariness of the former and the exteriorized extraordinariness of the latter.

Anna Deavere Smith has said of this character: "I'm not interested in who's responsible. I'm interested in catching this particular agent, who wears Armani suits and is a neat guy. Where is he? That inability to express is itself a reality."[60] Her statement could be interpreted as a disingenuous apoliticalism, akin to Adrian Piper saying that she doesn't have an "aesthetic program," akin to Diana Son saying that she does not want "to condemn." However, the "not interested" in responsibility might also show Smith's interest in something other than locating an individuated and sovereign culpability. Certainly the question of culpability is at issue for the Anonymous Agent, something broached and suspended as he struggles to make himself the subject of his own sentences.

> Whether well-intentioned or not,
> somebody got the short shift,
> and they did,
> and I started to
> absorb a little guilt
> and say, uh,
> "I deserve,
> I deserve it!"
> I don't mean I deserve to get my house burned down.

The us
did
not in . . .
not,
I like to think, not intentionally,
but
maybe so . . .[61]

In contemporary liberal American society, the intentionlessness
of racial privilege and the urge to avoid culpability brace against
the structure of a grammatical sentence, particularly in the first-
person, particularly in the present tense. It might be helpful to
ask what an ideal performative sentence would be – really – and
upon sensing the inevitability of imperfect uptakes and the lure of
self-deferral, to think more judiciously and pragmatically about
language's impure performativity. Until that moment, the experience of race and class privilege will return to the positions that
always seem happier, that of the "white unlike me," or that are often too readily available, that of hidden, normalized anonymity.

Performing professions

The vexed and productive relationship between theatricality and
performativity offers a structure for understanding the dynamics
of identity-based theatre. In turn, instances of racialized and anti-
racist theatre give contemporary rhetoricians a useful site with
which to explore the dynamics of intra-racial and cross-racial
exchange. Such racialized deflections and infelicities appear in
a variety of American public spheres, including the sphere of
the post-1990s university classroom. As it happens, the issue of
imputed intention and sovereign subjectivity turns out to be fundamental to understanding a triangulated conversation amongst
the discourses of race, theatre, and performativity. In theatrical
exchanges, different spectators not only "have different views"
but also posit addressive effects as the intended goal of the performer. An uptake is posited as a send-out; his disorientation
is cast as her misfire. That process is exacerbated in racialized
theatres where injuries are narrated, imputed, deflected, and exchanged in circuitous currents and with alarming force. Infelicity
is the occupational hazard of anti-racist theatre where the possibility of "getting it right" is quite low even as the stakes for *not*

getting it right are quite high. To take a rhetorical and performative stance on race and theatre makes it possible to see these dilemmas as formal operations and, perhaps, to put less pressure on the dream of complete felicity or unproblematic success. That stance might also help politicized critics and artists to navigate their relationship with each other. It offers a different way of approaching instances of artist self-deflection, those "I don't try" and "I wasn't thinking" responses that frustrate critics' attempts at interpretation. Before calling such responses "apolitical" or "anti-intellectual," it might be helpful to examine the highly individuated terms with which critics identify an artist's "program." Rather than questioning the political commitment of an artist who says that she is "not trying to condemn" a specified opponent or that she is not interested in "who's responsible," the performativity critique asks us to reconsider the models of subjectivity and the dynamics of locution with which artists experiment. From this view, a number of performance-based artists might turn out to be "performativity coordinators" after all.

Thinking about theatrical production and reception through the addressive operations of speech has more implications from the standpoint of institutional history. To bring discourses of performativity and discourses of theatrical performance into conversation is simultaneously to join rhetorical and dramatic legacies that became disconnected from each other in the United States over the course of the last 100 years. A theatricality and performativity debate might thus offer the chance for a different kind of reunion between theatre and rhetoric. This version of the rhetorical is a far cry from the "briefs" that George Pierce Baker once offered in rhetorical argumentation. However, this theatre is also a far cry from Baker's "how to make a play" pedagogy and from the rather simplistic assumptions of free will on which so much academic drama relied.[62] Writing *Excitable Speech* from a Rhetoric department traditionally centered on the act of persuasion, Judith Butler's elaboration of the role of "bodily demeanor" in producing the effects of speech is a reminder of the relationship between the theatrical and the rhetorical; as she says, "any theory of acting knows this."[63] One theatre critic's account of Anna Deavere Smith gestures, however off-handedly, to a rhetorical genealogy as well: "This is as close as our culture can come to the impact of Homer, enacting his 'Iliad' to a

rapt audience in the days when the medium was the person."[64]
And Anna Deavere Smith's own dramaturgical sense displays an
active interest in the creation of a public sphere. "I believe the
audience's response and presence is as important as my speaking.
For instance, people may hear a line and experience it as moving – that same line may cause others to laugh. My hope is that
in the physical experience of seeing *Twilight* – sitting in a room
with 700 other people and everyone having different responses –
a kind of integrative thinking will begin to happen."[65] Such connections can revitalize the now tired relationship between Speech
and Theatre – the two words that still hang unhappily next to
each other above the stone entrances of several university departments. Similar connections might prompt reassessment along
other axes as well, such as those that plot the opposition between
"theory" and "practice" or between "humanistic" and "technical" knowledge. They might traverse the geographic distance that
separates so many humanities departments from so many theatre
departments, an infrastructural preoccupation that both required
and maintained their epistemological separation. Whether or not
it offers alternative, if historic, principles of connection between
diverse persons who occupy different university buildings, something provocative can be gleaned by acknowledging our shared
disciplinary interest in language as action.

Those shared disciplinary interests, however, will not necessarily resolve institutional obstacles. To conclude not only this
chapter but also this book, it is important to acknowledge that
almost all of the artists whom I considered (and many, many
others who I could have considered) have had complicated relationships with academia. "I've realized that people in academic
circles aren't really talking to me. They're trying to figure out if
I'm smart or not," Anna Deavere Smith noted in an interview.[66]
As a professor of acting at Stanford who ended up with another
full-time career, Smith offered brief reflections on her university
work environment. Those occasions rapidly diminished when
the time-space requirements of professional performance inter-
fered with the time-space requirements of professional teaching and service. The difficulty of managing not simply interdisciplinarity but also "inter-professionality" ultimately proved
to be overwhelming, and Smith resigned from Stanford. Such lo-
gistical disparities between the world of the artist and the world of

the intellectual constantly recur. More recently, they reappeared in Adrian Piper's suit against Wellesley College. There, Piper accused college administrators of being insidiously unsupportive of her artistic career, despite their public celebration of her innovation. "Wellesley has used my public visibility to enhance its multicultural public image while in reality actively preventing me from doing the multicultural work it publicly claims to welcome."[67] In an open letter to Wellesley's president, published on her website, she argued that the college had not granted necessary leaves, funding support, or reduced teaching loads. Despite the pressures assorted with her "public visibility," she was told that she needed to do college committee work in order "to keep the institution running."[68] As a professor of performance and, on occasion, a performing professor, I am sympathetic to Piper's sense of betrayal and to her frustration at not having time to complete her own work. As a professor of performance and, on occasion, a performing professor, I am also sympathetic, not only to the idea that someone has to keep the place running, but that that running is also part of "my own work."

For many of us who hold out the possibility of unifying research and art-making – so-called "theory" and "practice" – Adrian Piper has been a much-touted example. Hence, to see this philosopher and artist ultimately admit and publicize her institutional quandary is profoundly unsettling. Indeed, "quandary" seems an apt word for the situation, for the question of professional injury and culpability is quite complicated. In a piece of semi-parodic writing entitled, "My Job Description," Piper laid out the demands of teaching, departmental service, and professional research next to those of the art theorist and art-maker, including "preparing lectures," "holding office hours," "writing letters of recommendation," "arranging conferences," "reviewing books," "reading PhD dissertations," "delivering specialized papers," "creating and fabricating," "photo-, slide-, or video-documenting," "labeling; inventorying," "writing explanatory statements," "coordinating promotional efforts with dealers and curators," "installing; exhibiting," "marketing through mailings," and the list continued.[69] The need to create such a description stemmed from her perception not only that her Wellesley colleagues could not fathom the demands of an art career but also that her art colleagues had (like most of the non-academic public) very little idea of what it meant to be a professional scholar. As unsettling as it is to recognize that the job description of the artist-and-academic is still so unclear, it is more unsettling to realize how long this mutual ignorance has persisted despite the inter-dependence of art and academic institutions. As Howard Singerman notes, "[t]he university too has its representations, its discourses of service and citizenship, of independent research and *Bildung*, and there are types and legends of the artist that it cannot easily include . . . The artist, or artistic subjectivity, is the university's problem and its project. From the turn of the century on, it has offered a series of new artistic subjects, written over and over in the likeness of the university professional."[70] The problem of artistic subjectivity has had particular impact on the project of performance in the academy. Performance's problems and projects have manifested themselves disciplinarily as well as institutionally. Its "writing over" has meant simultaneous incorporation and deflection from major critical schools and politicized intellectual projects – philology, New Criticism, cultural studies, deconstruction, New Historicism, and identity politics to name a few of those explored in this book. It has meant the embrace and rejection of legitimating pedagogies and curricular terms that divided its knowledges, its objects, its practices, and its faculties into different technical, humanistic, and occupational spheres. At the same time, the partiality of the incorporating embrace and the reluctance of the deflecting rejection have also provided opportunities for analysis; they expose and render intelligible the principles, divisions, and occupational conventions of academic knowledge. My hope is that by investigating the partial spaces of university inscription we might imagine performance's "writing over" into a different kind of likeness.

Notes

CHAPTER ONE

1. Marjorie Garber, *Academic Instincts* (Princeton University Press, 2001), p. 57.
2. Michel Foucault, *Archaeology of Knowledge and the Discourse on Language*, Trans. A.M. Sheridan Smith (New York: Pantheon, 1972), p. 44.
3. J.L. Austin, *How to Do Things with Words* (Cambridge: Harvard University Press, 1962, 1975), p. 22.
4. Foucault, *Archaeology* 32.
5. Foucault, *Archaeology* 33.
6. John Guillory, "Literary Critics as Intellectuals," *Rethinking Class: Literary Studies and Social Formations*, eds. Wai Chee Dimock and Michael T. Gilmore (New York: Columbia University Press, 1994), pp. 110, 111.
7. Jon McKenzie, *Perform or Else: From Discipline to Performance* (New York: Routledge, 2001), p. 47.
8. Peggy Phelan, "Introduction," *The Ends of Performance* (eds.) Peggy Phelan and Jill Lane (New York University Press, 1998), p.3.
9. Richard Schechner, "A New Paradigm for Theatre in the Academy," *The Drama Review* 36.4 (1992), 7–10.
10. See, for instance, Josephine Lee, "Disciplining Theater and Drama in the English Department: Some Reflections on 'Performance' and Institutional History," *Text and Performance Quarterly* 19 (1999), p. 3. Lee considers some of the early figures who will appear in the next chapter. While she focuses on the conservative dimensions of early pro-theatre discourse to challenge the radical claims of contemporary performance discourse, I will be more interested in remembering the radicality of early pro-theatre efforts to counter the present tendency in performance studies to see such figures as necessarily conservative and conventional. See also, Jill Dolan, "Geographies of Learning: Theatre Studies, Performance, and the 'Performative,'" *Theatre Journal* 45 (1993), 417–41.
11. Foucault, *Archaeology*, p. 33.

12. Philip Auslander also criticized the use of the term "paradigm" to describe performance studies. See, "Evangelical Fervor," *The Drama Review* 39.4 (1995), 169–80.

13. Gerald Graff, *Beyond the Culture Wars: How Teaching the Conflicts Can Revitalize American Education* (New York and London: W.W. Norton and Co., 1992).

14. Marvin Carlson, *Performance: A Critical Introduction* (New York: Routledge, 1996).

15. Joann Kealiinohomoku, "An Anthropologist Looks at Ballet as a Form of Ethnic Dance," *What is Dance?: Readings in Theory and Criticism* (eds.) Roger Copeland and Marshall Cohen (Oxford University Press, 1983), p. 533.

16. Kealiinohomoku, "An Anthropologist Looks," p. 534. See also, Eli Rozik, *The Roots of Theatre: Rethinking Ritual and Other Theories of Origin* (University of Iowa Press, 2002).

17. Laurence Veysey, *The Emergence of the American University* (University of Chicago Press, 1965).

18. Frederick Rudolph, *The American College and University: A History* (New York: Vintage Books, 1962), pp. 247, 264.

19. Julian B. Roebuck and Komanduri S. Murty, *Historically Black Colleges and Universities: Their Place in Higher Education* (Westport CN: Praeger, 1993).

20. Andrew Abbott, *The System of Professions: An Essay on the Division of Expert Labor* (University of Chicago Press, 1988).

21. For discussions on the professionalization of the intellectual, see Bruce Robbins's edited collection, *Intellectuals: Aesthetics, Politics, Academics* (Minneapolis: University of Minnesota Press, 1990).

22. Bruce Kuklick, "The Emergence of the Humanities," *South Atlantic Quarterly* 89.1 (1990), 205–6.

23. For discussions of the idea of the amateur, see Wendy Lesser, *The Amateur: An Independent Life in Letters* (New York: Pantheon, 1999), and Marjorie Garber's first chapter of *Academic Instincts*.

24. Abbott, *System of Professions*, p. 197.

25. Abbott, *System of Professions*, p. 198.

26. Rudolph, *American College and University*, p. 272.

27. Rudolph, *American College and University*, p. 281.

28. Sally Banes, "Institutionalizing Avant-Garde Performance: A Hidden History of University Patronage in the United States," *Contours of the Theatrical Avant-Garde: Performance and Textuality* (ed.) James M. Harding (Ann Arbor: University of Michigan Press, 2000), pp. 217–38; Howard Singerman, *Art Subjects: Making Artists in the American University* (Berkeley: University of California Press, 1999).

29. William Bennett, "To Reclaim a Legacy," 1984 Report on Humanities in Education, *Chronicle of Higher Education* (January 13,

1988), A52; Dinesh d'Souza, *Illiberal Education: The Politics of Race and Sex on Campus* (New York: Free Press, 1991); Roger Kimball, "'Tenured Radicals': A Postscript," *The New Criterion* 9.5 (January 1991), 4–13; Graff, *Beyond the Culture Wars*, p. 16.

30. Richard Hornby, "The Death of Literature and History," *Theatre Topics* 5.2 (September 1995), 145–6.

31. Ted Wendt, "The Displacement of the Aesthetic: Problems of Performance Studies," *Text and Performance Quarterly* 10 (1990), 248–56.

32. Hornby, "Death of Literature and History," 145–6.

33. Stephen Bottoms, "Titillating the Impotent," Unpublished Essay delivered at American Society for Theatre Research, 2001.

34. Pierre Bourdieu, *Homo Academicus* (trans.) Peter Collier (Cambridge UK: Polity Press, 1988), p. 36.

35. Andrew Ross, "Defenders of the Faith and the New Class," *Intellectuals* (ed.) Bruce Robbins, p. 122.

36. Ross, "Defenders of the Faith," p. 125.

37. MacKenzie, *Perform or Else*, p. 49.

38. Sigmund Freud, *Civilization and Its Discontents* (1930), in *The Standard Edition of the Complete Psychological Works of Sigmund Freud*, ed. James Strachey (London: Hogarth Press and the Institute of Psycho-Analysis, 1986) 21:114. See also Garber's discussion of "Discipline Envy" in *Academic Instincts*, pp. 53–96.

39. Sverre Sjølander, "Long-Term and Short-Term Interdisciplinary Work: Difficulties, Pitfalls, and Built-In Failures," *Inter-Disciplinarity Revisited* (eds.) Lennart Levin and Ingemar Lind (Stockholm: OECD, SNBUC, Linkoping University, 1985), pp. 85–101.

CHAPTER TWO

1. Michael Bérubé, *The Employment of English: Theory, Jobs, and the Future of Literary Studies* (New York University Press, 1998), p. 101.

2. Joseph Roach, "Reconstructing Theatre/History," *Theatre Topics* 9.1 (March 1999), 3–10, 9.

3. George Lyman Kittredge to George Pierce Baker (March 19, 1905), Papers of George Pierce Baker, Harvard Theatre Collection, Pusey Library, Harvard University.

4. Roach, "Reconstructing Theatre/History," 3.

5. Paul Edwards, "Unstoried: Teaching Literature in the Age of Performance Studies," *Theatre Annual* 52 (1999), 1–147; Alexandra Carter, "General Introduction," *Routledge Dance Studies Reader* (ed.) Alexandra Carter (New York: Routledge, 1998), pp. 1–18.

6. James Hatch, "Some African Influences on the Afro-American Theatre," *Theatre of Black Americans* (ed.) Erroll Hill (New York: Applause, 1987), pp. 13–29.

7. Julian B. Roebuck and Komanduri S. Murty, *Historically Black Colleges and Universities: Their Place in American Higher Education* (Westport, CN: Praeger, 1993), p. 61.

8. See Josephina Niggli, *Mexican Folk Plays* (ed.) Frederick Koch (Chapel Hill: University of North Carolina Press, 1938); Walter Spearman, *The Carolina Playmakers: The First Fifty Years* (Chapel Hill: University of North Carolina Press, 1970), p. 71.

9. George Pierce Baker, "The Mind of the Undergraduate," *Educational Review* 30 (Sept 1905), 189–200, 193.

10. George Pierce Baker, "The Theatre and the University," *Theatre Arts Monthly* 9.1 (Jan 1925), 99–108, 99.

11. Alexandra Oleson and John Voss, *The Organization of Knowledge in Modern America, 1860–1920* (Baltimore: Johns Hopkins University Press, 1979), pp. x–xi.

12. Barbara and John Ehrenreich, "The Professional-Managerial Class," *Between Labor and Capital* (ed.) Pat Walker (Boston: South End Press, 1979), pp. 5–49, 12.

13. Charles Eliot to George Pierce Baker (April 25, 1895), Harvard Theatre Collection.

14. Barbara and John Ehrenreich, "The PMC," p. 26.

15. Richard Moulton, *Shakespeare as a Dramatic Artist: A Study of Inductive Literary Criticism* (original publisher not listed, 1888), excerpted in Gerald Graff and Michael Warner (eds.) *The Origins of Literary Studies in America* (New York: Routledge, 1989), pp. 61–74, 61–2. Moulton's italics.

16. Moulton, *Shakespeare as a Dramatic Artist*, p. 63.

17. Laurence Vesey, "The Plural Organized Worlds of the Humanities," *Organization of Knowledge*, pp. 51–106; Laurence Vesey, *The Emergence of the American University* (University of Chicago Press, 1965).

18. Stuart P. Sherman, "Professor Kittredge and the Teaching of English," *The Nation* (1913) reprinted in Graff and Warner, *Origins* (cf. notes 36 and 37), pp. 147–55: 152.

19. Sherman, "Professor Kittredge," p. 152.

20. Sherman, "Professor Kittredge," p. 155.

21. John Guillory, *Cultural Capital: The Problem of Literary Canon Formation* (University of Chicago Press, 1993), p. 80.

22. Michael Quinn, "*Theatrewissenschaft* in the History of Theatre Study," *Theatre Survey* 32 (1991), 123–36; Marvin Carlson, "Theatre and Performance at a Time of Shifting Disciplines," *Theatre Research International* 26.2 (2001), 137–44. For a related discussion of literature, performance, and philology see, Shannon Jackson, "Professing Performance: Disciplinary Genealogies," *The Drama Review* 45.1 (Spring 2001), 84–95.

23. Kittredge to Baker (Dec 20, 1894), Harvard Theatre Collection.

24. Review Materials, passim, Papers of George Pierce Baker, Harvard Theatre Collection.

25. Barrett Wendell to Baker (December 20, 1894), Harvard Theatre Collection.

26. Graff and Warner, *Origins* (cf. notes 36 and 37), p. 4.

27. Edwards, "Unstoried"; Margaret Robb, "The Elocutionary Movement and Its Chief Figures," *History of Speech Education in America* (ed.) Karl R. Wallace (New York: Appleton-Century-Crofts, 1954), pp. 178–201. See other chapters in this edited collection for a diverse disciplinary history of speech and rhetoric.

28. Edwards, "Unstoried," 77.

29. Wisner Payne Kinne, *George Pierce Baker and the American Theatre* (Cambridge: Harvard University Press, 1954), p. 7.

30. Elizabeth Bell, "Performance Studies as Women's Work," *Text and Performance Quarterly* 13 (October 1993), 362.

31. Harry P. Kerr, "Baker's *Principles of Argumentation*," *The Speech Teacher* (March 1962), 120.

32. Kerr, "Baker's *Principles*," 121.

33. Kerr, "Baker's *Principles*," 122.

34. Review Materials, passim, Papers of George Pierce Baker, Harvard Theatre Collection.

35. Eliot to Baker (April 25, 1895), Harvard Theatre Collection.

36. William Lyons Phelps, *Autobiography with Letters*, 1939, excerpted in Graff and Warner, *Origins*, pp. 156–67, 159.

37. Phelps, in Graff and Warner, *Origins*, p. 160.

38. James Berlin, *Rhetoric and Reality: Writing Instruction in American Colleges, 1900–1985* (Carbondale, IL: Southern Illinois University Press, 1987).

39. Wendell to Baker (Feb 11, 1899), Harvard Theatre Collection.

40. James Morgan Hart, "The College Course in English Literature, How it May Be Improved," *PMLA* (1884–85), reprinted in Graff and Warner, *Origins*, pp. 34–7, 35.

41. Kinne, *George Pierce Baker and the American Theatre*, pp. 3–4.

42. Ibid.

43. Brander Matthews, *The Development of Drama* (New York: Scribner, 1904), pp. 1–9.

44. George Pierce Baker, *The Development of Shakespeare as a Dramatist* (New York: Macmillan, 1923), p. 4.

45. Roach, "Reconstructing Theatre/History," 5.

46. Kittredge to Baker (September 28, 1902), Harvard Theatre Collection.

47. Kittredge to Baker (March 8, 1905), Harvard Theatre Collection.

48. Thomas Wood Stevens, "Carnegie Tech: First Phase," lecture delivered in 1915, p. 3, Thomas Wood Stevens Collection, Manuscripts, The University of Arizona Library.

49. Thomas Wood Stevens, "Carnegie Tech: First Phase," p. 2.
50. John Mason Brown, "The Four Georges," *George Pierce Baker* (New York: Dramatists Play Service, 1939), p. 9; George Pierce Baker Collection, Sterling Memorial Library, Yale University.
51. John Mason Brown, "Four Georges," pp. 13–14.
52. Wendell to Baker (June 21, 1902); Wendell to Baker (August 3, 1902), Harvard Theatre Collection.
53. Elizabeth H. Hunt to George Pierce Baker (Dec 9, 1920), Harvard Theatre Collection.
54. John Mason Brown, "Four Georges," p. 16.
55. Donald Oenslager, "Mr. Baker in His Theatre," *George Pierce Baker* (New York: Dramatists Play Service, 1939), p. 26.
56. Lawrence Lowell to George Pierce Baker (May 21, 1923), Harvard Theatre Collection.
57. Baker to Lowell (May 13, 1924), Harvard Theatre Collection.
58. Lowell to Baker (May 14, 1924), Harvard Theatre Collection.
59. Baker, "The Theatre and the University," 100.
60. George Pierce Baker to Phillip Barry (October 6, 1925), Box 1, Folder 10, George Pierce Baker Papers, Sterling Memorial Library, Yale University.
61. George Pierce Baker to Harley Granville-Barker (October 30, 1925), Box 4 Folder, 79, George Pierce Baker Papers, Sterling Memorial Library, Yale University.
62. Baker to Barry (April 10, 1930), Box 1, Folder 10, George Pierce Baker Papers, Sterling Memorial Library, Yale University.
63. Lee Simonson, "Faith and Works," *Theatre Arts Monthly* 17.7 (July 1933), 509.
64. Baker, "The Theatre and the University," 103.
65. Baker, "The Theatre and the University," 103.
66. Thomas Wood Stevens, "A School of the Theatre Arts," undated publication, Thomas Wood Stevens Papers, Manuscripts, The University of Arizona Library.
67. Thomas Wood Stevens, "The Theatre Goes to School," undated lecture, Thomas Wood Stevens Papers, Manuscripts, The University of Arizona Library.
68. Stevens, "Carnegie Tech: First Phase," p. 1.
69. Wendell to Baker (November 9, 1899), Harvard Theatre Collection.

CHAPTER THREE

1. Robert Brustein, "Why American Plays Are Not Literature," *American Drama and Its Critics* (ed.) Alan Downer (University of Chicago Press, 1965), pp. 245–55; originally appeared in *Harper's Magazine* (1959), p. 209.

2. Raymond Williams, *Keywords: A Vocabulary of Culture and Society* (New York: Oxford University Press, 1984), p. 20.
3. Raymond Williams, "Preface," *Modern Tragedy* (London: Chatto and Windus, 1961), p. iv.
4. See Cary Nelson, Paula A. Treichler, and Lawrence Grossberg, "Cultural Studies: An Introduction," *Cultural Studies* (New York: Routledge, 1992), pp. 1–16; Stuart Hall, "Cultural Studies and Its Theoretical Legacies," *Cultural Studies*, pp. 277–85; Cary Nelson, "Always Already Cultural Studies," *Manifesto of a Tenured Radical* (New York University Press, 1997), pp. 52–74.
5. Richard Schechner, "A New Paradigm for Theatre in the Academy," *The Drama Review* 36.4 (1992), 10.
6. Eric Bentley, *The Life of the Drama* (New York: Atheneum, 1967).
7. Paul Gilroy, *The Black Atlantic: Modernity and Double Consciousness* (Cambridge: Harvard University Press, 1993), p. 75.
8. For an example of such a debate, see William Worthen's "Disciplines of the Text/Sites of Performance," *The Drama Review* 39.1, 13–28 and the responses from Richard Schechner, Joseph Roach, and Jill Dolan that follow.
9. Anthony Easthope, *Literary into Cultural Studies* (London and New York: Routledge, 1991).
10. Brustein, "Why American Plays Are Not Literature," p. 247.
11. John Guillory, *Cultural Capital: The Problem of Literary Canon Formation* (University of Chicago Press, 1993), p. 28.
12. George Pierce Baker, "The Dramatist and His Public," *The Lamp* (1903–4), 329.
13. Brander Matthews, *The Development of Drama* (New York: Charles Scribner's Sons, 1903), pp. 4, 6.
14. Laurence Veysey, *The Emergence of the American University* (University of Chicago Press, 1965), pp. 186, 191. Internal quotation is from C.F. Thwing (president of Western Reserve Academy), *The College of the Future* (Cleveland, 1897), pp. 12–13.
15. Terry Eagleton, *Literary Theory: An Introduction* (1983, Minneapolis: University of Minnesota Press, 1996), p. 39.
16. Eagleton, *Literary Theory*, pp. 40, 42.
17. See Guillory, *Cultural Capital* and Gerald Graff, *Professing Literature: An Institutional History* (University of Chicago Press, 1987).
18. Northrop Frye, *Anatomy of Criticism* (Princeton University Press, 1967).
19. Eagleton, *Literary Theory*, p. 80.
20. Cleanth Brooks and Robert Penn Warren, *Understanding Poetry* (New York: Holt, Rinehart, and Winston, Inc., 1960).
21. Cleanth Brooks and Robert Heilman, *Understanding Drama* (1945, New York: Henry Holt, 1948), p. 24.

22. Cleanth Brooks, John Purser, and Robert Penn Warren, *An Approach to Literature* (New York: Appleton-Century, 1952).
23. Eric Bentley, *The Playwright as Thinker* (1946, New York: Harcourt, Brace, and World, 1967), pp. xix, 75.
24. Bentley, *Playwright as Thinker*, p. xxii.
25. John Gassner, "There is No American Drama," *Theatre Arts* (September 1952), 24–5, 84.
26. Gassner, "No American Drama," 24.
27. Gassner, "No American Drama," 25.
28. Gassner, "No American Drama," 84.
29. Gassner, "An Answer to the New Critics," *Theatre Arts* (November 1952), 59.
30. Gassner, "No American Drama," p. 24; Gassner, "An Answer," 60.
31. Gassner, "An Answer," 60.
32. Gassner, "An Answer," 60.
33. Gassner, "An Answer," 61.
34. Gassner, "An Answer," 61.
35. Gassner, "An Answer," 61.
36. Gassner, "An Answer," 61.
37. A.M. Drummond and Richard Moody, "Indian Treaties: The First American Dramas," *Quarterly Journal of Speech* 39.1 (February 1953), 15–24.
38. Edith Isaacs, *The Negro in the Theatre* (New York: Theatre Arts Incorporated, 1947), p. 15.
39. Bernard Hewitt, *Theatre U.S.A* (New York: McGraw-Hill, 1959); Walter Meserve, *An Emerging Entertainment* (Bloomington: Indiana University Press, 1977); See Joseph Roach, *Cities of the Dead* (New York: Columbia University Press, 1996), pp. 186–7.
40. Francis Fergusson, *The Idea of the Theater: The Art of Drama in Changing Perspective* (Princeton University Press, 1949), p. 21.
41. Fergusson, *Idea of the Theater*, p. 22.
42. Clifford Geertz, "Blurred Genres: The Refiguration of Social Thought," *Local Knowledge* (New York: Basic Books, 1983), pp. 19–35; Stephen Greenblatt, "Toward a Poetics of Culture," *New Historicism* (ed.) Aram Veeser (New York: Routledge, 1989), pp. 1–14.
43. Eagleton, *Literary Theory*, pp. 27–8.
44. Eagleton, *Literary Theory*, p. 32. He elaborates on the reproduced if occasionally unrecognized legacy: "The fact remains that English students in England today are 'Leavisites' where they know it or not, irremediably altered by that historic intervention. There is no more need to be a card-carrying Leavisite today than there is to be a card-carrying Copernican" (p. 27).
45. T.S. Eliot, *Notes Towards the Definition of Culture* (1948, London: Faber, 1962).

46. In fact, his list was akin to the kind drawn by Drummond and Moody in 1953: "charades, initiations, parades, costume dances, football celebrations, snake dances, and the life... burials, marriages, commencements, church services, courtroom trials," p. 15.

47. For a discussion of Hoggart's indebtedness to practical criticism in his study of the "lived experience" of working-class English families, see Andrew Goodwin's introduction to *The Uses of Literacy* (1957, New Brunswick and London: Transaction, 1998), pp. xiii–xxxiv.

48. Raymond Williams, *Culture and Society* (1958, New York: Columbia University Press, 1983), p. 234.

49. John Higgins, *Raymond Williams: Literature, Marxism, and Cultural Materialism* (London: Routledge, 1999), 21–45.

50. Raymond Williams, *Sociology of Culture* (New York: Schocken, 1982).

51. Jill Dolan, "Geographies of Learning," *Theatre Journal* 45 (1993), 417–41.

52. Fred Inglis, *Raymond Williams* (London and New York: Verso, 1995), p. 233.

53. Raymond Williams, *Problems of Materialism in Culture* (London and New York: Verso, 1980), p. 29.

54. Raymond Williams, *Drama from Ibsen to Brecht* (London: Chatto and Windus, 1968), pp. 18, 20.

55. Raymond Williams, "Drama in a Dramatised Society," Professorial address (Cambridge University Press, 1975); Reprinted in *Writing in Society* (London: Verso, 1983), pp. 20–1.

56. Williams, *Modern Tragedy*, p. 43.

57. Williams, *Modern Tragedy*, p. 45.

58. Williams, *Modern Tragedy*, p. 46.

59. Williams, *Sociology of Culture*, p. 204.

60. Inglis, *Raymond Williams*, p. 241

61. Inglis, *Raymond Williams*, p. 105.

62. Stuart Hall, "Communities, Nation, and Culture," *Cultural Studies* 7.3 (1993), 349–63.

63. Paul Gilroy, '*There Ain't No Black in the Union Jack': The Cultural Politics of Race and Nation* (University of Chicago Press, 1991), pp. 49–50; Gilroy quotes Williams's *Towards 2000* (Harmondsworth: Pelican, 1983), p. 195.

64. Paul Gilroy, "Black Music and the Politics of Authenticity," *The Black Atlantic: Modernity and Double Consciousness* (Cambridge: Harvard University Press, 1983), p. 75.

65. Gilroy, *The Black Atlantic*, p. 77.

66. Gilroy, *The Black Atlantic*, p. 78.

67. Gilroy, *The Black Atlantic*, p. 77.

68. Gilroy, "Black Music," p. 74; James Hatch, "Speak to Me in Those Old Words, You know, Those La-La Words, Those Tung-Tung Sounds," *Yale/Theatre* 8.1 (Fall 1976), 25–34.

69. Eleanor W. Traylor, "Two Afro-American Contributions to Dramatic Form," *The Theatre of Black Americans* (ed.) Errol Hill (New York: Applause, 1980), pp. 45–60.

70. James Hatch, *Black Image on the American Stage: A Bibliography of Plays and Musicals, 1770–1970* (New York: Drama Book Specialists, 1970); Eileen Southern, *The Music of Black Americans: A History* (New York: W.W. Norton, 1971); Errol Hill (ed.) *The Theatre of Black Americans* (New York: Applause, 1980); Edith Isaacs, *The Negro in the Theatre*, p. 15.

71. Meagan Morris, "A Question of Cultural Studies," unpublished paper cited in Lawrence Grossberg, *Bringing It All Back Home: Essays on Cultural Studies* (Durham and London: Duke University Press, 1997), p. 14.

72. Dorothy Hale, *Social Formalism: The Novel from Henry James to the Present* (Palo Alto: Stanford University Press, 1998), p. 13.

73. Hale, *Social Formalism*, p. 5.

74. Hale, *Social Formalism*, p. 12.

75. Catherine Gallagher, "The New Materialism in Marxist Aesthetics," *Theory and Society: Renewal and Critique in Social Theory* 9 (1980), 633–46, 635.

76. Grossberg, *Bringing It All Back Home*, p. 16.

CHAPTER FOUR

1. Deb Margolin, "A Perfect Theatre for One: Teaching Performance Composition," *The Drama Review* 41.2 (Summer 1997), 81.

2. Allan Kaprow, "Education of the Un-Artist, Part I," *Essays on the Blurring of Art and Life* (Berkeley: University of California Press, 1993), p. 109.

3. Nick Kaye, "Elizabeth LeCompte: Interview," *The Twentieth-Century Performance Reader*, ed. Michael Huxley and Noel Witts (London: Routledge, 1996), pp. 228–36, p. 230.

4. Nick Kaye, "Elizabeth LeCompte: Interview," p. 231.

5. Howard Singerman, *Art Subjects* (Berkeley: University of California Press, 1999), p. 130. See also, Judith Adler, *Artists in Offices: An Ethnography of an Academic Art Scene* (New Brunswick, NJ: Transaction Books, 1979).

6. Sally Banes, "Institutionalizing Avant-Garde Performance: A Hidden History of University Patronage in the United States," *Contours of the Theatrical Avant-Garde: Performance and Textuality* (ed.) James M. Harding (Ann Arbor: University of Michigan Press, 2000), pp. 217–38.

7. Kaye, "Elizabeth LeCompte," p. 234.
8. Jacques Derrida, *Of Grammatology*, trans. Gayatri Chakravorty Spivak (Baltimore and London: Johns Hopkins University Press, 1974), pp. 97–164. Originally published in France in 1967 by Les Editions de Minuit.
9. Barbara Johnson, "Translator's Introduction," in Jacques Derrida, *Dissemination* (University of Chicago Press, 1981), p. viii.
10. Jacques Derrida, "The Theater of Cruelty and the Closure of Representation," *Writing and Difference* (trans.) Alan Bass (University of Chicago Press, 1978), p. 232.
11. Derrida, "Theater of Cruelty," p. 234.
12. Derrida, "Theater of Cruelty," p. 238.
13. Derrida, "Theater of Cruelty," p. 239.
14. John Locke, *An Essay Concerning Human Understanding* (ed.) John W. Yolton, 2 vols (London: Dent and New York: Dutton, 1961) Book 3, pp. 87–8.
15. Locke, *An Essay*, Book 3, p. 87–8.
16. De Man quotes Locke, *An Essay*, Book 3, p. 105.
17. De Man, "The Epistemology of Metaphor," *Critical Inquiry* 5 (1978), 16.
18. De Man, "Epistemology," 17.
19. De Man, "Epistemology," 28.
20. Lucy Lippard, "Questions to Stella and Judd," *Minimal Art* (ed.) Gregory Battcock (New York: E.P. Dutton, 1968), p. 149.
21. Michael Fried, "Art and Objecthood," *Art and Objecthood: Essays and Reviews* (University of Chicago Press 1998), p. 151.
22. Clement Greenberg, "After Abstract Expressionism," *Art International* 6.5 (Summer 1962), 25.
23. Greenberg, "After," 25.
24. Greenberg, "After," 25.
25. Fried, "Art and Objecthood," p. 153.
26. Robert Morris, quoted in Fried, "Art and Objecthood," p. 153; see also, Robert Morris, "Notes on Sculpture, Part I," *Artforum* 4.6 (February 1966), 42–4.
27. Fried, "Art and Objecthood," p. 154.
28. Fried, "Art and Objecthood," p. 155.
29. The suspicion of the theatrical also came from the criticism of the Frankfurt School, where a theatrical terminology was used to characterize the invasion of mass culture sensibilities and processes on the artistic object.
30. Fried, "Art and Objecthood," p. 164.
31. Clement Greenberg, "Modernist Painting," *Art and Literature* (1965), 193–201, 194.
32. Fried, "Art and Objecthood," p. 164.
33. Robert Morris, quoted in Fried, "Art and Objecthood," p. 150.

34. Donald Judd, quoted in Fried, "Art and Objecthood," p. 165.
35. Fried, "Art and Objecthood," p. 152.
36. Fried, "Art and Objecthood," p. 165.
37. Fried, "Art and Objecthood," p. 158.
38. Derrida, "Theater of Cruelty," p. 238.
39. Jerzy Grotowski, *Towards a Poor Theatre* (Odin Teatrets Forlag, 1968), p. 123.
40. Grotowski, *Towards*, pp. 124–5.
41. Grotowski, *Towards*, p. 257.
42. Grotowski, *Towards*, p. 210.
43. Grotowski, *Towards*, p. 258.
44. Grotowski, *Towards*, pp. 20, 21.
45. Sally Banes, *Judson Dance Theatre: Democracy's Body, 1962–1964*, PhD Thesis (New York University Press, 1980), pp. xv–xvi.
46. Michael Kirby, *Happenings: An Illustrated Anthology* (London, Sidgwick and Jackson, 1965), p. 27.
47. Kirby, *Happenings*, p. 27.
48. Kirby, "The Activity: A New Art Form," *The Art of Time: Essays on the Avant-Garde* (New York: E.P. Dutton, 1969), pp. 160–5.
49. Kirby, *Happenings*, p. 43.
50. Kirby, *Happenings*, p. 30.
51. Kirby, *Happenings*, p. 32.
52. Rebecca Schneider, *The Explicit Body in Performance* (London and New York: Routledge, 1997).
53. James Hatch, "Some African Influences on the Afro-American Theatre," *The Theatre of Black Americans* (ed.) Erroll Hill (New York: Applause, 1980), pp. 19–20.
54. Rosalind Krauss, "Pictorial Space and the Question of Documentary," *Artforum* 10.3 (November 1971), 63.
55. Singerman, *Art Subjects*, p. 178.
56. It is telling that a recent issue of *October* on the "Obsolescence" of professional art criticism cited the anti-academic histories of "first generation Conceptualists." See George Baker *et al.*, "Round Table: The Present Conditions of Art Criticism," *October* 100 (Spring 2002), pp. 200–28.
57. Kaprow, "Un-Artist," (details already given in n. 2), p. 107.
58. Jon McKenzie, *Perform or Else: From Discipline to Performance* (New York: Routledge, 2001), p. 49.
59. Andrew Ross, "Defenders of the Faith and the New Class," *Intellectuals: Aesthetics, Politics, Academics* (ed.) Bruce Robbins (Minneapolis: University of Minnesota Press, 1990), p. 128; Alvin Gouldner, *The Future of Intellectuals and the Rise of the New Class* (New York: Continuum, 1979).
60. Kaprow, "Un-Artist," p. 107.

61. Allan Kaprow, "The Artist as a Man of the World," *Essays on the Blurring of Art and Life*, p. 55.

62. Lucy Lippard, *Six Years: The Dematerialization of the Art Object from 1966 to 1972* (New York: Praeger, 1973), p. 8.

63. Rosalind Krauss, *The Originality of the Avant-Garde and Other Modernist Myths* (Cambridge, MA and London: The Massachusetts Institute of Technology Press, 1999), p. 209.

64. Quoted in Sally Banes, *Greenwich Village, 1963* (Durham and London: Duke University Press, 1993), pp. 92–3.

65. De Man, *Allegories of Reading: Figural Language in Rousseau, Nietzsche, Rilke, and Proust* (New Haven: Yale University Press, 1979), p. 9.

66. Barbara Johnson, "Gender Theory and the Yale School," *A World of Difference* (Johns Hopkins University Press, 1988), p. 41.

67. Trisha Brown, "An Interview," *The 20th Century Performance Reader*, eds. Noel Witts and Michael Huxley (Routledge, 1996), p. 125.

68. Grotowski, *Towards*, p. 15.

69. Grotowski, *Towards*, p. 24.

70. Greenberg, "Modernist Painting," p. 194.

71. Grotowski, *Towards*, p. 15.

72. Greenberg, "After," 27.

73. Philip Auslander, *From Acting to Performance: Essays in Modernism and Postmodernism* (London and New York: Routledge, 1997), p. 56.

74. Singerman, *Art Subjects*, p. 156; he quotes Jurgen Habermas, "Modernity-an Incomplete Project," *The Anti-Aesthetic: Essays on Postmodern Culture* (ed.) Hal Foster (Port Townsend, WA: Bay Press 1983), p. 9.

CHAPTER FIVE

1. Catherine Gallagher and Stephen Greenblatt, *Practicing New Historicism* (University of Chicago Press, 2000), p. 17.

2. Victor Turner, *From Ritual to Theatre* (New York: Performing Arts Journal Publications, 1982), p. 97.

3. Clifford Geertz, "Blurred Genres: The Refiguration of Social Thought," (reprinted) *Local Knowledge* (New York: Basic Books, 1983), p. 19.

4. Clifford Geertz, "Thick Description: Toward an Interpretive Theory of Culture," *The Interpretation of Cultures* (New York: Basic Books, 1973).

5. Joseph Roach and Janelle Reinelt, *Critical Theory and Performance* (Ann Arbor: University of Michigan Press, 1992), pp. 9–15, 293–8.

6. Michael Quinn, "*Theatrewissenschaft* in the History of Theatre Study," *Theatre Survey* 32 (1991), 123–36; Marvin Carlson,

"Theatre and Performance at a Time of Shifting Disciplines," *Theatre Research International* 26.2 (2001), 137–44.

7. Stephen Greenblatt, *Renaissance Self-Fashioning* (University of Chicago Press, 1980).

8. Catherine Gallagher, *The Industrial Reformation of English Fiction* (University of Chicago, Press, 1985); Walter Benn Michaels, *The Gold Standard and the Logic of Naturalism* (Berkeley: University of California Press, 1987); D.A. Miller, *The Novel and the Police* (Berkeley: University of California Press, 1987).

9. Catherine Gallagher and Stephen Greenblatt, *Practicing New Historicism* (University of Chicago Press, 2000), p. 2.

10. Stephen Greenblatt, "Invisible Bullets: Renaissance Authority and Its Subversion," *Glyph* 8 (1981), 42–56.

11. Carolyn Porter, "Are We Being, Historical yet" *The South Atlantic Quarterly* 87:4 (Fall 1988), 765.

12. Clifford Geertz, *Interpretation of Cultures* (New York: Basic Books, 1973), p. 9.

13. Catherine Gallagher and Stephen Greenblatt, *Practicing New Historicism* (University of Chicago Press, 2000), p. 21.

14. James Clifford, *Predicament of Culture: Twentieth-Century Ethnography, Literature, and Art* (Cambridge: Harvard University Press, 1988), p. 94.

15. Michael Warner, "Literary Studies and the History of the Book" *The Book* 12 (1987), p. 5.

16. Stephen Greenblatt, "Introduction," *The Forms of Power and the Power of Forms in the Renaissance* (Norman, OK: Oklahoma University Press, 1982), p. 5.

17. Donald R. Kelley, "Practicing New Historicism (Review)," *Journal of Interdisciplinary History* 32.1 (2001), 99–101, 99.

18. Joan W. Scott, "The Evidence of Experience," *Critical Inquiry* 17 (Summer 1991), 773–97. For a discussion of the linguistic turn in relation to performance history, see Shannon Jackson, *Lines of Activity* (Ann Arbor: University of Michigan Press, 2000), pp. 18–35.

19. Carolyn Porter, "Are We Being Historical Yet?," *The South Atlantic Quarterly* 87:4 (Fall 1988), 743–86, 780.

20. Porter, "Are We Being," 779.

21. Carolyn Porter, "History and Literature: 'After the New Historicism'" *New Literary History* 21.2 (Winter 1990), 255.

22. Thomas Postlewait and Bruce McConachie, *Interpreting the Theatrical Past* (University of Iowa Press, 1989).

23. Bruce McConachie, "New Historicism and Theatre History," *The Performance of Power* ed. Sue-Ellen Case and Janelle Reinelt (University of Iowa Press, 1991), pp. 265–71. Roach and Reinelt, *Critical Theory and Performance*, p. 295.

24. Porter, "Are We Being," 770.
25. Roach and Reinelt, *Critical Theory and Performance*, p. 295.
26. Geertz, "Blurred Genres," 25.
27. Geertz, "Blurred Genres," 24.
28. Erving Goffman, *The Presentation of Self in Everyday Life* (New York: Doubleday, 1959).
29. Goffman, *Presentation*, p. 21.
30. Goffman, *Presentation*, p. 12.
31. Goffman, *Presentation*, p. 126.
32. Goffman, *Presentation*, p. 127.
33. Goffman, *Interaction Ritual: Essays on Face-to-Face Behavior* (New York: Anchor Books, 1967); *Frame Analysis: An Essay on the Organization of Experience* (New York: Harper & Row, 1974).
34. Goffman, *Gender Advertisements* (New York: Harper & Row, 1979).
35. Geertz, "Blurred Genres," 28.
36. Victor Turner, *Dramas Fields, and Metaphors* (Ithaca: Cornell University Press, 1974), p. 37.
37. Dwight Conquergood, "Poetics, Play, Process, and Power: The Performative Turn in Anthropology," *Text and Performance Quarterly* 1 (1989), 82–95.
38. Naomi Schor, *Reading in Detail: Aesthetics and the Feminine* (New York: Methuen, 1987), p. 3.
39. Schor, *Reading in Detail*, p. 4.
40. Sherry Ortner, "Is Female to Male as Nature is to Culture?" *Woman, Culture, and Society* (eds.) Michelle Zimbalist Rosaldo and Louise Lamphere (Stanford University Press, 1974), pp. 79, 81.
41. Schor, *Reading in Detail*, p. 17.
42. Schor, *Reading in Detail*, p. 20.
43. Hannah More, *Strictures on the Modern System of Female Education* (Boston: Joseph Bumstead, 1802), p. 61.
44. Catharine Beecher, *Treatise on Domestic Economy* (New York: March, Capen, Lyon, and Webb), pp. 36–7.
45. Lora Romero, *Homefronts: Domesticity and Its Critics* (Durham: Duke University Press, 1999), p. 64.
46. Nancy Armstrong, *Desire and Domestic Fiction: A Political History of the Novel* (Oxford University Press, 1989).
47. D.A. Miller, *The Novel and the Police*, p. 10.
48. Romero, *Homefronts*, p. 50.
49. Quote in Romero, *Homefronts*; Ann Douglas, *Feminization of American Culture* (New York: Anchor/Doubleday, 1978), p. 81.
50. Schechner, "Restoration of Behavior," p. 110.
51. Schechner, "Restoration of Behavior," p. 113.
52. Rebecca Schneider, *The Explicit Body in Performance* (New York: Routledge, 1997), p. 4 and elsewhere.

53. Laura Levin, "Masculinist Rites: Ritual Models and Gender Identity," Unpublished Essay.

54. Richard Schechner, *Environmental Theater* (New York and London: Applause, 1994), p. 100.

55. Schechner, *Environmental Theater*, 99.

56. Pierre Nora, "Between Memory and History: *Les Lieux de Memoire*," *Representations* 26 (Spring 1989), 7–24.

57. Paul Connerton, *How Societies Remember* (Cambridge University Press, 1989), pp. 72–104.

58. Paul Gilroy, *The Black Atlantic: Modernity and Double Consciousness* (Cambridge: Harvard University Press, 1993).

59. Richard Schechner, "Ritual, Violence, Creativity," *Creativity/ Anthropology* (eds.) Smadar Lavie, Kirin Narayan, Renato Rosaldo (Ithaca: Cornell University Press, 1993), pp. 297, 298.

60. Joseph Roach, *Cities of the Dead* (New York: Columbia University Press, 1996), pp. 218, 220.

61. Roach, *Cities of the Dead*, p. 218.

62. Dion Boucicault *The Octoroon, Plays by Dion Boucicault* (Cambridge University Press), p. 138.

63. Roach, *Cities of the Dead*, p. 218.

64. Claudia Tate, *Domestic Allegories of Political Desire* (New York and Oxford: Oxford University Press, 1992), p. 66.

65. Claudia Tate, *Domestic Allegories of Political Desire* (New York and Oxford: Oxford University Press, 1992), p. 67.

CHAPTER SIX

1. Brander Matthews, *The Development of the Drama* (New York: Scribner, 1904), p. 96.

2. Quoted in Tejumola Olaniyan, *Scars of Conquest/Masks of Resistance* (New York: Oxford University Press, 1995), p. 128.

3. Adrian Piper, "Passing for White, Passing for Black," First published in *Transition* 58 (1992), 4.

4. Adrian Piper, "Xenophobia and the Indexical Present: Lecture I," *Out of Order Out of Sight* (Cambridge, MA: The Massachusetts Institute of Technology Press, 1996), p. 247.

5. Piper, "Xenophobia and the Indexical Present: Lecture I," *Out of Order*, p. 248.

6. Piper, "On Wearing Three Hats," Originally presented at the Third Annual Tillie K. Lubin Symposium, *Who Is She? Conversations with Multi-Talented Women* (with Mary Catherine Bateson, Perri Klass, Kristin Linklater, and Sherry Turkle) at Brandeis University/Rose Art Museum on March 17, 1996. Available at <http://adrianpiper.com>

7. Piper, "On Wearing Three Hats."
8. Piper, "On Wearing Three Hats."
9. Shoshana Felman, *The Literary Speech Act: Don Juan with J.L. Austin, or Seduction in Two Languages* (Ithaca, NY: Cornell University Press, 1983), p. 17.
10. Ibid.
11. Jacques Derrida, "Signature/Event/Context," *Margins of Philosophy* (University of Chicago Press, 1982).
12. Judith Butler, *Bodies That Matter: On the Discursive Limits of Sex* (New York: Routledge, 1993), p. 234.
13. Adam Shatz, "Black Like Me: Conceptual Artist Adrian Piper Gets Under Your Skin," *Lingua Franca* 8.8 (November 1998), 40; quotes and ellipses added by Piper in (January 1999) response.
14. Adrian Piper, "Ways of Seeing: Letter to the Editor," *Lingua Franca* (January 1999), 7.
15. Piper, "Ways of Seeing", 94.
16. Judith Butler, *Excitable Speech* (New York: Routledge, 1997), p. 119.
17. Butler, *Excitable Speech*.
18. J.L. Austin, *How to Do Things with Words*, 2nd Edition (1962, Cambridge, MA: Harvard University Press, 1975), p. 22.
19. *Webster's New Collegiate Dictionary* (Springfield, MA: Merriam, 1958).
20. William Worthen, "Drama, Performativity, and Performance," *PMLA* 113.5 (October 1998), 1095.
21. Butler, *Bodies That Matter*, p. 234.
22. Jill Dolan, "Geographies of Learning: Theatre Studies, Performance, and the 'Performative,'" *Theatre Journal* 45 (1993), 420.
23. Elin Diamond, *Unmaking Mimesis* (London and New York: Routledge), p. 47.
24. Dolan, "Geographies of Learning," 434.
25. Elin Diamond, "Brechtian Theory/Feminist Theory" *TDR* (November 1988), 85.
26. Butler, *Excitable Speech*, p. 199.
27. José Esteban Munoz, *Disidentifications: Queers of Color and the Performance of Politics (Cultural Studies of the Americas, V.2)* (Minneapolis: University of Minnesota Press, 1999).
28. Butler, *Excitable Speech*, p. 99.
29. Eve Kosofsky Sedgwick, "Queer Performativity: Henry James's *The Art of the Novel*," *Gay and Lesbian Quarterly* 1.1 (1993).
30. Anne Cheng, *The Melancholy of Race: Psychoanalysis, Assimilation, and Hidden Grief* (Oxford and New York: Oxford University Press, 2000), p. 188.
31. Cherrie Moraga, "Preface," *This Bridge Called My Back* (New York: Kitchen Table Women of Color Press, 1981), p. xvii.
32. Moraga, "Preface," p. xvii.

33. Cherrie Moraga, "La Guera," *This Bridge*, pp. 28, 29.
34. Yvonne Yarbro-Bejarano, "Cherríe Moraga's *Shadow of a Man*: Touching the Wounds in Order to Heal," *Acting Out: Feminist Performances* (eds.) Lynda Hart and Peggy Phelan (Ann Arbor: University of Michigan Press, 1993), p. 87. Yarbro-Bejarano cites Wright, *Daily-Ledger-Post Dispatch* and Steven Winn, *San Francisco Chronicle* (November 11, 1990).
35. Diana Son, "R.A.W. ('Cause I'm a Woman)," *Contemporary Plays by Women of Color* (eds.) Kathy Perkins and Roberta Uno (New York: Routledge, 1996), p. 292.
36. Diana Son, "Artistic Statement," *Contemporary Plays by Women of Color*, p. 289.
37. Son, "R.A.W.," p. 291.
38. Cheng, *The Melancholy of Race*, p. 4.
39. Cheng, *The Melancholy of Race*, p. 5.
40. Ntozake Shange, *for colored girls who have considered suicide/when the rainbow is enuf* (New York: MacMillan, 1977).
41. Butler, *Excitable Speech*, p. 199.
42. Ntozake Shange, *Spell #7* (New York: Samuel French, 1980), p. 9.
43. Shange, *Spell #7*, p. 9
44. Shange, *Spell #7*, p. 44.
45. Richard Eder, "Stage: Ntozake Shange in her "Spell #7" at the Public," *New York Times* (June 3, 1979); David Gelman, "This Time Shange Casts No Spell," *Newsweek* (July 30, 1979); Deborah Geis, "Distraught Laughter: Monologue in Ntozake Shange's Theater Pieces," *Feminine Focus* (ed.) Enoch Brater (New York: Oxford University Press, 1989), p. 221.
46. Peggy Phelan, *Unmarked: The Politics of Performance* (New York: Routledge, 1993), p. 96.
47. Sandra Richards, "Conflicting Impulses in the Plays of Ntozake Shange," *Black Literature Forum* 17.2 (Summer 1983), 76.
48. Geis, "Distraught Laughter," 77.
49. Anna Deavere Smith, *Twilight Los Angeles, 1992* (New York: Anchor Books, 1994), p. 139.
50. Richard Stayton, "A Fire in a Crowded Theatre," *American Theatre* (July/August 1993), 73.
51. John Lahr, "Under the Skin," *The New Yorker* (June 28, 1993), 90.
52. Ibid.
53. Christopher Meeks, "Twilight: Los Angeles 1992," *Legit* (June 28, 1993), 30.
54. Jack Kroll, "Fire in the City of Angels," *Newsweek* (June 28, 1993), 62.
55. Smith, *Twilight*, p. 152.
56. Tania Modleski, "Doing Justice to the Subjects," *Female Subjects in Black and White: Race, Psychoanalysis, Feminism* (eds.) Elizabeth

Abel, Barbara Christian, and Helene Moglen (Berkeley: University of California Press, 1997), p. 70.

57. Smith, *Twilight*, p. 134.
58. Smith, *Twilight*, p. 135.
59. Smith, *Twilight*, p. 136.
60. Lahr, "Under the Skin," 93.
61. Smith, *Twilight*, p. 140.
62. Joseph Roach, "Reconstructing Theatre/History," 9.
63. Butler, *Excitable Speech*, p. 11.
64. Kroll, "Fire in the City of Angels," 62.
65. Bob Blanchard, "Drama of L.A.'s Anguished Soul," *The Progressive* (December 1993), 36.
66. Deavere Smith, "Anne Deavere Smith: The Word Becomes You," interview with Carol Martin, *TDR* 37.4 (Winter 1993), 49.
67. "PERSONAL REPORT" From Professor Adrian M.S Piper to President Diana Chapman Walsh (July, 3 2000) Wellesley College. Available at <http://adrian.piper.com> Piper's italics.
68. "PERSONAL REPORT" From Professor Adrian M.S. Piper to President Diana Chapman Walsh.
69. Piper, "My Job Description". Available at <http://www.adrian.piper.com>
70. Howard Singerman, *Art Subjects*, p. 5.

Select bibliography

Abbott, Andrew, *The System of Professions: An Essay on the Division of Expert Labor* (University of Chicago Press, 1988).

Adler, Judith, *Artists in Offices: An Ethnography of an Academic Art Scene* (New Brunswick, NJ: Transaction Books, 1979).

Armstrong, Nancy, *Desire and Domestic Fiction: A Political History of the Novel* (Oxford University Press, 1989).

Auslander, Philip, "Evangelical Fervor," *The Drama Review* 39.4 (1995), 169–80.

  From Acting to Performance: Essays in Modernism and Postmodernism (London and New York: Routledge, 1997).

Austin, J.L., *How to Do Things with Words*, 2nd Edition (1962, Cambridge, MA.: Harvard University Press, 1975).

Banes, Sally, "Institutionalizing Avant-Garde Performance: A Hidden History of University Patronage in the United States," *Contours of the Theatrical Avant-Garde: Performance and Textuality* (ed.) James M. Harding (Ann Arbor: University of Michigan Press, 2000), pp. 217–38.

  Judson Dance Theatre: Democracy's Body, 1962–1964, PhD Thesis (New York University Press, 1980).

Bell, Elizabeth, "Performance Studies as Women's Work," *Text and Performance Quarterly* 13 (October 1993), 362.

Bentley, Eric, *The Life of the Drama* (New York: Atheneum, 1967).

  The Playwright as Thinker (1946, New York: Harcourt, Brace, and World, 1967).

Berlin, James, *Rhetoric and Reality: Writing Instruction in American Colleges, 1900–1985* (Carbondale, IL: Southern Illinois University Press, 1987).

Bourdieu, Pierre, *Homo Academicus* (trans.) Peter Collier (Cambridge UK: Polity Press, 1988).

Brooks, Cleanth and Robert Heilman, *Understanding Drama* (1945, New York: Henry Holt, 1948).

  and Robert Penn Warren, *Understanding Poetry* (New York: Holt, Rinehart, and Winston, Inc., 1960).

John Purser and Robert Penn Warren, *An Approach to Literature* (New York: Appleton-Century, 1952).

Brown, Trisha, "An Interview," *The 20th Century Performance Reader*, eds. Noel Witts and Michael Huxley (London: Routledge, 1996).

Brustein, Robert, "Why American Plays Are Not Literature," *American Drama and Its Critics* (ed.) Alan Downer (University of Chicago Press, 1965), pp. 245–55; originally appeared in *Harper's Magazine* (1959), 209.

Butler, Judith, *Bodies That Matter: On the Discursive Limits of Sex* (New York: Routledge, 1993).

Excitable Speech (New York: Routledge, 1997).

Carlson, Marvin, *Performance: A Critical Introduction* (New York: Routledge, 1996).

"Theatre and Performance at a Time of Shifting Disciplines," *Theatre Research International* 26.2 (2001), 137–44.

Carter, Alexandra, *The Routledge Dance Studies Reader* (ed.) Alexandra Carter (New York: Routledge, 1998).

Cheng, Anne, *The Melancholy of Race: Psychoanalysis, Assimilation, and Hidden Grief* (Oxford and New York: Oxford University Press, 2000).

Clifford, James, *The Predicament of Culture: Twentieth-Century Ethnography, Literature, and Art* (Cambridge: Harvard University Press, 1988).

Connerton, Paul, *How Societies Remember* (Cambridge University Press, 1989).

Conquergood, Dwight, "Poetics, Play, Process, and Power: The Performative Turn in Anthropology," *Text and Performance Quarterly* 1 (1989), 82–95.

De Man, Paul, "The Epistemology of Metaphor," *Critical Inquiry* 5 (1978).

Allegories of Reading: Figural Language in Rousseau, Nietzsche, Rilke, and Proust (New Haven: Yale University Press, 1979).

Derrida, Jacques, *Of Grammatology*, trans. Gayatri Chakravorty Spivak (Baltimore and London: Johns Hopkins University Press, 1974), p. 97–164. Originally published in France in 1967 by Les Editions de Minuit.

Writing and Difference (trans.) Alan Bass (University of Chicago Press, 1978).

Margins of Philosophy (University of Chicago Press, 1982).

Diamond, Elin, *Unmaking Mimesis* (London and New York: Routledge).

Dolan, Jill, "Geographies of Learning: Theatre Studies, Performance, and the 'Performative,'" *Theatre Journal* 45 (1993), 417–41.

Douglas, Ann, *The Feminization of American Culture* (New York: Anchor/Doubleday, 1978).

Eagleton, Terry, *Literary Theory: An Introduction* (1983, Minneapolis: University of Minnesota Press, 1996).

Easthope, Anthony, *Literary into Cultural Studies* (London and New York: Routledge, 1991).

Edwards, Paul, "Unstoried: Teaching Literature in the Age of Performance Studies," *Theatre Annual* 52 (1999), 1–147.

Ehrenreich, Barbara and John, "The Professional-Managerial Class," *Between Labor and Capital* (ed.) Pat Walker (Boston: South End Press, 1979), pp. 5–49.

Felman, Shoshana, *The Literary Speech Act: Don Juan with J. L. Austin, or Seduction in Two Languages* (Ithaca, NY: Cornell University Press, 1983).

Fergusson, Francis, *The Idea of the Theater: The Art of Drama in Changing Perspective* (Princeton University Press, 1949).

Foucault, Michel, *The Archaeology of Knowledge and the Discourse on Language*, Trans. A.M. Sheridan Smith (New York: Pantheon, 1972).

Freud, Sigmund, *Civilization and Its Discontents* (1930), in *The Standard Edition of the Complete Psychological Works of Sigmund Freud*, ed. James Strachey (London: Hogarth Press and the Institute of Psycho-Analysis, 1986) 21:114.

Fried, Michael, "Art and Objecthood," *Art and Objecthood: Essays and Reviews* (University of Chicago Press, 1998).

Frye, Northrop, *Anatomy of Criticism* (Princeton University Press, 1967).

Gallagher, Catherine, "The New Materialism in Marxist Aesthetics," *Theory and Society: Renewal and Critique in Social Theory* 9 (1980), 633–46.

   The Industrial Reformation of English Fiction (University of Chicago Press, 1985).

   and Stephen Greenblatt, *Practicing New Historicism* (University of Chicago Press, 2000).

Garber, Marjorie, *Academic Instincts* (Princeton University Press, 2001).

Geertz, Clifford, *The Interpretation of Cultures* (New York: Basic Books, 1973).

   "Blurred Genres: The Refiguration of Social Thought," *Local Knowledge* (New York: Basic Books, 1983).

Gilroy, Paul, '*There Ain't No Black in the Union Jack*': *The Cultural Politics of Race and Nation* (University of Chicago Press, 1991).

   The Black Atlantic: Modernity and Double Consciousness (Cambridge: Harvard University Press, 1993).

Goffman, Erving, *The Presentation of Self in Everyday Life* (New York: Doubleday, 1959).

   Interaction Ritual: Essays on Face-to-Face Behavior (New York: Anchor Books, 1967).

Frame Analysis: An Essay on the Organization of Experience (New York: Harper & Row, 1974).

Gender Advertisements (New York: Harper & Row, 1979).

Gouldner, Alvin, *The Future of Intellectuals and the Rise of the New Class* (New York: Continuum, 1979).

Graff, Gerald, *Beyond the Culture Wars: How Teaching the Conflicts Can Revitalize American Education* (New York and London: W.W. Norton and Co., 1992).

Professing Literature: An Institutional History (University of Chicago Press, 1987).

and Michael Warner (eds.) *The Origins of Literary Studies in America* (London: Routledge, 1989).

Greenberg, Clement, "After Abstract Expressionism," *Art International* 6.5 (Summer 1962).

"Modernist Painting," *Art and Literature* (1965).

Greenblatt, Stephen, *Renaissance Self-Fashioning* (University of Chicago Press, 1980).

"Invisible Bullets: Renaissance Authority and Its Subversion," *Glyph* 8 (1981), 42–56.

The Forms of Power and the Power of Forms in the Renaissance (Norman, OK: Oklahoma University Press, 1982).

"Toward a Poetics of Culture," *New Historicism* (ed.) Aram Veeser (New York: Routledge, 1989).

Grotowski, Jerzy, *Towards a Poor Theatre* (Odin Teatrets Forlag, 1968).

Guillory, John, *Cultural Capital: The Problem of Literary Canon Formation* (University of Chicago Press, 1993).

Hale, Dorothy, *Social Formalism: The Novel from Henry James to the Present* (Palo Alto: Stanford University Press, 1998).

Hall, Stuart, "Communities, Nation, and Culture," *Cultural Studies* 7.3 (1993), 349–63.

"Cultural Studies and Its Theoretical Legacies," *The Stuart Hall Reader*, 277–85.

Hatch, James, "Some African Influences on the Afro-American Theatre," *The Theatre of Black Americans* (ed.) Erroll Hill (New York: Applause, 1980).

Black Image on the American Stage: A Bibliography of Plays and Musicals, 1770–1970 (New York: Drama Book Specialists, 1970).

"Speak to Me in Those Old Words, You know, Those La-La Words, Those Tung-Tung Sounds," *Yale/Theatre* 8.1 (Fall 1976), 25–34.

Higgins, John, *Raymond Williams: Literature, Marxism, and Cultural Materialism* (London: Routledge, 1999).

Hill, Errol (ed.) *The Theatre of Black Americans* (New York: Applause, 1980).

Hornby, Richard, "The Death of Literature and History," *Theatre Topics* 5.2 (September 1995).

Inglis, Fred, *Raymond Williams* (London and New York: Verso, 1995).

Isaacs, Edith, *The Negro in the Theatre* (New York: Theatre Arts Incorporated, 1947).

Jackson, Shannon, *Lines of Activity* (Ann Arbor: University of Michigan Press, 2000).

"Professing Performance: Disciplinary Genealogies," *The Drama Review* 45.1 (Spring 2001), 84–95.

Johnson, Barbara, "Translator's Introduction," in Jacques Derrida, *Dissemination* (University of Chicago Press, 1981).

A World of Difference (Johns Hopkins University Press, 1988).

Kaprow, Allan, *Essays on the Blurring of Art and Life* (Berkeley: University of California Press, 1993).

Kaye, Nick, "Elizabeth LeCompte: Interview," *The Twentieth-Century Performance Reader*, ed. Michael Huxley and Noel Witts (London: Routledge, 1996).

Kealiinohomoku, Joann, "An Anthropologist Looks at Ballet as a Form of Ethnic Dance," *What is Dance?: Readings in Theory and Criticism* (eds.) Roger Copeland and Marshall Cohen (Oxford University Press, 1983).

Kirby, Michael, *Happenings: An Illustrated Anthology* (London: Sidgwick, and Jackson, 1965).

The Art of Time: Essays on the Avant-Garde (New York: E.P. Dutton, 1969).

Krauss, Rosalind, "Pictorial Space and the Question of Documentary," *Artforum* 10.3 (November 1971).

The Originality of the Avant-Garde and Other Modernist Myths (Cambridge, MA and London: The Massachusetts Institute of Technology Press, 1999).

Kuklick, Bruce, "The Emergence of the Humanities," *South Atlantic Quarterly* 89.1 (1990).

Lee, Josephine, "Disciplining Theater and Drama in the English Department: Some Reflections on 'Performance' and Institutional History," *Text and Performance Quarterly* 19 (1999), 3.

Lesser, Wendy, *The Amateur: An Independent Life in Letters* (New York: Pantheon, 1999).

Lippard, Lucy, "Questions to Stella and Judd," *Minimal Art* (ed.) Gregory Battcock (New York: E.P. Dutton, 1968).

Six Years: The Dematerialization of the Art Object from 1966 to 1972 (New York: Praeger, 1973).

Margolin, Deb, "A Perfect Theatre for One: Teaching Performance Composition," *The Drama Review* 41.2 (Summer 1997).

McConachie, Bruce, "New Historicism and Theatre History," *The Performance of Power* (ed.) Sue-Ellen Case and Janelle Reinelt (University of Iowa Press, 1991).

McKenzie, Jon, *Perform or Else: From Discipline to Performance* (New York: Routledge, 2001).

Michaels, Walter Benn, *The Gold Standard and the Logic of Naturalism* (Berkeley: University of California Press, 1987).

Miller, D.A., *The Novel and the Police* (Berkeley: University of California Press, 1987).

Modleski, Tania, "Doing Justice to the Subjects," *Female Subjects in Black and White: Race, Psychoanalysis, Feminism* (eds.) Elizabeth Abel, Barbara Christian, and Helene Moglen (Berkeley: University of California Press, 1997).

Moraga, Cherrie, "Preface," *This Bridge Called My Back* (New York: Kitchen Table Women of Color Press, 1981), p. xvii.

Morris, Robert, "Notes on Sculpture, Part I," *Artforum* 4.6 (February 1966), 42–4.

Munoz, José Esteban, *Disidentifications: Queers of Color and the Performance of Politics (Cultural Studies of the Americas, V. 2)* (Minneapolis: University of Minnesota Press, 1999).

Nelson, Cary, Paula A. Treichler, and Lawrence Grossberg, "Cultural Studies: An Introduction," *Cultural Studies* (New York: Routledge, 1992).

Nelson, Cary, "Always Already Cultural Studies," *Manifesto of a Tenured Radical* (New York University Press, 1997), pp. 52–74.

Niggli, Josephina, *Mexican Folk Plays* (ed.) Frederick Koch (Chapel Hill: University of North Carolina Press, 1938).

Nora, Pierre, "Between Memory and History: *Les Lieux de Memoire,*" *Representations* 26 (Spring 1989), 7–24.

Olaniyan, Tejumola, *Scars of Conquest/Masks of Resistance* (New York: Oxford University Press, 1995).

Oleson, Alexandra and John Voss, *The Organization of Knowledge in Modern America, 1860–1920* (Baltimore: Johns Hopkins University Press, 1979), pp. x–xi.

Ortner, Sherry, "Is Female to Male as Nature is to Culture?" *Woman, Culture, and Society* (eds.) Michelle Zimbalist Rosaldo and Louise Lamphere (Stanford University Press, 1974).

Phelan, Peggy, "Introduction," *The Ends of Performance* (eds.) Peggy Phelan and Jill Lane (New York University Press, 1998).

Unmarked: The Politics of Performance (New York: Routledge, 1993).

Piper, Adrian, "Passing for White, Passing for Black," First published in *Transition* 58 (1992).

Out of Order, Out of Sight, Vols. 1 and 2 (Cambridge MA: Massachusetts Institute of Technology Press, 1996).

Porter, Carolyn, "Are We Being Historical Yet?," *The South Atlantic Quarterly* 87:4 (Fall 1988), 743–86, 780.

"History and Literature: 'After the New Historicism'" *New Literary History* 21.2 (Winter 1990).

Postlewait, Thomas and Bruce McConachie, *Interpreting the Theatrical Past* (University of Iowa Press, 1989).

Quinn, Michael, "*Theatrewissenschaft* in the History of Theatre Study," *Theatre Survey* 32 (1991), 123–36.

Richards, Sandra, "Conflicting Impulses in the Plays of Ntozake Shange," *Black Literature Forum* 17.2 (Summer 1983).

Roach, Joseph and Janelle Reinelt, *Critical Theory and Performance* (Ann Arbor: University of Michigan Press, 1992).

Roach, Joseph, *Cities of the Dead* (New York: Columbia University Press, 1996).

"Reconstructing Theatre/History," *Theatre Topics* 9.1 (March 1999), 3–10.

Robb, Margaret, "The Elocutionary Movement and Its Chief Figures," *History of Speech Education in America* (ed.) Karl R. Wallace (New York: Appleton-Century-Crofts, 1954), pp. 178–201.

Robbins, Bruce, ed. *Intellectuals: Aesthetics, Politics, Academics* (Minneapolis: University of Minnesota Press, 1990).

Roebuck, Julian B. and Komanduri S. Murty, *Historically Black Colleges and Universities: Their Place in Higher Education* (Westport CN: Praeger, 1993).

Romero, Lora, *Homefronts: Domesticity and Its Critics* (Durham: Duke University Press, 1999).

Ross, Andrew, "Defenders of the Faith and the New Class," *Intellectuals: Aesthetics, Politics, Academics* (ed.) Bruce Robbins (Minneapolis: University of Minnesota Press, 1990).

Rudolph, Frederick, *The American College and University: A History* (New York: Vintage Books, 1962).

Schechner, Richard, "A New Paradigm for Theatre in the Academy," *The Drama Review* 36.4 (1992), 7–10.

"Ritual, Violence, Creativity," *Creativity/Anthropology* (eds.) Smadar Lavie, Kirin Narayan, Renato Rosaldo (Ithaca: Cornell University Press, 1993).

Between Theater and Anthropology (Philadelphia: Pennsylvania University Press, 1985).

Schneider, Rebecca, *The Explicit Body in Performance* (London and New York: Routledge, 1997).

Schor, Naomi, *Reading in Detail: Aesthetics and the Feminine* (New York: Methuen, 1987).

Scott, Joan W., "The Evidence of Experience," *Critical Inquiry* 17 (Summer 1991), 773–97.

Sedgwick, Eve Kosofsky, "Queer Performativity: Henry James's *The Art of the Novel*," *Gay and Lesbian Quarterly* 1.1 (1993).

Shange, Ntozake, *for colored girls who have considered suicide/when the rainbow is enuf* (New York: MacMillan, 1977).

Spell #7 (New York: Samuel French, 1980).

Singerman, Howard, *Art Subjects: Making Artists in the American University* (Berkeley: University of California Press, 1999).

Sjølander, Sverre, "Long-Term and Short-Term Interdisciplinary Work: Difficulties, Pitfalls, and Built-In Failures," *Inter-Disciplinarity Revisited: Re-assessing the Concept in the Light of Institutional Experience* (eds.) Lennart Levin and Ingemar Lind (Stockholm: OECD, SNBUC, Linkoping University, 1985), pp. 85–101.

Smith, Anna Deavere, *Twilight Los Angeles, 1992* (New York: Anchor Books, 1994).

Son, Diana, "R.A.W. ('Cause I'm a Woman)," *Contemporary Plays by Women of Color* (eds.) Kathy Perkins and Roberta Uno (New York: Routledge, 1996).

Southern, Eileen, *The Music of Black Americans: A History* (New York: W.W. Norton, 1971).

Spearman, Walter, *The Carolina Playmakers: The First Fifty Years* (Chapel Hill: University of North Carolina Press, 1970), p. 71.

Stayton, Richard, "A Fire in a Crowded Theatre," *American Theatre* (July/August 1993), 73.

Tate, Claudia, *Domestic Allegories of Political Desire* (New York and Oxford: Oxford University Press, 1992).

Traylor, Eleanor W., "Two Afro-American Contributions to Dramatic Form," *The Theatre of Black Americans* (ed.) Errol Hill (New York: Applause, 1980), pp. 45–60.

Turner, Victor, *Dramas Fields, and Metaphors* (Ithaca: Cornell University Press, 1974).

  From Ritual to Theatre (New York: Performing Arts Journal Publications, 1982).

  The Ritual Process (Cornell University Press, 1969).

Veysey, Laurence, *The Emergence of the American University* (University of Chicago Press, 1965).

  "The Plural Organized Worlds of the Humanities," *Organization of Knowledge in Modern America*, 1860–1920, eds. Oleson, A. and J. Voss (Johns Hopkins University Press, 1979).

Warner, Michael, "Literary Studies and the History of the Books," *The Book* 12 (1987).

Wendt, Ted, "The Displacement of the Aesthetic: Problems of Performance Studies," *Text and Performance Quarterly* 10 (1990), 248–56.

Williams, Raymond, *Culture and Society* (1958, New York: Columbia University Press, 1983).

  "Preface," *Modern Tragedy* (London: Chatto and Windus, 1961).

  Drama from Ibsen to Brecht (London: Chatto and Windus, 1968).

  "Drama in a Dramatised Society," Professorial address (Cambridge University Press, 1975); Reprinted in *Writing in Society* (London: Verso, 1983).

Problems of Materialism in Culture (London and New York: Verso, 1980).

Sociology of Culture (New York: Schocken, 1982).

Keywords: a Vocabulary of Culture and Society (New York: Oxford University Press, 1984).

Worthen, William, "Disciplines of the Text/Sites of Performance," *The Drama Review* 39.1 (1995), 13–28.

"Drama, Performativity, and Performance," *PMLA* 113.5 (October 1998), 1095.

Index

Abbott, Andrew 16
Abstract Expressionism 112, 130
Alarcon, Norma 180
amateurism *see* professionalism
American G.I. Bill 88
American Repertory Theatre (ART) 1
anthropology 4, 7, 8, 9, 36, 100, 105, 147, 149, 153
    gender and 162–163
Anzaldua, Gloria 180
Armstrong, Nancy 166
Artaud, Antonin 118–119, 120, 126, 127–128
Auslander, Philip 143
Austin, J.L. 2, 3, 12, 182, 186, 188, 207
    How to Do Things with Words 2–3, 182

Bacon, Wallace 9
Bahktin, Mikhail 12
Baker, George Pierce 35, 40–41, 43, 44–45, 47–48, 51–53, 55–56, 57, 58–59, 61, 63–64, 65, 74, 75, 85, 150, 216
    "The Mind of the Undergraduate" 44
    Shakespeare as a Dramatist 61
    Specimens of Argumentation 55
Banes, Sally 113, 128
Barry, Phillip 71
Bateson, Gregory 12
Bauman, Richard 12
Beecher, Catherine 165, 168
    Treatise on Domestic Economy 165
Bell, Elizabeth 55, 68
Benjamin, Walter 139
Bennett, William 22

Bentley, Eric 86, 88, 89–91
    The Playwright as Thinker 89
Berlin, James 57
Bérubé, Michael 29, 40
Bhabha, Homi 181
Bildung 18–19, 21, 22, 25, 219
Black Mountain College 127, 130
Blackmur, R.P. 88
Bloom, Harold 22
Boucicault, Dion
    The Octoroon 172–173
Bourdieu, Pierre
    Homo Academicus 27
Brecht, Bertolt 190, 205
Brecht, George
    Recipe 136
Breen, Robert 9
British Education Act 88
Brooks, Cleanth 88–89, 92
    An Approach to Literature 88–89
    Understanding Drama 88
    Understanding Poetry 88–89
Brown v. Board 198
Brown, Trisha 139–140
Brustein, Robert 79–80, 81, 84–85, 86–87, 89, 209
    "Why Plays Are Not Literature" 79
Burke, Kenneth 12
Butler, Judith 12, 14, 183–184, 189–190, 199, 205
    Bodies That Matter 189
    Excitable Speech 184, 186–187, 190, 216
    Gender Trouble 189

Cage, John 110, 129
Carlson, Marvin 51, 151
    Performance: a Critical Introduction 12

Carter, Alexandra 41
Chaiken, Joseph
  The Presence of the Actor 127
Chekhov, Anton 99
  Three Sisters 110
Cheng, Anne 198
  The Melancholy of Race 192
class 25–29, 37–38, 43, 45, 48, 51,
  58, 69, 74–75, 85, 86, 97, 102,
  131–132, 180
  domesticity and 165
  literality and 132
  race and 213–215
  racialization and 211
  see also professionalism
Clifford, James
  Predicament of Culture 153
Conquergood, Dwight 9, 23, 161
Crenshaw, Kimberlé 180, 193
cultural studies 23, 35, 36, 80–83, 90,
  94, 97, 149, 150, 219
Cunningham, Merce 110, 129
Curry, Samuel 54

D'Souza, Dinesh 22
Dada 130
dance 5, 7, 8, 11, 12–13, 36, 41, 64,
  74, 103, 114, 129, 142, 188,
  189
deconstruction 112, 113, 115, 117,
  120, 124–125, 127, 134, 138,
  144, 182, 219
  class and 139–141
  feminism and 139
  gender and 139–141
  literality and 139
DeMan, Paul 116–117, 124–125,
  126, 128–129, 131, 134, 138
  Allegories of Reading 138
  "Epistemology of Metaphor"
  119–120
Derrida, Jacques 12, 14, 112,
  116–119, 120, 121, 124–127,
  128–129, 134, 139, 182,
  188
  De la Grammatologie 117, 126
Dewey, John 12
Diamond, Elin 189, 190
Dickinson, Thomas 41
Dolan, Jill 98, 189, 190
Douglas, Ann
  Feminization of American Culture
  167

Douglas, Mary 9
drama 5, 23, 25, 35, 40, 42, 44, 51,
  59, 60–61, 63, 64, 65–66, 75–76,
  77, 79–87, 88–108, 150, 158,
  159, 178, 188, 189, 191, 192,
  216
  dramatic arts 61
  dramatic literature 24, 51, 60,
  64
Drummond, A.M. 93
DuBois, W.E.B. 43, 103

Eagleton, Terry 96
  Literary Theory 87
Easthope, Anthony 83
Edwards, Paul 41, 54
Ehrenreich, John and Barbara 46–47,
  56
  "The Professional-Managerial
  Class" 26, 46–48
Eliot, Charles 45, 47, 50, 56, 57
Eliot, T.S. 90, 92–93, 94, 96–97
  *Notes Towards the Definition of
  Culture* 97
Emerson, Charles Wesley 54
Empson, William 88, 91
  Seven Types of Ambiguity 94

Felman, Shoshana 182
feminism 7, 9, 23, 25, 37, 81, 125,
  167, 169–170, 190, 192
  anthropology and 150, 163–164
  deconstruction and 139
  domesticity and 174–175
  race and 179–180, 193, 209–210
Féral, Josette 143
Fergusson, Francis 94–95, 105
  The Idea of the Theater 95
Fletcher, John 67
Foucault, Michel 1, 4–5, 6, 10, 11,
  30, 38, 77, 82, 148, 150, 160,
  164–168, 180
  Language, counter-memory, practice
  4–5
Freud, Sigmund 31
Fried, Michael 116–117, 120–127,
  128–129, 130, 131, 134, 135,
  136, 137, 139, 141,
  143–144
  "Art and Objecthood" 117, 121,
  136, 142
Frye, Northrop
  Anatomy of Criticism 88

Gallagher, Catherine 106, 107, 146, 153
The Industrial Reformation of English Fiction 151
Garber, Marjorie 1
Gassner, John 90–94, 95, 96, 99, 103
"There is No American Drama" 90
Gates, Henry Louis 106
Geertz, Clifford 146–148, 152–153, 156, 159, 160–161, 164
"Blurred Genres" 146
"Common Sense is a Cultural System" 164
The Interpretation of Cultures 152
Geis, Deborah 205
gender 29, 36, 37–38, 43, 48, 54, 58, 65–69, 70, 72, 76, 86–87, 92, 93, 106, 131–132, 150, 162–173, 180, 190, 196, 198
domesticity and 165–168
institutionalization of performance and 43–44, 48, 51, 54–55, 58
literality and 132
performance studies and 174–175
performativity and 183
university enrollment and 15, 22, 45, 48
whiteness and 203
Gilroy, Paul 81, 102, 103–105, 173
The Black Atlantic 82, 171
There Ain't No Black in the Union Jack 102
Glissant, Edouard 103
Goffman, Erving 12, 159–160, 164, 168
Frame Analysis 160
Gender Advertisements 160
Interaction Ritual 160
Presentation of the Self in Everyday Life 160
Gouldner, Alvin 26, 135
Graff, Gerald 11, 29, 48
"The Great Color Purple Hoax" 23
The Origins of Literary Studies in America 53
Gramsci, Antonio 5
Granville-Barker, Harley 71
Greenberg, Clement 116–117, 121, 122, 123, 125, 126, 128–129, 130, 134, 137, 141, 142, 143
Greenblatt, Stephen 146, 152–153
"Invisible Bullets" 152

Renaissance Self-Fashioning 151
Grotowski, Jerzy 127–128, 141
Towards a Poor Theatre 127
Grossberg, Lawrence 81, 106
Guillory, John 4–5, 25, 29, 48, 50, 84

Hale, Dorothy 106–107
Hall, Stuart 81, 97, 102, 103
Hansen, Al 131
Happenings 128, 130, 137
Harkness, Edward 71
Hart, James Morgan 58
Harvard University 15, 40, 44, 45, 56, 64, 65, 67, 69–73, 76, 176
Hatch, James 104
Hewitt, Bernard 93
Hill, Errol 104
Hirsch, E.D. 22
Hoggart, Richard 97
Uses of Literacy 97
Hornby, Richard 24
"The Death of Literature and History" 23
Hunt, Elizabeth 68
Hutcheon, Linda 14

Ibsen, Henrik 63, 101
Inglis, Fred 98, 101
interdisciplinarity 4, 7–8, 14, 23, 30, 32, 77, 79, 81–108, 114, 117, 123–124, 130, 134, 143, 147, 149, 154, 155, 156, 158, 217
anti-disciplinarity 123
disciplinarity 6, 7, 38, 82, 123
gender, race, class and 25
intra-disciplinarity 7
textuality and 155
Isaacs, Edith
The Negro in the Theatre 93, 104

Johnson, Barbara 106, 117, 139
Johnston, Jill 132
Jonson, Ben 49
Judd, Donald 121, 124, 126
Judson Dance Theater, the 127

Kaprow, Allan 109, 110, 131, 132, 135
18 Happenings in 6 Parts 130, 131
"Education of the Un-Artist" 134
Kaye, Nick 110–111, 113, 125, 139
Kealiinohomoku, Joann 12

"An Anthropologist Looks at Ballet
    as a Form of Ethnic Dance" 12
Kelley, Donald 154
Kerr, Harry 55–56
Kershaw, Baz 23
Kimball, Roger 22
King, Deborah 180
Kinne, Wisner Payne 59
Kirby, Michael 110, 129–131, 147
Kittredge, George Lyman 40, 44–45,
    47, 49–52, 58, 63–64, 70
Koch, Frederick 41, 44
Krauss, Rosalind 133, 135–136
Kuklick, Bruce 8

Lacan, Jacques 12, 180
Lahr, John 208
Lasch, Christopher
    Feminization of American Culture
    167
Leavis, F.R. 95
    The Great Tradition 96
Leavis, Q.D. 96, 97
    Fiction and the Reading Public 96
LeCompte, Elizabeth 110–115, 125,
    137
Levin, Laura 169
Lippard, Lucy 135
literary studies 2, 4, 12, 44, 48, 53,
    54, 57, 66–67, 76, 94–101,
    105–108, 116
    English 21, 24, 42, 44, 48–51, 52,
        55, 58, 59, 64, 65, 69, 74, 83,
        87
    gender and 163, 167
    Literature 8, 30, 36, 42, 54, 55, 60,
        62, 66, 67, 70, 75, 77, 79,
        81–93, 114, 149, 150
    new historicism and 151–155
    text 62, 157–158, 159
Living Theatre, the 127
Locke, Alain 43, 103
Locke, John 125, 131, 138
    Essay Concerning Human
    Understanding 119–120
Lowell, Lawrence 70–71
Lyly, John
    Endymion 51

McConachie, Bruce 156, 158
    Interpreting the Theatrical Past 156
McKenzie, Jon 8, 10, 30, 135

McNamara, Brooks 156
McRobbie, Angela 81
Margolin, Deb 109
Matthews, Brander 41, 60–61, 64,
    85, 150, 176, 179, 189
    The Development of Drama 60
Merleau-Ponty, Maurice 28
Meserve, Walter 93
Michael, Walter Benn
    The Gold Standard the Logic of
    Naturalism 151
Miller, D.A.
    The Novel and the Police 151, 166
Miller, Harriett 55
Mills, C. Wright 29
Minimalism 121–126, 133, 136, 142
    literalist art 122–126, 130, 133
Modleski, Tania 209
Moody, Richard 93
Moraga, Cherríe 193–195
    Giving Up the Ghost 194
    Shadow of a Man 194–195
    This Bridge Called My Back 193
More, Hannah 165
Morrill Federal Land Grant 16
Morris, Meagan 105
Morris, Robert 110, 121, 122, 124,
    126
Moulton, Richard 49, 52, 60
multiculturalism 7, 22, 23, 179
Muñoz, José 191, 205

Nelson, Cary 29
new criticism 87–92, 94–96, 100,
    101, 106, 116, 151, 154, 156,
    219
new historicism 149, 150–155, 161,
    165, 167, 219
    literary studies and 151–155,
        157–158
    theatre and 156–159
New Lafayette Theatre
    Ritual To Bind Together and
        Strengthen Black People So That
        They Can Survive the Long
        Struggle That Is To Come 132
New York University (NYU) 8, 9
    Tisch School of the Arts 8
Niggli, Josephina 44
Noh Theatre 110–112
Northwestern University 8, 9,
    147

Ohmann, Richard
  English in America 40
Oldenburg, Claes
  Washes 131, 132
Ortner, Sherry 163–164
  "Is Female to Male as Nature is to
    Culture?" 162

performance art 11, 82, 188
performance studies 2, 3–10, 11, 15,
    22, 23–24, 25, 30, 32, 36,
    77–78, 80–83, 95, 103–105,
    107–108, 110, 111, 113, 129,
    130, 135, 136, 147–148, 156,
    159, 173–175, 178, 199
  class and 25–29
  feminism and 25
  interdisciplinarity and 7, 24
  origins of 7, 8–11, 23, 36, 144, 161
  theatre and 3–10, 15, 22, 23–24,
    35, 59, 143, 173
performativity 1–2, 3–10, 36,
    177–179, 216–217
  gender and 183
  race and 181–197, 199
  theatre and 178, 188–191
  theatricality and 178, 188, 192–197
  textuality and 188
Performing Garage, the 110, 127
Phelan, Peggy 8, 14, 204
  *Unmarked: The Ontology of
    Performance* 191
Phelps, William Lyons 57
philology 35, 48–52, 59, 60, 61–62,
    75, 88, 116, 150–151, 219
  new historicism and 154
Piper, Adrian 184–188, 195, 214,
    218–219
  "calling card" piece 185, 186
  Cornered 185
  "Passing for White, Passing for
    Black" 176–179
Plato 3
Pollock, Jackson 130
Pop Art 128
Porter, Carolyn 157–158, 168
postcolonial studies 181
Postlewait, Tom
  Interpreting the Theatrical Past
    156
postmodernism 110–114, 121,
    137–141
  literality and 132–134, 136

professionalism 45–49, 51, 54, 58,
    60, 67, 68, 76, 83, 89, 95, 109,
    113, 114, 133, 151, 217
  amateurism and 17–18, 28, 62
  class and 5, 134–136
  "Professional-Managerial Class"
    26, 45, 56, 57, 75
  postmodernism and 133–134,
    145

Quinn, Michael 51, 151

race 29, 37, 93–94, 106, 131–132,
    167, 175
  anti-racist politics 37–38, 81,
    176–177
  class and 213–215
  critical race studies 180
  domesticity and 165, 172
  identity and 177–181, 202–206,
    208–210
  institutionalization of performance
    and 43–44
  nation and 102–105, 173, 196
  performativity and 181–197, 199,
    204–216
  racial injury 197–206
  racialization 179, 192, 203, 206,
    211
  theatricality and 204–216
  university enrollment and 16, 22,
    45
Rainer, Yvonne 110, 132
  Dance for 3 People and 6 Arms 131
Ransom, John Crowe 88
Reinelt, Janelle 153, 156, 158
  Critical Theory and Performance 150
Representations 151–153, 158
Reuben Gallery 127
rhetoric 4, 7, 9, 44, 51, 52, 53, 56,
    58, 69, 116, 178, 182, 216
  anti-rhetorical prejudice 119
  oratory and 53, 54, 63, 66
Richards, I.A. 87
Richards, Sandra 205
Roach, Joseph 40, 41, 62, 153, 156,
    158
  Cities of the Dead 170–173
  Critical Theory and Performance 150
Robb, Margaret 54
Romero, Lora 166, 169
  *Homefronts: Domesticity and Its
    Critics* 166–167

Ross, Andrew 29, 135
Rousseau, Jean Jacques 120, 121
  Confessions 117
Rudolph, Frederick 19
Ryle, Gilbert 153

San Francisco Actors Workshop, the
  127
Schechner, Richard 8, 9, 14, 23, 80,
  97, 110, 129, 131, 143, 147,
  161, 168–169, 171
Schneemann, Carolee 110, 132
Schneider, Rebecca 132, 139,
  169
Schor, Naomi 170
  Reading in Detail 162
Scott, Joan Wallach 155
Sedgwick, Eve Kosofsky 12, 106,
  183–184, 192, 201
Shakespeare, William 24, 52, 53, 61
  Hamlet 24
Shange, Ntozake 176, 198–206
  *for colored girls who have considered
    suicide when the rainbow is enuf*
    198, 202
  Spell #7 198–206
Shatz, Adam
  "Black Like Me" 185, 186
Shaw, Bernard 89
Singerman, Howard 112, 133, 144,
  219
Sjølander, Sverre 31
Smith, Anna Deavere 216, 217
  Twilight: Los Angeles 1992 207–215,
  217
Smith, Tony 121, 125, 132
Son, Diana 214
  R.A.W. ('Cause I'm a Woman)
  195–197
Southern, Eileen 104
speech 4, 9, 10, 24, 36, 42, 54–59,
  77, 200, 217
  identity and 194–195
  oratory 3–10, 11, 41, 53, 54
  School of 9
speech-act theory 3, 4, 175, 182, 184,
  189, 199
Spivak, Gayatri Chakravorty 180
Stebbins, Elizabeth 54
Steiner, George 99
Stevens, Thomas Wood 41, 64–65,
  74–75
Surrealism 130, 169

Tate, Claudia 165, 173
The Drama Review (TDR) 8, 23,
  147
Theaterwissenschaft 20, 51, 151
theatricality 114, 126, 141, 143–145
  anti- 3, 76, 144, 188
  anti-theatrical prejudice 3, 12, 38,
    69, 114, 116, 121, 144
  figural, and the 115–118, 126, 128,
    144
  literality, and 116, 118, 122–124,
    127, 128, 142–144
  performativity and 178, 188,
    192–197, 204–217
Thomas, Brook
  "The New Historicism and Other
    Old-Fashioned Topics" 155
Traylor, Eleanor 104
Tulane Drama Review *see* The Drama
  Review
Turner, Victor 8, 12, 146, 160–161

Veysey, Lawrence
  *The Emergence of the American
    University* 85

Walker, Alice 24
Warner, Michael 53, 54, 154
  *The Origins of Literary Studies in
    America* 53
  Letters of the Republic 54
  Fear of a Queer Planet 54–74
Washington-DuBois debate, the 16
Wendell, Barrett 52–53, 56–57, 67,
  76
  English Composition 56, 57
Wendt, Ted 23, 24
Williams, Emmett
  Ten Arrangements for Five Performers
  131
Williams, Patricia
  Alchemy of Race and Rights 180
Williams, Raymond 79–81, 92,
  97–103, 106–108
  Culture (or, The Sociology of Culture)
  98
  Culture and Society 79, 97
  Drama in Use 79, 98
  Drama from Ibsen to Brecht 79, 98
  Drama from Ibsen to Eliot 79
  Keywords 79
  Modern Tragedy 79, 99, 100
  The Long Revolution 98

Williams, Raymond (*cont.*)
  "structure of feeling" 98–100, 102,
    107
Winnicott, D.W. 168
Wooster Group, the
  Brace-Up! 110
  Nayatt School 110
  Route 1 and 9 110
  Sakonnet Point 110
  To you, the Birdie 110
  also see LeCompte, Elizabeth
Worthen, William 188, 190

Yale University 15, 59, 71
  School of Drama 44
Yarbro-Bejarano, Yvonne 194–195